THE TRIBAL SITUATION IN INDIA
STRUCTURE, CHANGE AND CONTINUITY

THE TRIBAL SITUATION IN INDIA

STRUCTURE, CHANGE AND CONTINUITY

Ashim Kumar Adhikary

ABHIJEET PUBLICATIONS

DELHI 110094

ABHIJEET PUBLICATIONS
2/46 Tukhmeerpur Extension
Delhi-110 094
Phone: 011-22960492, 65698474
E-mail: abhijeetpublication@gmail.com

THE TRIBAL SITUATION IN INDIA

First Published 2009

ISBN 978-81-89886-90-5

PRINTED IN INDIA

Published by J.K. Singh for Abhijeet Publications, Delhi-110 094, Lasertypeset by Gaurav Graphics, New Delhi and Printed at Himanshu Printers, Delhi.

Preface

When I began my doctoral research work among the Birhor, a nomadic hunting and gathering tribe moving in and around the forest-clad zones of Bihar, Orissa and West Bengal in eastern India in early seventies of the last century I was, at first, shocked at the grim reality of their life situations. They seemed to have not even the minimum numerical and material strength to maintain their social representation in a significant way. They were small in numbers, and had only a little control over their traditional home base in the forest. After a few months of my moving with the people about the jungles, the peasant villages and the markets I, however, discovered that the people had a natural capability to construct and reconstruct social realities through a careful manipulation of the material and non-material things inside and outside the forests and maintain a distinct self-image.

In the changing contexts of their resource base in the forest, the Birhor organized their society and culture based on an idiom of 'universal kinship' with man, nature and super-nature; they developed beliefs, notions and ideas about the jungle as well as the world outside their immediate jungle environment as a viable 'material' as well as 'power' base in the construction of their socio-cultural identity. In this process of identity formations the Birhor showed a strong sense of morality and spirituality as well as rationality, that helped them not only construct their own social representation but also communicate the same meaningfully to the larger world of man and society. The life-situations of the Birhor thus intrigued me to probe further deeply into the making of 'cosmologies' both objectively and subjectively among the many other tribes of India. The tribes covered in the present volume are some hunter-gatherer, shifting cultivator and settled agriculturalist tribes of central-east India, and in my delineation of them the emphasis has been given more on individual actors, their actions, ideas, the ways they construct their society and culture in the changing context of modernization rather than 'social structure' as a straight totalizing entity.

The essays presented here were spread over a number of journals and books; they are brought together partly, on requests from my research scholars, P.G. students and my anthropologist colleagues and partly, on my academic interest in anthropological theories. In the process of compilation, some moderation and updating of the articles have been made with an introductory discourse on the social significance of tribal culture in the wider sphere of humanity. It suggests that the tribes of India are not an archaic base of human civilization; they are a particular variety of Homo sapiens having the essential capability of culture-construction like all other human beings.

Prof. (Dr.) Ashim Kumar Adhikary

Contents

Preface v

Introduction 1

1. The Concept of 'Primitive' and the 'Primitive Tribal Groups' in India 13
2. Hunter-Gatherer Tribes of India: Survival Strategies 40
3. Hunting and Gathering Societies in India: Structure and Transformations 63
4. The Nomadic Mankria: Aspects of Their Articulation with the Settled Peasantry 75
5. Nomadism, Economy and World View of the Birhors of Orissa 87
6. Status and Role of Women in Birhor Society 99
7. Social Structure of a Dongria Kondh Village (Khambesi) 106
8. The Juangs of Orissa: An Ethnographic Note 117
9. Social Organization and Change: A Study of the Santal in a Village of West Bengal 132

10. Systems of Exchange in Tribal Society: A Case Study of the Santal 159

11. Tribal Groups of Eastern India: Changing Aspects of their Land and Economy 176

12. Ethnic Plurality, Nation-States, and the Changing Tribal Identities in India 193

13. Ritual and Cosmology of the Birhor, a Hunter-Gatherer Tribe 213

14. Gods, Spirits and Ghosts: A Study of Santal Cosmology 227

15. The Tribal Worldview: Changing Perspectives 255

Bibliography 279

Index 291

Introduction

The term 'tribe' with a connotation of 'primitive' was brought to India by the British colonists to designate the numerous prefarming population groups in forests and hills living outside the mainstream of the Hindu society. Following the nineteenth-century European intellectual trend in natural history and curiosity for the exotic the British administrator-scholars in India listed the number of tribes, and made general descriptions of their life and culture. In the ethnographic descriptions the primary tendency of the scholars was to show in the tribal cultures an archaic base of humanity. The British colonists, however, designated the tribes as 'primitive' or' native' and tried to keep them more or less in isolation from any intrusion of non-tribal peoples. A systematic character of designating and scheduling the tribes took its form in the 1931 Census of India, and in 1936, a list of 'backward tribes' was prepared. In the decolonized new state of India more or less a similar strategy of designation, classification and segregation of the tribes in small pockets was adopted. In 1950 when the new Constitution of Independent India was adopted, the President of India also promulgated a list of Scheduled

Tribes that was more or less in congruence with the list of Backward Tribes prepared under the colonial administration. The scheduling of tribes, and also other backward communities has been a recurrent process in modern India. The separation of a category of 'primitive tribal groups' from and among 'Scheduled Tribes' is a recent innovation in the process of modernization.

In the pre-British, pre-modern India there was, however, no common tribal identity. In ancient India the indigenous peoples and their inhabited territories were designated by the Aryan immigrants respectively as 'janas' and 'janapadas'. The term *jana* broadly referred to the indigenous peoples whom we now call 'tribes' while the term janapad denoted the land inhabited by those people. Later, in the history of ancient India we find another pair of terms, *Arya* and *Dasyu*. The term *Arya* denoted the Aryans themselves while the term *Dasyu* was used to refer to the indigenous inhabitants of the land. The Hindu civilization of India is, indeed, one of ancient civilizations in the world, and the characteristic feature of it is its 'unity in diversity'. Many peoples and cultures, of both exogenous and endogenous origins, together formed the structure of the civilization, and yet maintained their individual ethnic and cultural identities. The so-called indigenous tribal peoples were slowly accommodated and absorbed into the grand structure of Hindu civilization. There were regional systems of symbiosis between the tribes and Hindu caste-peasants as well as a pattern of socio-economic consensus, specifically in the mainland of India. These regional and particular dimensions of tribal life and culture were slowly universalised to a culture of humanity within the broad framework of Hindu civilization.

The post-British modern India ignored this historical process of tribal absorption in Hindu India. Instead, she followed the Western model of modernization and development. The development of Western civilization with new technologies, huge money and matter, massive buildings, big cities and towns as well as intellectual repositories of science and knowledge led the people therein to deliberately distinguish themselves from those who are not like them and who are very different from them not merely in terms of materials but also in terms of the scientific rationality they possess. The Western civilization considered itself the 'most developed', and subsequently, felt it a necessity, among other things, to develop the 'other' blacklisted peoples. This led ultimately to the irreconcilable division of the mankind into the 'subject' and the 'object'. The dialectical difference of 'subject' and 'object' was, indeed, implicated into the whole process of human development.

In India, 'modernization' was, and is still equated to Westernization, and involved in developing her diverse traditional and rural societies in the model of the Western modernity. Industrial economy based on an open system of market and the participatory political democracy constituted the 'mainstream' of modern India while all the traditional-rural societies were considered 'objects' to be developed to, and integrated into the modernity of India. The tribal societies were, in this way, constituted a part of the traditional-rural stream. The 'tribal' identity is given a legal sanction, and in this respect, it is a unique identity. In this process of legalization, not only their multiple identities of tribes were ignored but also the socio-economic consensus prevailing in the regional systems was undermined. Andre Beteille, a sociologist of international repute, argued how the legal sanction of a definite tribal identity has created a boundary between 'tribe' and 'non-tribe', and subsequently, inculcated a political interest in the tribal mind to strategically maintain the tribal identity (Beteille, 1991). Peoples normally go by multiple identities and the ascription of a unique identity to any people often creates problems. Amartya Sen, a Nobel Laureate, thus argues that 'conflict and violence are sustained today, no less than in the past, by the illusion of a unique identity' (Sen, 2006).

In anthropological discourses, the term 'tribe' has been used broadly to refer to 'two realities, two fields of facts'—one, 'a type of society' and the other, 'a stage of evolution' in the development of humanity (Godelier 1977:70). Although analytically the concepts are separate, in practice they are mutually inclusive. It is, however, not that anthropologists did not use the word 'primitive' at all. They used it but broadly with a sense of 'the primary' or the other. In an effort to avoid the derogatory implications of the term 'primitive' they variously designated them as 'preliterate', 'simple' or 'folk' societies.

Anthropologists working in India initially studied the 'tribal' societies as representing evolutionary sequences in the development of the Hindu civilization in India, but later, they viewed the diversity of tribal economy, society and culture as 'a mosaic' of tribal identities and cultures in Indian situation. As a result, we find different classifications of Indian tribes'. One of them is the economic classification of tribes by Vidyarthi (1983)[1976]: *(i)* forest hunting type, *(ii)* hill cultivation type, *(iii)* settled agricultural type, *(iv)* simple artisan type, *(v)* cattle-herder type, *(vi)* labour: agricultural and industrial type, *(vii)* folk artist type, and *(viii)* white-collar jobs and trader type. Bose in his Tribal life of India (1979) [1971] made a four-fold classification of Indian tribes: *(i)* hunters, fishers and gatherers, *(ii)* shifting cultivators, *(iii)* peasants, artisans and caste, and *(iv)* nomadic groups. The Ministry of Welfare, Government of India has, however, carved out a new category of 'primitive tribal groups' with some hunters and gatherer, shifting cultivator, artisan tribes from the list of 'Scheduled Tribes'.

Hunter-gatherer and shifting cultivator tribes constitute an important segment in this new category of PTGs in India. Hunters and gatherers are hardly 2 percent of India's total tribal population. As a means of livelihood hunting and gathering or in a broad sense, foraging, however, covered about 90 percent of the history of human development, and all humans, in fact, lived this way until 12000 years ago. It is reported that 'one-third of the globe including all of Australia, most of North America, as well as large tracts of South America, Africa, and Northeast Asia' was occupied by hunters and gatherers as recently as A.D. 1500 (Lee and Daly, 1999: 2-3). In India, the available archaeological remains suggest for the existence of hunter-gatherers back to a period between twenty-sixth and nineteenth century B.C.

'Foraging' ideally refers to the means of subsistence 'based on hunting wild animals, gathering of wild plants, and fishing, with no domestication of plants, and no domestication of animals except the dog' (*ibid*: 3) though the contemporary foragers are found to adopt a variety of pathways. One pathway in which the contemporary hunter-gatherers persist is represented by the aboriginal peoples of Australia, northwestern North America, the southern core of South America, the Jarwas, and the Sentinelese of the Andaman and Nicobar Islands. They have persisted hunting and gathering in the more or less traditional way. Another way is reflected in the centuries-old symbiosis of the hunter-gatherer groups in central Africa, East Africa, South and Southeast Asia with their neighbouring horticulturalists, peasants, and markets of the larger society. There is also another situation in which hunting and gathering has been a 'secondary adaptation' and/ or, a case of 'secondary primitivization'. In the mainland of India as well as South America the colonial rules compelled many traditional farmers of the forest to adopt foraging as their means of livelihood.

Persistence of hunting and gathering in the contemporary situation is thus a process of adaptation of a people not only to its immediate natural environment but also to the economic, socio-political and cultural environments of the larger society. On many occasions, hunter-gatherer groups have expanded their resource base in the larger society, and added new dimensions to their traditional means of subsistence. Lee and Daly report, 'almost all tropical South American foragers today plant gardens as one part of their annual trek'. There are parallels here with Siberia, where most the "small peoples" classified as hunter-gatherers also herded reindeer, a practice which greatly expanded during the Soviet period' (ibid: 3). In South-east Asia the Birhor, besides hunting and gathering, have also specialized themselves in the art of 'rope-making', and 'occult performance' based on their traditional knowledge of jungles, and operate like a specialized caste group of the Hindu society. The recently sedentary Paliyans in south India still stick to their traditional values of nomadic life-style to avoid conflict with the sedentary non-hunter peoples (Gardner, 2000).

Hunting and gathering has thus been a highly adaptive strategy for humanity, and not totally lost its significance in the process of human development. Hunting and gathering societies persisted, and still persist well with multiple technologies and scales of society in traditional and modern civilizations. In the traditional Hindu civilization of India hunting and gathering, precisely speaking foraging, transcended its material dimension was raised to a sublime status.

This symbolic significance of hunting and gathering is, however, not appreciated by the modernists of India; it is viewed primarily in economic terms, and treated as a non-viable, inferior technology in the context of modernity. The peoples attached to this means of livelihood are considered irrational, and unaware of the material reality. Hunting and gathering peoples of India are thus identified as 'primitive' ignoring their centuries-old adaptations, and enduring social process of identity formations.

The survival strategies of the hunting and gathering peoples over time and space reflect, among other things, a unity of man and nature. Despite essential productive relations with their immediate natural environment they value moral ties to hills, forests, lands, animals, fellow humans and non-human entities within a universal framework of kinship over space and time. The hunting and gathering peoples combine meaningfully material or rational understanding of their physical environment with transcendental, metaphysical, spiritual understanding for the realization of a culture of humanity.

Barnard (2001) thus gives an emphasis 'on the ideological basis of a hunting and gathering economy'. To him the value on the immediacy of economic returns, mutual sharing, and the idea of universal kinship with hills, forests, lands, animals, humans and non-human entities reflect the general mode of thought of hunter-gatherer peoples.

There are two broad views on the 'hunting and gathering' society: 'traditionalist' (Lee, 1979) and 'revisionist' (Wilmsen, 1989b). The traditionalists argue for the independent existence of a hunter-gathering society while the revisionists argue for centuries-old contacts of hunter-gatherers with herders and cultivators. Barnard's (2001) view is worth noting in this context. He says, 'Rather than contact, trade, and mixed subsistence strategies negating the notion of a hunting-and-gathering society, I see them as enabling a vision of hunter-gatherer's thought as transcendent of material forces—at least in the short term. If I am right, it should be the goal of those accumulators who are in power over hunter-gatherers and recent former hunter-gatherers, both to respect hunter-gatherer's values and to work towards a social order based on a merging of conflicting ideologies' (*ibid* :87).

The tribal peoples who have been traditionally living in hills and hill-slopes with shifting cultivation as their primary means of livelihood are also included into the category of PTGs. In historical terms, shifting cultivation as a means of livelihood came earlier to settled plough cultivation, and the available archaeological remains have traced the antiquity of the technology back to a period between 7000 and 3000 B.C. Shifting cultivation was, and is still in practice in many countries other than India. According to 1960-61 and, in some cases, 1971-75 estimates by the Census of India there are about one hundred and ten shifting-cultivator tribes with varying numerical strengths that are spread over a wider region of the country. In all, seventeen distinct areas where shifting cultivation is practised have been identified. Based on altitude, rainfall, geological formation, vegetation and the population density their areas of their distribution can be divided into three major zones: *(1)* North-eastern Sub-Himalayan Area, *(2)* The Central Plateau, and *(3)* The Southern Hill Tracts. The North-eastern Sub-Himalayan Area includes the States of Arunachal Pradesh, Nagaland, Sikkim, Tripura, and Sub-Himalayan west Bengal. The Central Plateau includes Keonjhar-Bonai-Pallahara of Orissa, and Madhya Pradesh while the districts of Palghat, Kottayam, and Quilon of Kerala and the south Canara districts of Karnataka, Nilgiri region of Tamil Nadu form the Zone of Southern Hill Tracts are included in the zone of the Southern Hill Tracts.

The maximum concentration of the tribes is in the states of Orissa, Andhra Pradesh, Assam, Meghalaya, Nagaland and Mizoram. The population of shifting cultivator tribes is nearly 12 percent of the total tribal population in India, and the estimated area which comes under shifting cultivation is nearly 9,29,480 hectares (Bose et al: 1982 quoted from Danda, 1998). Shifting Cultivation is technically known 'Extensive Agriculture' since in this practice the 'field' is periodically left fallow and the people move to new plots of land for cultivation instead of using a particular plot intensively year after year. Technically, 'shifting cultivation' is also termed as 'swidden cultivation', 'slush and burn' cultivation, and 'hoe-cultivation'. In local dialects of India shifting cultivation is termed variously as *jhum* (in Assam), *tekeonglu* (in Nagaland) *odiabik* (in Arunachal Pradesh) *hookuismong* (in Tripura), *badaga, taila, koman, dahi* or *podu* (in Orissa), *penda, bewar, dahiya, dipa* or *dahi* (in Madhya Pradesh), *kumri,* or *kumari* (in Western Ghats of south India), *kurari* and *khallu* (in Bihar), *watra* (in south-east Rajasthan), *waler* (in Gujarat) and *podu* (in Andhra Pradesh).

Shifting cultivation in India has been practised invariably in combination with hunting and gathering. In some cases, terrace cultivation with plough is also pursued along with hoe-cultivation on hill-slopes. Land ownership has been collective as well as individual. Right to land is normally usufructory, and passed on to individuals through the decision of the village council or the chief, and sometimes, through hereditary principle. The density of population in the areas under shifting cultivation is generally low although middle and high density of population is found in some areas. The reason of low density of population has, among other things, been often ascribed to the low 'carrying capacity' of the land and the inferior quality of the technology of shifting cultivation, thereby raising a pertinent question of economic viability of the production technology under increasing population (Bose, 1989).

A close probe in the historical situations of the peoples would, however, reveal that the shifting cultivators in India had traditionally maintained economic and socio-political consensus with other tribal communities, neighbouring caste-peasants and the former Royal states of the region. Unlike the hunter-gatherer groups the shifting cultivators were more privileged in their control over forest resources. They have, in fact, a stronger sense of territory than the hunter-gatherer tribes, and in many instances, the chiefs of these tribes had functioned as vassals of their neighbouring Hindu kings. Besides perpetuating a systematic network of relations with certain service castes of the neighbouring Hindu society these tribes had maintained an elaborate territorial organization in the forest. The territorial organization of the people was perpetuated through a careful manipulation of the political power and authority conferred on them by the kings of the Royal Hindu States and the jural power of their traditional kinship system.

Under the pressure of forest regulation and the development programmes in Independent India there has occurred much change in the habitat, the economy and the society of the concerned tribes. The development programmes have been oriented broadly to stop soil erosion under shifting cultivation, arrest the decline of the vegetation in the forest and rehabilitate the people in suitable alternative habitat and economy. The programmers and development workers, however, seemed to be inclined more to preserve and develop forest environment for national economy and politics than to help the people develop modern agriculture and forest ecology. The material resources were given priority over the concerned human resources.

In the process of economic and political modernization of India the shifting cultivator tribes, with their linkage to the former Princely states as well as identity with the forest was ignored. Precisely speaking, the morally integrated nature of the tribes with their natural environment was left unnoticed. The plants, the animals, the land of hills and forests, and even the water and the air therein are all animated with supernatural spirits and these still play important roles in process of formation of their identity with the forest. Tyler (1974), an anthropologist, for instance, shows the way and the manner the productive activities of the Koya, a shifting cultivator group, are woven together with their religious values to form an integrated view of self-image and identity with the forest.

Many individuals have, however, positively responded to the moderning forces of the new state of India and entered into the wider world of modern economics and politics. In the new contexts, some educated tribal personalities have emerged as leaders who carefully manipulate the legally sanctioned tribal identity and Constitutional provisions accompanying it in an effort to reinforce their traditional identity with the forest.

Some of the new states in the Northeastern zone were already formed in this way, and some are in the process. The process does not seems to be an outright negation of the modernity but a merging of material forces of the modern and the ideological forces of the traditional societies for a meaningful world of communication. To Jurgen Habermas, for instance, modernity is an unfinished product. Full potential of modernity is yet to be realized not through social movements but through communicative action that would mediate between different positions. Habermas takes the stance neither of universalism of the modern nor of particularity of the postmodern. Instead, he would like to make a search for means to mutual understanding and a listening that respects the other.

There are many agriculturalist tribes who in pre-British Hindu India developed elaborate state systems in their forest areas with effective articulation with the peasant economy and state polities of the Hindu. The systems started breaking down with the colonial administration of the British, and finally came an end in modern India. A careful study of the historical functioning of those tribal states reveals that the break-down could do away with neither moral relationship with the forest not could it take away the idiom of their kinship. The hierarchical structure of economic and political institutions of tribal states in the past did not make any deep implication in the community spirit of the peoples. The studies on the Santals included here shows the way they are still producing and reproducing their socio-cultural identity in the context of moderning forces.

The tribal peoples who are well exposed to modern education, white collar jobs, and other opportunities in modern India oscillate between the civic world of the larger society and their primordial ties to kinship, religion and morally ordered world of man, nature, and supernature. They seem to lack a world of meaningful communicative action as well as a distinct self-identity of social significance in the decision-making process of modern nation and states. The tribes at all levels of techno-economy seem to assert consciously or unconsciously a self-image with social significance. The cosmologies and world-views of the peoples are in the constant process of construction that involves together the intellectual as well as spiritual dimensions of natural mental faculty. The spiritual dimension of their mental faculty helps them realize their communion with the wider world of man and nature.

1

The Concept of 'Primitive' and the 'Primitive Tribal Groups' of India

Conceptualizing the 'Primitive'

'Primitive Tribal Groups' (PTGs) is a new classification of the tribal population in India made from and among the category of 'Scheduled Tribes' by the Ministry of Welfare, Govt. of India. In the process of re-designating the peoples as PTGs the emphasis was on aspects of the relative backwardness of the peoples compared to other tribes, specifically, smallness of their numbers, illiteracy, pre-farming subsistence economy and marginal position to the peasant economy.

According to the latest available record of the Ministry of Welfare, there are 74 groups that have been enlisted as PTGs in India. The exact number of the groups as well as their numbers would, however, need further scrutiny and, there are some overlaps and other anomalies in the classification. The major concentration of the tribes is in south India and Orissa. There are four Negrito, and one Mongoloid group in the Andaman and Nicobar Islands.

The category, PTGs, identified by the Govt. of India is, however, not a homogeneous one and the tribes included under this category are of different techno-economic levels and scales of society (defined in terms of maximal size of the population involved in significant networks of social relationship). There are included in this category, so-called 'primary' hunters, secondary hunters, swidden cultivators, and tribal artisans. This official identification as well as the numerical strength of the groups would also need scrutiny and there are overlaps and other anomalies in the documentation.

The Ministry of Welfare identified PTGs primarily to accord constitutional privileges to the groups and adopt special measures for their welfare in the process of national integration and modernization of India. The stigma 'primitive' is attached to the groups broadly with reference to their simple subsistence technology, traditional life style and comparative remoteness from the mainstream of modern India. It may be noted in this context that the term 'tribe', with 'primitive' connotation, was first brought to India by the British colonists broadly to designate the peoples generally inhabiting the hills, forests, and the plains outskirting peasant villages, eking out their subsistence through hunting, gathering, and shifting cultivation outside the mainstream of the Hindu society.

Anthropologists and many other scholars working in India also looked upon the tribal peoples in general broadly with a connotation of 'primitive' although they identified different levels of economy and social-cultural integration among them. The scholars have, however, argued variously for the use and non-use of the term 'primitive' for the tribal peoples in India. Sachchidananda (1981), for instance, describes the academic reasons as to why the ethnographers in general used the term 'primitive' and then argues to designate certain tribal groups as 'primitive'. Sachchidananda restricts the term 'primitive' to 'hunters and food gatherers, nomadic pastorals or shifting cultivators' and notes that they are very small in size and have a greater degree of isolation with an optimum equilibrium with their ecology. In his conception Sachchidananda follows broadly the criteria pointed out by Dozier (1955:188). The criteria noted by Dozier are as follows: "*(1)* absence of written language, *(2)* a relatively simple technology, *(3)* social institutions which are cast in a simpler mould, *(4)* smaller numbers, *(5)* relative isolation, and *(6)* societies whose cultures are characterized by a slower rate of change." The list of the criteria was based on the observations of the contemporary peoples of the kind made in sharp contrast with large population, written tradition, a complex technology with varied social institutions, and whose cultures are fast changing.

Singh (1998) brings in the "the factor of ecology" to define the 'primitive'. In terms of the peoples' participation into the forest ecology he makes a distinction between 'primary primitives' and 'marginal communities'. He notes that primitive tribal groups possess a special quality of community life with their habitat and subsistence in the forest ecology. They 'draw their sustenance from it and move forward'. Marginal communities, on the other hand, seek 'their nourishment from an impoverished environment, living on the periphery—geographical, economic, social, psychological, cultural and so on'. (1988:80). Singh's association of the 'primitive' with forests is reminiscent of the classical notion of the natural state of humanity.

It may, however, be noted here that the 'Hindu civilization' of India itself was conceptualized and developed in the midst of forest. In ancient India the Hindu literatii *(rishis)* who universalized the social and cultural norms of the diverse peoples and framed a unified pattern of society, culture, education, law and administration of the land had their normal habitat in the forest. The forest was not merely a site for habitation, economy, and learning for the people; it provided an essential cultural space of initiation in one's life and was integrated with the social system of the Hindus. In the development of the most of the world's traditional civilizations the cities played important cultural roles while in the development of the Hindu civilization in India the forests played the essential cultural roles. The forest in India has thus not only provided an appropriate ambience for the codification of complex culture or civilization of India but also been deeply integrated with the life and society of the Hindus.

In lieu of 'primitive' Vidyarthi (1981) suggests to use 'such positive terms which help us in understanding the total temper, the ethos or the nature-man-spirit complex of a hunting and/or food gathering or pre-farming communities'. He cites Julian Steward's 'primary subsistence band' and Gisbert's 'food-gatherers' (that include marginals and lower hunters) and 'food producers' (that include pastoral and incipient agriculturalists) as examples of such 'positive terms'. In his opinion, these terms denote the social structure and the method of acquiring food of the peoples and hence, are not offensive. Vidyarthi thus combines cultural criteria with subsistence techniques to classify the tribal peoples.

In his study of the historical reconstruction of Indian civilization in materialistic terms Kosambi (1970) viewed the food gatherers of the land as 'primitive survivals'. He considered their 'means of production' as well as the super-structure or 'relations of production' to designate them as 'primitive'.

Fox (1969) conceptualized the hunter-gatherer groups of nuclear South Asia—the Kadar, the Birhor, the Chenchu, the Vedda and the Nayadi—as 'professional' primitives. He observed that 'Indian hunters and gatherers' are 'marginal economic specialists for traditional Indian Civilization' and resemble, in many ways, the artisan castes in Hindu villages. Their nucleated social organization, according to Fox, is an adaptation to trade. He also notes that the primitive peoples hunt and gather only because of this 'professional' occupation, which requires them to live in the forest. This conceptualization privileges the wider market economy and pays little attention to 'the local economic and social consensus' as well as the peoples' moral attachment to forests. The occupational specialization of these tribal groups fits well into the structural framework of the caste-based Hindu society. The socio-economic framework of the Hindu society is such that any group may articulate itself to it on economic and social consensus, with ample scope for freedom and cultural autonomy.

Sinha (1958) defines an ideal-typical 'tribe' broadly as a people characterized by isolation, homogeneity, cultural autonomy, a value system of equality, closeness of the human, the natural and the supernatural world, and lack of systematisation of ideas. Here, Sinha conceptualizes 'tribe' in terms of Redfield's ideal 'folk' society, and investigates into the process of development of Hindu civilization in India from the tribal base. He also conceptualises an idea of 'tribe-caste and tribe-peasant' continuum in the model of 'folk-continuum' of Redfield. Here, Sinha's approach was essentially 'evolutionary'. Although Sinha did not make any explicit use of the term 'primitive', there was implicit in his conception of tribe a connotation of 'primitive'.

In a later writing Sinha (1973), however, changes his view and looks upon the contemporary tribal cultures of India broadly as dependent 'historic structures'. Sinha draws our attention specifically to the Birhor and the Hill-Kharia of eastern India, who are broadly known as 'primitive' hunter-gatherer tribes, and points out their long symbiosis with the Hindu caste-peasants as well as the level of their socio-cultural integration. Sinha describes the life-situations of the tribes as an instance of secondary primitivization or devolution. He observed that the Birhor and the Hill-Kharia, like many other tribes in Chotanagpur were, in the past, shifting cultivators on hill slopes. But 'penetration of the caste-based economy into these areas and extensive de-forestation' forced these peoples to adopt a 'hunting and gathering' mode of subsistence (1969:184). Here, Sinha seems to be viewing 'primitivity' in terms of 'simple technology' and 'small-scale' society.

This technoeconomic adoption of hunting, gathering and foraging of the people may, however, be looked upon as a 'significant strategy of resistance' to external forces in an effort to preserve their self image and be interpreted as a natural process of social production and reproduction. The people who practiced shifting cultivation combined with hunting and gathering, later adopted hunting and gathering for subsistence still perpetuating their kinship bondage with the forest. Hunting and gathering that was secondary in material terms became 'primary' in the new situation. An ethno-historical study of the Kung in the Kalahari region revealed a similar situation (Gordon 1984). Myers (1988) also noted that the prehistoric hunters and gatherers of the Connecticut River Valley took refuge from, or actively resisted, intensification. A close probe into such trend of 'primitivization' reveals, among other things, a process of cultural construction of a 'self-image' or 'ethnic identity'.

The 'primitive' has, thus, been variously defined and re-defined to evade the value-bias implicit in it. Since 1990s an attempt has been made to replace the term 'primitive tribe' by 'indigenous people'. The term 'indigenous' denotes the original inhabitants, or the heritage people; in other words it refers to the original human condition. Roy Burman who made attempts to replace the term 'primitive' first, by 'post-primitive', and later, by 'primal', ultimately decided to identify the people as a primordial type of socio-cultural formation; in his opinion the term convivial social formation is a suitable replacement of 'primitive', 'primal', 'indigenous' and even of 'tribe'. Roy Burman looks upon the so-called peoples as 'repositories of the values of altruism, mutual cooperation, equity and sharing at the level of ethos' (Roy Burman 2003: 335).

Although the term 'primitive' is now considered offensive, and alternative terms signifying the peoples' actual socio-economic institutions and cultural values are suggested to get rid of the possible value-bias, it cannot be denied that the concept 'primitive' has been in vogue in the ethnographic description of non-literate societies since the very beginning of the anthropological enterprise. In the traditional ethnographic literature the non-literate peoples were viewed more or less as a natural state of humanity, and their cultures, as important source of information for understanding human variation over time and space. Benedict notes that primitive cultures 'are a laboratory in which we may study the diversity of human institutions. With their comparative isolation, many primitive regions have had centuries in which to elaborate the cultural themes they have made their own. They provide ready to our hand the necessary information concerning the possible great variations in human adjustments.' (1934: 17).

In the evolutionary thinking of the nineteenth-century anthropologists pre-literate societies were considered 'survivals' or 'degenerated' societies. "Such societies were most often and most consistently thought to represent 'stages' in the cultural growth of mankind that culminated in the so-called 'advanced' traditions of Europe. 'Psychic unity' also characterized the thinking of the day so that the work of the early anthropologists was done largely in the belief that primitives represented the backwaters in the historical stream." (Dozier 1955:189).

Many anthropologists investigated the nature of 'primitive mind', and tried to construct the 'elementary' structure of human thought from and among the primitive or folk societies for an understanding of society in general and of our own modern urbanized society in particular (Redfield 1962: 231). In his *The Primitive World and Its Transformations* (1953) Redfield brings in, among other things, the concept of worldview. According to him the worldview of a people is the sum total of ideas and notions about the world in and around which the members live. It is the 'total vision and conception of everything' from inside. Redfield mentions Man, Nature and God or Super-nature as three basic elements of every worldview, and observes that in the primitive worldview these elements are not separate; the man-nature-supernature relationship is morally bounded to form the unitary cosmos of the primitive people. He further notes that 'the predominant attitude of the primitive or primary worldview is one of participant maintenance'.

'Primitive man's intellectual faculty has also been discussed by many scholars. Levy-Bruhl (1923) considers the thought of primitive man as 'pre-logical' by which he means that it fails to conform to the laws of classical logic. Primitive man cannot distinguish properly between subject and object, and the relation between them involves mystic participation (participation mystique). Evans-Pritchard, however, observes that Levy-Bruhl's notion of 'pre-logicality' is not an exclusive mentality; he shows that it is an intellectually pre-critical attitude peculiar to certain social and cultural contexts, and that it is neither unintelligible nor unreasonable for all practical purposes (Evans-Pritchard 1940).

Durkheim and Mauss (1963)[1903] observe that 'primitive classifications are...not singular or exceptional, having no analogy with those employed by more civilized peoples; on the contrary, they seem to be connected, with no break in continuity, to the first scientific classifications...like all sophisticated scientific classifications they are systems of hierarchized notions' and 'have a purely speculative purpose' (1963:81). They further note that the object of primitive classification 'is not to facilitate action, but to advance understanding, to make intelligible the relations which exist between things'. Primitive classifications, according to the authors, 'are intended to connect ideas, to unify knowledge', and they constitute the 'first philosophy of nature' (*ibid*: 81).

Radin in his *Primitive Man as Philosopher* (1957) makes quite an elaborate description of philosophical thinking of primitive peoples. He notes that there is, in almost every primitive as well as civilized society, a few 'thinkers' and a large group of common mass as 'men of action'. The 'thinker' makes a sharp differentiation between the subject and the object; he also discerns their respective relation to each other. The 'man of action' is, on the other hand, interested primarily in the object. Radin also finds that there is an inordinate urge among certain primitive thinkers to systematize and harmonize ideas.

It becomes evident now that many of the aspects of the worldview and philosophical thinking of the primitive peoples also characterize the so-called civilized peoples. The similarities indicate, not merely a 'psychic unity' of mankind but a natural process of human thought and action. "Primitive man' was constructed as our anthropological 'other' not only to learn something about him but also from him—in which we rediscover our participation in its being (Evens, 1982:390). There are enormous ethnographic writings on the so-called 'primitive other' highlighting the 'elementary' process of thought and action in which we also participate.

The concept of 'primitive man' has, however, been misunderstood for its use in anthropology as 'an essentially backward and irretrievable other'. It is mistaken; we simply fancy ourselves as the exemplar of civilization, and there is enough commensurable space that the 'modern' or the 'civilized' people share with the so-called 'primitive'. We are yet to have a measure of what is 'primitive'. "What is primitive is not only what is first in time but also what is fundamental. It is not simply, like say, *Pithecanthropus alalus,* that from which we once (historically) began, but like, say, upright posture, that from which we begin. It is the horizon of our perception and the radical of our being. It is...our embeddedness in a lived and generative All" (Evens 1982: 390-1). Primitive man is thus not a backward and irretrievable other but a model representative of the plane upon which we project ourselves.

We may note here Boas' observation. Boas treats 'primitive' people in a non-judgemental way and notes, 'Primitive are those whose forms of life are simple and uniform, and the contents and form of whose culture are meagre and intellectually inconsistent' (Boas 1938:197) [1911]. He observes that different peoples are primitive or advanced in different respects. For instance, Australian Aborigines have a complex social structure but are poor in material culture. He adds that no people are untouched by foreign influences. It is, therefore, pointless to assign a whole culture to a uniform category of 'primitive' or 'civilized'. It was, indeed, Franz Boas through whose work emerged the paradigm of cultural relativism.

Levi-Strauss (1963), somewhat in a similar vein, says, 'a primitive people is not a backward or retarded people; indeed it may possess, in one realm or another, a genius for invention or action that leaves the achievements of civilized peoples far behind. One might cite as illustrations the true 'sociological planning' evident in the study of family organization among the Australian societies; the integration of emotional life within a complex system of rights and obligations in Melanesia; and, almost everywhere, the utilization of religious feeling to establish a viable, if not always harmonious, synthesis of individual aspirations and the social order' (*ibid*: 102).

Although the anthropological conception of 'primitive' was primarily analytical, and varied with the particular field contexts of the scholars, it always involved a perspective of the 'primitive' and the 'civilized' dichotomy. Some scholars, however, tried to get rid of the ethnocentric bias of the 'civilized', and showed that the 'primitive' and the 'civilized' were not mutually exclusive; and there were elements of complex society in 'primitive' cultures as there were elements of 'primitive' society in modern civilizations or cultures. In some instances the social and cultural planning of the primitive was found to be more complex than that of the civilized. The label 'primitive' to a particular human group, therefore, does not go well with the anthropological perspective of humanity. Man is distinguished from other animals for his capability to construct culture, and it is 'culture' that shaped all men, primitive or civilized, as a single species, *Homo sapiens*. Culture has also been shaping men as separate individuals. Man, however, cannot be defined by his innate capacity to build culture or by his actual behaviour. He is to be defined 'by the link between them, by the way in which the first is transformed into the second, his generic potentialities focussed into his specific performances' (Geertz 1993:52) [1973]. This is the most enduring natural process of culture construction that has always been in man's career.

In our conceptualization of 'primitive' we emphasized mainly the specific performances of a people, focussed on their technology, society, culture and intellectual faculty, and designated them as 'simple', 'primary', 'primordial' or 'preliterate' in contrast to modern peoples. There is obviously an impact of the concept of our own culture on such conceptualization, and little attention is given to the generic potentialities of the people as culture-constructionists, as a group of *Homo sapiens*. The primitive peoples like all other human groups on the globe are constructing and reconstructing cultures to cope with time and space, and it is this underlying process of culture construction in the context of the actual life-life-situations of people on which we need to project ourselves.

As anthropologists our task would thus be 'to uncover the conceptual structures that inform our subjects' acts, the 'said' of social discourse, and to construct a system of analysis in whose terms what is generic to those structures, what belongs to them because they are what they are, will stand out against the other determinants of human behaviour' (Geertz 1993:27).

Primitive Tribal Groups in India

The 'primitive tribal groups' of India have, since long, been in a network of trade, barter and exchange with peoples different in their economies and scales of social organization, markets, and urban centres of great antiquity occupying complementary ecological niches. Despite diversified occupations and essential articulation to the surrounding societies in the region the peoples keep up a distinct socio-cultural identity with the surrounding natural ecology, the forest and the sea, fellow humans, and supernatural beings.

The network of communication of the so-called 'primitive tribal groups' of India, however, extends much beyond their immediate local environment. The primitive tribal groups have considerable historical depth and are well exposed to, and integrated with, by implication, the civilization of India, which by common estimates dates to the third millennium BC. All the primitive tribal groups in the mainland of India had been in the midst of Hindu civilization. The socio-economic pattern of interaction and articulation of these tribes to the Hindu caste-peasants, their position in the local social milieu, the preponderant animistic faith, and their holistic life-form with forest are all embedded in the civilization of India.

Regional Systems in the Andaman and Nicobar Islands

The Great Andamanese and the Onges in the Andaman and Nicobar Islands have had sporadic contacts with outside world since long. Both these groups are now well exposed to induced development programmes from the government. They, however, hang around the forest and the natural ecology and seem to carve out a distinct world of their own. The Onges 'live by hunting, fishing and the collection of wild produce, like berries or honey from forest' (Pandit 1990:268). They have two endogamous clusters, forest-dwellers and coast-dwellers who exploit respectively two different ecological terrains, the interior forest and the sea. The clusters are also related to each other through barter and exchange. The Great Andamanese who now live in an officially constructed settlement on the Strait Island off the eastern coast of Middle Andaman, combine their hunting, gathering and fishing with pig rearing and horticulture; the latter activities were introduced by the government.

The Shompen live in the Great Nicobar Island. They too combine hunting, gathering and fishing with pig rearing and horticulture. They have a long tradition of trade and barter with the coastal Nicobarese (Kloss 1903). At present the Shompen barter honey, lemons, megapode eggs, seashells and the like with the coastal Nicobarese as well as the local administration. The Shompen of Alexandra and Degmar barter with Nicobarese of Kopenheat while those of Badueyon and Dakoyen exchange with the villagers living between Kosintooth in the north and Kotinjong in the south (Rizvi 1990: 45).

Jarawas live in the western coast and forest reserves in South and Middle Andaman Islands. They had experienced, in the past, several unpleasant encounters and in the course of time, developed an attitude of hostility towards outside people. The Sentinelese had virtually no regular contact with outside world, and thus no detailed information about their life-situation is available.

Although the 'primitive tribal groups' in these islands, like those in the mainland of India, had no contact with caste-peasants, they had a long tradition of barter and exchange among different ethnic groups occupying different ecological niches and having specialized skills and knowledge. Prevalence of a system of inter-island trade and ceremonial exchange in this region may also not be ruled out.

Regional Systems Embedded in Hindu Civilization

The primitive tribal groups in the mainland of India may be distinguished from those in the islands in their having a long tradition of symbiosis with the caste-peasants and of direct or indirect exposures to the religious ideology of Hindu civilization.

Many of these groups trace their descent from some royal ancestry, or claim to have connections with the ancient kings and their kingdoms. They remember also heritage from glorious past. For instance, the Nayaka food gatherer-groups of the Nilgiri Hills, south India claim their descent from the Kuruma (Pallavas).

The Pallavas fled to the forest when the Chola Dynasty came to power around 900A.D. (Bird-David 1999). The Hill Pandaram of Kerala and many other forest-dwelling foragers had been part of the early Dravidian kingdom. Royalties were levied on minor forest produce gathered by the foragers, especially exotic spices that were highly valued in European markets (Morris 1982).

The Birhor hunter-gatherer groups of Sundargarh district in Orissa often trace their descent from a Kherwar king in Chotanagpur, and feel proud often to narrate their royal heritage and identify themselves as 'nagbansi kherwar'. At present they, however, associate themselves with forests, and assert their self-image' as 'Birhor', meaning 'man of the jungle'. In the past, these people practised shifting cultivation combined with hunting and gathering. At present they pursue hunting, gathering, and jungle-based crafts, and strategically operate between the natural ecology of forests and a social ecology of neighbouring Hindu caste-peasants and markets.

The Raji of Uttar Pradesh, who until recently were nomadic hunters and gatherers, trace their ancestry to the feudal royalty of Askot, and call themselves 'Raji' meaning 'Royal' people. They also claim to have been a part of the ancient Kirata people. In the Kumaon Himalayas, they are popularly known as Ban Rawat, meaning 'king of forest'. At present Rajis are also engaged in animal husbandry, tailoring and other occupations along with their traditional hunting and gathering.

Some Palyans came very close to the old city of Madurai that had trade relations with Rome. Madurai is now a centre of modernization. They also had contacts with forest temples sites. Palyans even, officiate as hereditary guardians of a certain forest temple (Gardner 1982). For their guiding and escorting the pilgrims to the temple in the jungle the Chenchus were paid in cash. This system was known as *metta mirasi* (Chandrasekhar 1965). The Chenchu watch over the fields and guard the crops of the non-tribal cultivators' lands bordering the forest. The peasants pay them in grain for these services. This practice has been in vogue for generations and the system is known as *mirasi*. Some Chenchus have also taken to agriculture, and rear goats, sheep and cattle for milk and meat. They are expert in weaving bamboo mats, wattle baskets, etc. These baskets are made mainly for their own use although in places they are also sold (Bhowmick 1989:92). A few Chenchus are also employed in government services.

Nayakas and Birhors serve the neighbouring Hindu

villagers as magico-religious experts. The Birhor also prepare rope and rope-made products with fibres of a jungle creeper, *Bauhinia valii* and barter or sell them to the caste-peasants in the neighbouring villages and markets. They also sell live games specifically, *Maccacus rhesus* to the traders who take them to big cities. During a few decades, Nayakas, Palyans, and Chenchus have sporadically engaged in plantation work, and Pandarams have taken up wage labour for the Forestry Department.

The Jenu Kuruba of Mysore and Coorg districts of Karnataka depended on food gathering and honey collection in the interior of dense forests. Now in lean periods they work for the peasants. They attend local shops and make purchases in both cash and kind. They take *ragi* or paddy in exchange for the tubers and honey that they collect in the forest. There are some permanent settlements in the area for the Jenu Kuruba, but the members always leave them for forests where they feel free (Misra 1977) and the wandering Hindu ascetics. There are century-old Hindu pilgrimage sites in the midst of the forest. Palyans and Chenchus had traditionally guided and escorted Hindu pilgrims to such pilgrim centres.

The Cholanaickan of Malappuram district in Kerala collect minor forest produce like dammer, honey, ginger, soap-seed, tree-bark, cardamom, astringent fruit, and the like and exchange in the neighbouring markets. Cholanaickans live in natural caves in interior forests and move about the forest ranges, Karulai and Chungathara of the Nilambur forest division. Each group moves about a particular territory, and is identified by the territory in which it operates. Besides gathering they also pursue fishing and hunting (Bhanu: 1989).

The Hill-Kharia of Purulia district in West Bengal now lead a sedentary life along with various Hindu peasant castes and communities, and are very much tied to the socio-political and economic network of the regional village society. They work as casual and contract labourers for the peasants and make handicrafts like brooms and fish-traps for sale and barter. They also resort to hunting, fishing and gathering and spend much of their time in the surrounding forest with which they have an intimate and moral relationship. Hill-Kharias are aware that the forest resources in the locality are exhausted; they, however, find the forest easy to adjust with because of their traditional relationship with the supernatural entities who are considered to be controlling it (Sinha: 1984:52).

Kadars were a food-gathering nomadic group in the adjacent hills and forests of Cochin and Coimbatore districts, which are now in Kerala and Tamil Nadu states. They were vassals of the kings; they guided the kings through the jungle and assisted them in hunting elephants. Kadars were expert elephant catchers. Some of them have now taken up cultivation, and work as agricultural labourer. Some are basket makers, mat weavers and petty shop owners. A few are engaged in government service as forest guard and peons.

The Asur, an artisan tribe of Chotanagpur areas of east-central India, claim to be descendants of the ancient Asur people. These ancient people were associated with the art of working in metals. They were also the makers of metal relics at the Asur sites in Chotanagpur (Leuva 1964). They were once engaged in hunting, gathering and shifting cultivation. At present, Asurs adopt, for survival, subsistence strategies like iron-smelting, agriculture, hunting and gathering.

The Baiga of Madhya Pradesh are distributed in the forest hill-tracts of Mandla and Balaghat districts. They are also found in small numbers in the districts of Seoni, Chhindwara, Bilaspur, Shadol and Durg. Traditionally they work as village priests and medicine men, catering their specialized service to the neighbouring tribal peoples. At present some of them are engaged in cultivation, animal husbandry, forestry and other occupations. The term 'Baiga' means a priest.

Juangs of Orissa, the swidden cultivators, also do hunting and gathering. They were, in the past, vassals of the kings of Keonjhar and had developed elaborate territorial organization. They used to pay annual tributes to their Rajas and supply choirs used for pulling the Cart of Lord Jagannath. The Rajas, in turn, offered turbans, clothes and other gifts to their Sardars. Some Juangs have now taken up basketry, a bamboo-craft as their occupation and live close to peasant villages; some have also switched over to settled plough cultivation in the plains where they live in multi-ethnic villages.

The Kondh, another shifting-cultivator tribe, living in the districts of Koraput and Kondhmal of Orissa is divided into different sections, each with a distinct ethnic identity. In the past the Kondh, like the Juang, also operated within the broad political framework of the regional Hindu kings and maintained their cultural autonomies with close links to forests. In the context of the nation-state organization of modern India the Kondhs have recently carved out a separate territory of their own, known as Kondhmal (land of the Kondh), in an effort to assert their new tribal identity, and are constructing a culture of their own in which their traditional links to the forests and the ancient kings of the area is reinforced.

Socio-Cultural Distinctiveness of the PTGs and Their Identity with the Forest

All the tribal groups described here adopt multiple survival strategies with specialization in one or two occupations and maintain an essential economic articulation with other tribal and non-tribal caste peoples with differing economies in a particular region. They occupy complementary ecological niches. Among many of these groups, hunting and gathering have formed the core of a mode of subsistence which is highly fluid. Fluidity in social organization is also obvious among other primitive tribal groups. All the groups allow individual as well as family autonomy and any individual or family may move from one place to another for work, for urge to meet relatives and also for freedom and pleasure. Foraging constitutes an integral part of their way of life.

The so-called 'primitive' tribal peoples have attachment not to any particular abode in the forest but to the forest itself, and this promotes, in a way, their mobility. In the Islands the particular settlements or hamlets are seen by the primitive tribal groups as parts of a mythic landscape where forests, animals, rocks, seas, winds, rains and storms are in a relation of contiguity. The frequency of movement among the hunters and gatherers range from weekly in Pandaram encampments, through every four weeks among the Birhor, seasonally among the Ongee and up to every year or so among the Nayakas.

The peoples' social organization, however, involves a bond of kinship, which Barnard (2001) would call 'universal kinship'. This kinship bondage with fellow humans and the forest and its beings help maintain their ethnic distinctiveness.

A close probe into the ethno-history of the contemporary primitive tribal groups of mainland India would reveal that many of them are off-shoots of large tribes who in the past practiced shifting cultivation in combination with hunting and gathering in the forest-hills. The social organization of shifting cultivator-tribes is characterized by a clan-lineage based segmentary social structure with an elaborate territorial system. The kin segments are simultaneously autonomous and complementary to one another. There is flexibility in the social organization, and individuals and families have freedom to move from one village to another. It is quite possible that many of the contemporary hunter-gatherer and other tribal groups, now designated as 'primitive tribal groups' were in the past the autonomous segments of some large tribes, and later formed individual ethnic identities with different occupations in complementary ecological niches. The Birhor, for instance, have clans similar to those of the Santal and other groups of Mundari family of tribes of Bihar, who in the past practiced shifting cultivation in the forest-hills of Chotanagpur. Each of the groups of the Cholanaickan is identified with the territory it occupies. The Cholanaickans who were ascribed by the local non-tribal as kings of forests divided the territories among themselves pursuing hunting and gathering in combination with other occupational strategies for survival. Naickan means kings. To the non-tribals of the region all the tribes in the forest-hills of Kerala, Tamil Nadu and Karnataka are Naickans. The non-tribals, Bhanu writes, 'never distinguish a Panyan from a Kattunaickan. All are Naickan to them' (1989:41). Bhanu also observes that in the initial stage the Kattunaickan were identified as the Cholanaickan. This points to a possibility of fissioning a large tribe into smaller groups.

Shifting cultivation in the mainland of India was pursued by the tribal peoples in combination not only with hunting and gathering but also with various sorts of jungle-based crafts, magico-religious expertise and service specializations of different sorts, with articulation to the neighbouring Hindu caste-peasants and the market economy of the larger society. But with the penetration of outside population and the introduction of the State's forest reservation policies into the tribal areas when shifting on hill slopes became untenable, some of the families took up foraging in the forests and other sorts of occupational strategies while a large number of families switched over to plough cultivation in the plains or other occupations within the broad framework of the agro-economic structure of the caste-based Hindu society. In different tribal belts these processes of expansion, displacement absorption and socioeconomic transformation have been going on since long. But the tribal groups have always operated as parts of the systems of the regional economy occupying complementary niche; they maintained essential economic articulation with caste-peasants and market economy of the larger society, yet perpetuated their intimate linkage to forests and sociocultural distinctiveness in the regional systems. The way and manner the people organize their life and activity reflects their social and cultural reflexivity. They carefully persisted their distinct identity with fellow humans, ancestors, forests, mythic landscape, time and heritage reflecting their social and cultural reflexivity.

Forest is manifest significantly in the habitat, economy, society and worldview of all the peoples. The peoples identify themselves with forests within and with which they live. The Birhor call themselves 'men of the jungle', Cholanaickans, kings of the forest, the Chenchu means 'a person who lives under a Chettu (tree)'.

These people perceive forests, hills, stones, as neighbouring moral agents and in a sense, as relatives and kin. They are regarded as entities with life and as con-substantial to themselves and other visible and non-visible objects. The Nayaka, the Pandaram and the Palyan are particularly concerned with mountains and hill beings (Morris 1981, Gardner 1991, Bird-David 1996). The Chenchu relate specially to stones. Onges show special concern with wind spirits, and spirits of such phenomena as earthquakes, thunder, rainbows and storms which signal the wind's departure and arrival (Pandya 1993). The Birhor are specifically concerned with the deities presiding over monkeys and langurs as well as those controlling rain and storms.

The 'primitive' tribal peoples share their lives with their ancestor-spirits and 'other-than-human persons' in neighbouring time and space. They commonly view their continuity and wellbeing as contingent upon such relations, neglect of which leads to disease and other mishaps. Health and wellbeing require communication with the spiritual realm, and the healing of such relationships. Spirit-possession is a practice associated with this goal. Typically, it involves frequent, spontaneous, and informal conversation with the spirits. Onges and Chenchus traditionally diagnose dreams; Onges, Nayakas, Palyans, and Chenchus also use divinatory means of various sorts to gear up most of their life-centric activities.

The principal ceremonial activities of the 'primitive' tribal groups, specifically the hunter-gatherer groups, involve socializing with forests and forest-beings. They express joy, and communicate with them through various gestures and feel communion with the forest. Through their various ceremonies a sense of collective identity is produced and reproduced: an identity woven from relationships with fellow-humans and forest-beings. The fabric of communal life, as much as the reproduction of a distinctive identity is embedded in their sustaining intimacy with the forest and its beings.

Although hunter-gatherer and other primitive tribal groups no longer draw their material subsistence solely from the forest, they lean heavily on it for moral support of their life and culture. The primitive tribal groups as stated above, in the course of their interaction with the caste-peasants and market economy of the larger society have developed economic, social and even political consensus at the local level. The neighbouring villagers, tribal as well as non-tribal, have a strong belief in supernaturalism and they consider these forest-dwelling peoples as 'mystic' and expert in divination. The people concede the rank accorded to them by the neighbouring peoples and simple reinforce the 'jungle image'. They strategically put on a mystic cover on their life-style, and carefully trade their magico-religious expertise to the neighbouring peoples. Many of the Birhor families are found to develop ceremonial kinship ties as well as *guru-sishya* (patron-client) relationship with the peasant villagers. All these help the people reinforce their identity with the forest, and reproduce the social distinctiveness in a meaningful way.

It may be noted in this context that the animistic ideas of the tribal groups constitute a substantive part of popular Hinduism. The rural Hindus, like the 'primitive' tribes, regard the natural objects as incarnates of supernatural power or deities in themselves. Spirit-possession is also a common phenomenon prevalent in ritual performances of the Hindu caste-peasants in rural India. Animism, spirit-possession, and the forest thus provide a commensurable space for viable economic and socio-cultural interaction between the Hindu and the forest communities. The Palyans' austere forest life is looked upon by their Tamil neighbours as a path to purity (Gardner 1982). The Hindus' and the forest-peoples' perspectives do not clash; instead, these lead to a situation of syncretism, and provide a common cultural space for meaningful communication and participation.

We, indeed, do not have uniform ethnographic information about all the primitive tribal groups of India for comparison. It may, however, be noted from the above description that these people generally live at subsistence level with little desire for surplus production and accumulation of wealth. Their social organization is flexible and the people enjoy much autonomy of individual and family, yet valuing their kinship bondage with humans, neighbouring forests and their beings. In their perspective, Man, Nature and Super-nature are not separate entities; they are bounded together to form a moral community.

The worldview of the primitive peoples is, however, not static; it is dynamic and new experiences are constantly woven together to form their total worldview. Although worldview of the people is highly reflexive, it always involves an orientation of participation in the reality. Their participation to the reality conveys a felt relation between self and society, and all other elements of the phenomenal world. The primitive tribal groups, their kin, relatives, friends forests and also to quote Hallowell's phrase, the 'other-than-human persons', are not only in a relation of contiguity but also in one of existential immediacy, and their participation is geared primarily in terms of 'sympathetic immediacy, performative speech acts, and ritual actions'. The pattern of socioeconomic and cultural interaction of the primitive groups with neighbouring Hindu caste-peasants and other communities may also be framed meaningfully in terms of the dialogue of participation developed over time and space.

'Primitive' Tribal Groups in Nation-State Contexts

The primitive tribal groups who have shown tremendous resiliency yet participating in barter, trade and exchange within a developed economy and society have, however, been under great pressure in the modern nation-state organization of India. The situation described here continued almost as such till the British colonial rule in India when the tribal peoples in general were considered 'primitive' and hence, were kept more or less in 'isolation' or at the periphery of the mainstream of the British administration. The situation, however, became worse after India's Independence when we started to build our nation through rapid economic and political modernization in the Western-oriented perspective. This perspective of development ignored the historical depth of the tribal cultures of the land, their long participation in the structure and continuity of the Hindu civilization of India, and above all, the peoples' tremendous potentiality in social production and reproduction over space and time. For consideration of development the Government of Independent India, through its various Five-year plans and different Commissions, has identified 'primitive tribal groups' as a special category of backward people living in comparative isolation from, or marginal to, the economic and political mainstream of modern India. This Western-oriented perspective of India's development policy, however, ignored their century-old articulation to the regional as well as the classical level of the socio-economic and cultural organization of the Hindus in pre-British, pre-modern India. Occasional attempts were thus made to 'help them develop', usually into a settled agricultural modernity (by giving them permanent housing, plots of land, seeds, and instruction). Regional 'development' in the form of new plantations, roads, dams, and national parks and reserves was also taken up. All these policies and programmes only exerted pressures on these peoples distancing them from their home base in forest, and severing their prevailing economic, socio-political and cultural ties to the neighbouring ethnic groups of the locality.

In many 'new states', indigenous voices are raised to resist modernizing forces and to preserve the peoples' identity with the forest. The Vedda or Wanniyayala-aetto of Sri Lanka identify themselves as "forest beings". But towards the end of the last century when forest destruction started on the pretext of modernization and the people were forced out of the forest, they claimed at the United Nations in Geneva for 'the right to maintain their lives as "forest-beings": the right to formal recognition as a people and a culture, located back in the forest they call home' (Stegeborn, 1999: 272). Despite essential contact with outside peoples the Chenchu also had chosen 'to remain in the forest and subsist on wild roots, tubers and berries, and the occasional game killed with bow and arrow' (Furer-Haimendorf 1969: 17). The Birhor and the Pandaram resisted attempts to sedentarize them away from forest (Adhikary 1999; Morris 1999).

When Palyan, the Pandaram and the Onges have been provided with permanent housing by the government and welfare agents, most of them moved to forest huts. The Birhor have preferred to remain in the forest, even though it has been depleted by outside exploiters. Palyans sometimes move closer to the fringes of the forest and of Tamil society, but these are oscillations, movements from and back to forest life.

Concluding Remarks

It is evident from the above description that despite small numerical strength and scarce resource base the so-called tribal peoples of India had, and still have tremendous capability in social production and reproduction, and have continued to maintain an effective structure of participation with nature and other men in regional contexts. In the wider context of nation-state of India also they are, consciously or unconsciously, weaving their experiences to culturally construct a distinct self and society for recognition of the public as well as the State. There is, in fact, an enduring process of cultural construction for an identity of social significance. Considering the historical depth of their cultures and social dynamics these tribal groups can no longer be defined either as a primitive and marginal people or as an 'essentially backward and irretrievable other'. We are to project ourselves at the human plane and define them in terms of their potentiality as a group of Homo sapiens engaged in the process of culture construction in specific environmental contexts.

The Hindus of ancient India initiated a process of development and integration through conservation and adopted, among other things, a cultural policy for the developing of a socioeconomic consensus with the indigenous peoples of the land. The consensus was arrived at gradually through a process of universalization of the tribal customs and rules allowing ample scope for cultural autonomy of individual groups. Plurality in ancient Indian national policy for development was highly standardized, and made culturally significant. The tribal peoples' conceptualization of, and relationship with, man, nature and the supernature were conserved, and codified in the Great Tradition of the Hindu civilization. The Hindus like the tribal peoples had a predominant orientation of participation to the cosmos, and they both shared a culture of participation with other men, nature and supernature.

It may, however, be noted here that despite the economic and cultural consensus these tribal peoples often feel that they are looked down upon by the neighbouring Hindu caste-peasants, and are accorded low position in the local social hierarchy. They concede the rank but carefully construct their worldview to reinforce a distinct social-image and self-identity that can be publicly acknowledged in the neighbouring society. The Birhor of Orissa, for instance, strategically act as magico-religious experts to the local peasants who have strong belief in supernaturalism by careful manipulation of the peasants' impression about them as a mystic jungle people, and reinforce their life-style and linkage to forests. In the contexts of the constitutional provisions and welfare measures of modern nation-states of India these tribal groups show much resilience in the adaptation as well as rational thinking; in modern India the people seem to feel the lack not only of their distinct 'self-image' but also an arena of meaningful participation. They search for an identity and engage themselves in a process of culture construction for a secure social position in the larger economic and political milieu. Among the primitive tribal groups the position of the human person is perceived within a continuous relational universe, and the human person comes into being within a comprehensive field of relations with human as well as non-human universe including land and forests.

2

Hunter-Gatherer Tribes of India: Survival Strategies

Introduction

Studies of hunter-gatherers play a central position in the building of anthropological concepts and theory. Hunting and gathering as a strategy for survival has, in fact, been the human way of life for about 90 percent of human history (Lee, R.B. & I. DeVore 1968), and in the course of time there has developed an enormous body of ethnographic literature on hunting and gathering tribes. Hunter-gatherers are normally treated as an archaic base of human development and their manner of existence as a primitive mode of survival. This broad conceptual framework of social evolutionism led most of the earlier ethnographers to the reconstruction of an ideal-type of 'primitive society' from among the contemporary hunter-gatherers (Boas 1988; Furer-Haimendorf 1943; Kroeber 1925; Roy 1925; Seligmann and Seligmann 1911). Hunting and gathering has been said to have represented a state of 'original affluence' or a 'natural form' of human condition. Many scholars have also pointed to the possibility of 'primitive communism' or 'sexual egalitarianism' among hunter-gatherers (Begler 1978; Leacock 1978; Lee 1982).

Later on, the persistence of this mode of subsistence over a wide range of ecological conditions induced ethnographers to study particular cultures and their adaptation to natural ecology (Bichhieri 1972; Lee and DeVore 1968) Steward 1955; Service 1962). Unlike earlier ethnographers, who made an ideological construction of hunting-gathering society as 'natural form' these later scholars were interested in the organizational dynamics of techno-economic activities in the local contexts of ecology. The emphasis of these studies was on the delineation of hunting and gathering society as a structural-functional whole emerging from the interaction between its subsistence technology and the surrounding environment. In all these accounts hunter-gatherers have been treated primarily as 'primitive isolates' adapted to an undifferentiated natural environment. Subsequent descriptions were made as if to fit examples into the frame of the chosen 'ecological paradigm'.

Among the hunter-gatherers of the temperate zone there is noticed a mix of subsistence activities. But Lee (1968) explains the situation primarily in terms of changes in the natural ecology and points out that there is an emphasis among the people on gathering rather than hunting. Contact and economic interaction of hunter-gatherers with other groups and the resultant opportunistic changes in subsistence activities were not taken into consideration by these scholars. A careful reading of the ethnographic reports reveals, however, that hunting and gathering tribes in the contemporary situation cannot be treated in complete isolation and that their natural ecology has not been left undisturbed. Almost all hunting and gathering communities have been and are in contact with others that have different levels of techno-economic culture, and these have influenced their mode of livelihood. In many contexts the hunting and gathering mode of subsistence is also found to be a case of secondary adaptation.

Putnam (1950) points out an instance of regular economic symbiosis between the Pygmy hunters of the Ituri forest in Africa and their neighbours, Negro planters. The pygmies give honey and meat to the Negroes in exchange of plantains. He observes, however, that the relationship is based on an 'ethnic division of labour' and that 'there is no strict process of barter involved'. There are also hunters who are 'failed agriculturalists' or who 'devolved' from a higher level of techno-economic culture (Lathrap 1968; Sinha 1969). Sinha observes that the adoption of hunting and gathering mode of subsistence by tribal groups on the mainland of India is a case of 'secondary primitivization' or 'devolution'. He points out that the encroachment of the caste-based economy and forest regulations of the State forced many tribal groups that were shifting cultivators on the hill slopes in east-central India to adopt 'hunting and gathering' as a survival strategy.

Through a careful probe into the historical situation of hunter-gatherers in the tropical zones of South-America Lathrap points out that 'many, perhaps all of these simple and less sedentary groups are degraded descendants of people who, at one time, maintained an advanced form of tropical culture'. Recently, Gordon (1984), basing himself on an ethno-historical study of the Kung in the Kalahari region, notes that 'hunting- gathering may historically have represented a significant strategy of resistance' to external forces. Similarly, Myers (1988) considers that the prehistoric hunter-gatherers of the Connecticut River Valley took refuse from, or actively resisted, intensification.

The subsistence strategies of hunter-gatherers, therefore, need to be studied not only in the context of natural ecology but also in that of contact and interaction with the larger techno-economic environment. Reports that refer to hunter-gatherers' interaction with the outside world note primarily the manner in which they have perpetuated their hunting and gathering strategies or how they have responded to the contemporary social and physical environment. Such studies did not, however, take into consideration the peoples' attitudes and notions towards the outside world.

Recently some attempts have been made to investigate the local meanings of interaction with the outside world (Bird-David 1982, 1983; Gardner 1985; Morris 1982). But the persistence of a survival strategy cannot be properly understood merely as a system of material interaction. The outlook towards life, or world-view, in the context of which the people often persist with their strategies must also be considered (Adhikary 1984). The adoption of a strategy may be due to forces from the physical or social environment but a human group's persisting relationship with it must be backed by shared cultural values.

Two Categories of the Hunter-Gatherers and their Relation to the Environments

Hunter-gatherers in India do not constitute even one percent of her total tribal population. There are, however, 20-22 distinct tribal groups who still pursue, for their subsistence, hunting and gathering in some form. The numerical strength of these groups ranges from a few individuals to a few thousand, and their distribution is mainly along the forest-clad regions of northeastern and southern India. Hunter-gatherers are also found in east-central regions of India, and beyond the mainland, in the Andaman and Nicobar Islands. These communities appear to be more concentrated in the southern part of India.

The hunting and gathering tribes of India may be broadly categorized into two groups: the 'primitive' or 'primary' and the 'symbiotic' or 'secondary'. Although all of these hunting and gathering groups have some experience of contact with external forces, their exposure to them varies and there are differences in the extent and nature of contact and economic articulation with the larger society. While explicating the 'multicentric scales and networks of Indian Civilization' Sinha (1978) observes that there are two levels of scales among India's hunter-gatherers. He includes the hunter-gatherers of the Andaman Islands at the level of 'primitive' and those in the mainland of India, at the level of 'symbiosis'. He notes that hunter-gatherers of the Andaman Islands are, or until recently were, more or less isolated and self-sufficient in their economy, while those on the mainland have for long maintained a regular and essential economic symbiosis with the settled peasantry and the market economy of the surrounding larger society.

The hunting and gathering of the peoples of the Islands is, in fact, their primary means of subsistence adapted to the physical environment and has been traditionally descended to them while that of the mainland in India is necessarily a secondary adaptation of the peoples.

Primary Hunters

Of the hunter-gatherers in the Andaman and Nicobar Islands mention may be made of the Jarawa, the Sentinelese, the Onge, the Great Andamanese and the Shompen. Only a few ethnographic reports are available on these communities, which are also small in numbers. In an earlier estimation, the population of the Onge was recorded as 108 and that of the Jarawas as 250 (Pandit 1982 :183-184). Recently the population of the Onge is reported to have come down to 98 and that of the Jarawa, to 200 (Basu 1990; Pandit 1990).

The Jarawa live in the western coastal and forest reserves of the South and Middle Andaman Islands. They had experienced several unpleasant encounters in the past and in course of time developed an attitude of hostility towards outside people. The Sentinelese who live in the north Sentinel Island are 'yet in a condition when they have absolutely no contact with outsiders'. Their exact population is not known. 'Once, thirty eight adult men were counted when an attempt was made to land there' (Bose 1971: 269). Recently their population has been estimated at 80-100 (Pandit 1990).

Compared to the Jarawa and the Sentinelese the Onge are more exposed to the larger society. Their former ecology has also been disturbed to some extent. The exposure of the Onge is, in fact, due to measures introduced by the Government India. In spite of this contact, 'the Onge live by hunting, fishing and the collection of wild produce, like berries or honey from the forest. Formerly, and even now, they have no trade with any other people' (Pandit 1990: 268). The Onge seem to have divided themselves into two endogamous clusters: forest-dwellers and coast-dwellers. This strategic device gives ample scope for the appropriation of the available natural resources for their survival.

Similar adaptive strategies are found among other hunting and gathering groups of the Andaman and Nicobar Islands. Mention may also be made of the Great Andamanese and the Shompen. There are only 28 individuals among the Great Andamanese who now live in an officially constructed enclave on the Strait Island off the eastern coast of Middle Andaman. Under the changed environmental condition the people combine their hunting, gathering and fishing strategy with pig rearing and the care of plantations, activities introduced by the Government.

The Shompen whose population is estimated at 214, live in the Great Nicobar Island. They too combine hunting, gathering and fishing with pig rearing and horticulture. They are reported to have a long tradition of barter relations with the coastal Nicobarese (Kloss 1903). At present the Shompen barter honey, lemon, megapode eggs, sea-shells and so on with the coastal Nicobarese and the local administration. They maintain their material transactions with other communities in a very strategic manner. It is observed that the Shompen of Alexandria and Degmar barter with the Nicobarese of Kopenheat while those of Badueyon and Dakoyen exchange what they collect with the villagers living between Kosintooth in the north and Kotinjong in the south (Rizvi: 1990:45).

Secondary or Symbiotic Hunters

While the hunter-gatherers of the Andaman and Nicobar Islands live in a comparatively isolated natural habitat and maintain a self-sufficient economy, those of the mainland display a regular economic symbiosis with the peasants and the market-based economy of the larger society. Bose (1956) points out that 'the Birhor (literally, 'men of the forest') of southern Bihar and northern Orissa have now practically become an appendage of the rural economic system of the caste villages.' He observes that the Birhor, having come in contact with the peasants of the neighbouring villages, have specialized 'in some industries based on jungle produce'. Since they do not get permanent patronage in any one village they are converted into a 'nomadic caste' and form a complement to the 'non-competitive productive system' of the caste-based Hindu society. Similar observations were also made by Sinha (1968).

Based on secondary sources of ethnographic information Fox (1968) also points out caste-like occupational specializations among five hunting and gathering tribes of India: Birhor, Chenchu, Kadar, Nayadi, and Vedda.

A close probe into the nature of their articulation would, however, reveal that despite their essential economic interaction with the settled peasantry and market economy, many of the hunter-gatherers on the Indian mainland carefully maintain their social and cultural boundaries and retreat into their traditional jungle environment. This is possible where there is a suitable ecological base of jungle resource to fall back upon.

Mention may be made of the Birhor in the district of Sundargarh, Orissa, where I made an intensive field investigation during the period between 1971 and 1976. In the course of my study I found that, broadly, the Birhor operate between two ecological terrains: the natural ecology, comprising the jungle and the social ecology, comprising the settled peasantry around them. The whole range of their survival strategy is, in fact, centred on the collection of jungle produce and the perpetuation of a regular economic symbiosis with the neighbouring village society. The Birhor exchange jungle produce for cash and paddy But the forest ecology on which they depended for their resources is also exploited by the neighbouring village communities. In order to avoid any direct conflict and maintain their essential economic interaction with the settled peasantry the Birhor, therefore, exploit the forest resources in a selective, calculated manner and adopt diverse occupational strategies. All their occupations are, however, centred around forest resources, of which they have traditional knowledge based on intimate association (Adhikary: 1974).

The Birhor are now found to be concerned primarily with the collection of the jungle creeper, bauhinia, and with the hunting of wild monkeys, occupations in which other people are seldom involved. They prepare different kinds of ropes and rope-products from the bark of these creepers and are specialized in this craft. These products are then exchanged with the villagers for necessaries. The hunting of monkeys and other small wild games is pursued occasionally and that to procure meat for consumption. Live monkeys and langur skins are also sold when the opportunity presents itself. Hunting does not, in fact, contribute much to their economy; but the Birhor still keep up the spirit of hunting as a cultural norm (Adhikary: 1984:85). Their way of life is nomadic and they live in temporary leaf huts at the edge of some forest. While making an encampment they also keep in view the vicinity of peasant villages and market centres.

In the course of their regular economic interaction with the neighbouring Hindu peasantry the Birhor experience some odd encounters that insulate them and keep them at a distance. They have learnt that they are placed low in the local social hierarchy and looked down upon by the caste people. The larger society often ridicules them for eating the meat of monkeys and treats them as 'nasty' and 'unclean'. The Birhor carefully manage the impressions of the local people and strategically adjust with these situations. They accept the subordinate position accorded to them and cleverly maintain occupational and social distance from the low Hindu castes and avoid certain food items that are considered polluting in the local Hindu society. Owing to their simple way of life in close association with the forest they are also regarded as experts in magico-religious activities. The Birhor make careful and rational use of these notions and occasionally work for the villagers as magico-religious experts.

The worldview of the Birhor reveals that they clearly distinguish a world, *disum,* their own territory in forests from *muluk,* the world of the larger society. They identify themselves as *hor,* 'men' or 'people', as against *diku,* aliens and foreigners. Not all the people other than themselves are included in the category of *diku*. Ethnic groups like the Mundari, the Bhuiya, and the Kurmi Mahato are often called *horhon,* that is, akin to *hor.* Their adaptive strategies are determined by these two sets of environment: a morally ordered gemeinschaft in *disum,* their own forest territory, and a rationalist-utilitarian gesellschaft orientation in muluk, the territory dominated by caste-peasants and the market economy.

There is a significant continuity between the human world of the Birhor and the natural and supernatural universe of their conception. They consider the jungle their home and describe themselves as Birhor, "man of the jungle'. The different social segments of the Birhor still claim to have their traditional homes in forest-clad high ground. Every phenomenon in the jungle is considered animated and presided over by some supernatural deity or *bonga.* The ancestral spirits of the Birhor, *hapram,* live in close association with these *bonga.* The Birhor think that the *hapram* and the *bonga* are responsible for giving them children and prosperity.

It is evident that in the changing contexts of modernization the technoeconomic activities of the Birhor extend far beyond the natural universe of the jungle ecology into the environment of the larger market-based society. With this, elements of their worldview have undergone change. In the course of their confrontation with the larger society they have gathered much experience, but this is not meaningfully integrated into their traditional way of life. Instead, these new experiences help the Birhor reinforce their special relation with the jungle ecology, in the context of which they find their lives socially and culturally meaningful. Although there have been some significant changes in the nature of their dependence on the forest ecology, the Birhor still form a world of their own in which they are bound together with the jungle and with supernatural phenomena.

Anandabhanu observed two distinct spheres of subsistence activity among the Cholanaickan of Malappuram district in Kerala: one, geared to their own consumption and the other, to barter and exchange for cash and paddy. 'They gather tubers, roots, fruits, berries, leaves and also fish, and hunt small games for self-consumption. For exchange they collect minor forest produce like dammer, honey, ginger, soap-seed, tree-bark, cardamom, astringent fruit, etc.' (Anandabhanu 1982: 219). Many external agencies are found to have encroached upon their traditional jungle terrain, as a consequence of which their access to it has become somewhat restricted. The Cholanaickan, who have a fair knowledge of the forest ecology and habitual skill in hunting and gathering, have, however, carefully adapted themselves to their contact with the larger society. Despite their contact with the market-based economy, they still move in the interior of the forest and inhabit natural caves on the bank of the small tributaries there.

The Jenu Kuruba who live in the forest areas of Mysore and Coorg districts of Karnataka also operate within two sets of environment. Traditionally, they have depended on food gathering and honey collection in the interior of dense forests. But most of their forest habitat has come to be surrounded by peasant villages and they have to maintain an essential economic interaction with the larger society. During lean periods they work in the fields of the neighbouring peasants. They go to the local shops and make transactions both in cash and in kind. They take ragi or paddy in exchange for the tubers and honey that they collect in the forest. There are some permanent settlements in the area for the Jenu Kuruba, but their membership is constantly changing (Misra: 1977). In spite of changes these people maintain their intimate association with the forest.

The Hill Kharia in Purulia district of West Bengal, unlike the Birhor of Orissa and the Cholanaickan of Kerala, have no effective hold over resources in the forest ecology. They now 'find themselves in a situation where their anchorage to the forest economic base has been rudely uprooted and they have been thrown at the door step of the peasant societies as landless dependent communities' (Sinha 1984: 85-86). The Hill Kharia of this area have experienced, over the years, a gradual decrease of resources in forests, as a result of which there has been an erosion of technology and of the knowledge of ecology among them. They now lead a sedentary life along with various peasant castes and communities, and are very much tied to the socio-political and economic networks of the larger village society. In order to cope with the depleted condition of the forest as well as their present situation of contact, they have adopted various occupational strategies. They often work as casual and contract agricultural labourers for the villagers and make handicrafts like brooms and fish-traps for sale and barter. They also resort to hunting, fishing and gathering.

Mention may be made here of their specific adaptation to the collection of paddy grains from the rat-holes in the harvested fields. The annual calendar of the subsistence strategies of the Hill Kharia in this region shows that much of their time and energy are spent in hunting, fishing and gathering in the surrounding forest, with which they still seem to have an intimate and moral relationship. As Sinha observes, 'although the Hill Kharia realize that the forest resources are more or less exhausted, emotionally they find the forest (more easy) to adjust with because the supernatural power which reigns over the domain of food in the forest can easily be comprehended with the help of their cultural idioms' (Sinha 1984: 52).

In the course of their regular and essential economic articulation with the settled peasantry the Hill Kharia have learnt that they are stigmatized as a 'criminal people' by the larger society and are given a low social position in the local hierarchy. They also suffer from a sense of 'relative deprivation'. Although they lead a sedentary village life and participate in the local festivals of badhna parab (cattle worship) and gajan they do not belong to the moral order of the village society.

The Chenchu are a nomadic food-gathering tribe mainly concentrated in the Nallamalai forests and the plateau of Abradabad in Andhra Pradesh. However, they are, no longer, isolated. They live in close contact with Hindu caste-peasants and the market economy of the larger society, and have adopted diverse occupational pursuits to supplement their traditional food gathering economy. Besides working as forest labour some Chenchus have also adopted agriculture. They also rear animals like goats, sheep and cattle for ritual sacrifice as well as for milk and meat. They are expert in weaving bamboo mats, wattle baskets, etc. These baskets and mats are made mainly for household use, although in places they are also sold (Bhowmick 1989: 92). A few Chenchus are also employed by the government on a salary basis.

In the course of their long interaction with the larger world the Chenchu developed a kind of symbiotic relationship with the neighbouring caste-peasants and with the Hindu pilgrims who visited Srisailam. The Chenchus watch over the fields and guard the crops of the non-tribal cultivators' land bordering the forest. The cultivators pay them in grains for these services. This practice has been in vogue for generations, and the system is known as *mirasi*. In the past, before construction of the Srisailam-Dornal-Atmakur Highway, Hindu pilgrims used to come to Srisailam on foot through the jungle route. Pilgrimages took place especially at Mahashivaratri in February and Bramaramba in March. At that time the route was full of dangers and the Chenchu, who had a fair knowledge of the jungle terrain, were often employed to guide and protect the pilgrims and their belongings. For these services the Chenchu were paid in cash. This system was known as *metta mirasi* (Chandra

Sekhar : 1965). Since the construction of the State Highway, buses ply to Srisailam and pilgrims no longer need the help of the Chenchu. The government, however, continues to pay some *metta* fees to the Chenchu *mirasidars* through the Forest Department (Bhowmick: 1989).

Chenchus spend much of their time and energy in the collection of forest produce for direct consumption. Their food habits indicate the importance of their gathering and collecting economy (Bhowmick 1989:94, 98). Despite their essential articulation with the larger society 'they have chosen to remain in (the) forest and subsist on wild roots, tubers and berries, and the occasional game killed with bow and arrow' (Furer-Haimendorf 1969:17). The life-style of the neighbouring Hindu farmers has not had any considerable impact on their general worldview, which is integrated with their gathering economy in the jungle ecology.

Recently, Morris has shown how the religious worldview of the Hill Pandaram, a hunting and gathering tribe of southern India, is integrated with their jungle habitat and economy in spite of their economic and cultural articulation with the wider Hindu society. He notes the various gods and spirits as conceptualized by the Hill Pandaram and studies their nature of relationship with them. He finds that 'the spiritual agencies recognized by the Hill Pandaram fall into three broad categories: the ancestral ghosts or spirits *(chavu)*, the mountain spirits *(mala devi)* and the gods of the Hindu pantheon. The spiritual agencies of the third category and the myths and rites associated with them have little significance for the Hill Pandaram'. The Hindu deities are looked upon 'as alien spirits who have little concern for the welfare of the people' (Morris 1981: 214).

Adaptive Relevance of Socio-Cultural Integration

In the foregoing pages a description has been given of

the survival strategies of some of the so-called hunting and gathering tribes in contemporary India. It is evident from our description that most of the hunter-gatherer tribes in India are now exposed to the outside world and are pushed into situations of mixed economy. They can, no longer, depend exclusively on their traditional natural ecology. They have to adopt diverse occupational strategies for their survival.

However, two distinct spheres of subsistence activity are observed: one, geared to self-consumption based on hunting, gathering and fishing in their natural ecology and the other, the barter and exchange for food and cash in the milieu of the larger society. Their traditional resource base, the jungle, is either encroached upon or shared by other ethnic groups or, has become subject of government regulations. As a result of this the contemporary hunting and gathering tribes in the mainland of India have been thrown into the threshold of the techno-economic culture of the neighbouring caste-peasants and the market economy. In the midst of the new environment many of the hunter-gatherers are now found to work as agricultural labourers, magico-religious experts, and sometimes as stigmatized pawns in the village disputes among different rival groups of peasants.

It is observed that in situations of contact many hunter-gatherer groups often approximate the status of professional caste-groups. Bose (1941) notes that many tribal groups having found a suitable alternative for their techno-economy within the regional 'non-competitive productive system' of the Hindu caste society in villages, have either adopted settled cultivation in the plains or have taken caste-like occupational specialization. The adoption by the Birhor of jungle-based crafts combined with hunting and gathering is cited as an example. What Bose is emphasising here is that certain tribal groups are being slowly and spontaneously absorbed into the traditional Hindu caste mode of production in which they may retain their cultural autonomy.

From the available studies of hunting and gathering tribes in contact situations, however, we find that the interaction of these people with caste-peasants and the market economy is primarily instrumental and guided by material or economic interests. Their social relationships hinge around their economic transaction (Adhikary 1974). Though they have to maintain an essential economic interaction with the larger society, they seem to live in dynamic isolation and do not belong to the moral community of the caste-based village society.

In direct confrontation with the socio-cultural environment of the larger society the Birhor of Orissa have come to learn not only that they are looked down upon by the people there but also that they have little grip over the culturally defined meaning of life. They turn back towards their jungle terrain where they feel free and find a meaningful world of their own. Under the changing life-situations they often create myths keeping in consonance with their jungle-based activities. The Birhor are expert in hunting monkeys with nets; but the neighbouring peasants think that this is almost an impossible task. They say that the Birhor have magical powers, that they utter spells and touch the trees, as a result of which monkeys come down with folded hands and enter their nets. The Birhor are well aware of this and carefully sustain this mystical image.

The Birhor also create new myths to cope with changing life-situations. They often tell a story asserting their expertise in monkey hunting. It runs as follows: 'Long ago, Ram and Sita tried to catch monkeys in the jungle but could not succeed. The monkeys even broke through their iron nets. At last they came across the Birhor and asked for their help. The Birhor then made nets of fibres and trapped monkeys'. There is, in fact, a strong belief in the supernatural among the settled Hindu peasantry in the area, who consider the Birhor expert in magico-religious activities. Their knowledge of the large society helps the Birhor reinforce their special relation to the forest ecology in their contemporary life-situation.

The Hill Kharia of Purulia, do not have any resource base in their forest ecology to fall back upon. Although they lead a sedentary village life they remain at the fringes of the Hindu caste society and keep to their cultural idiom, their traditional survival strategy of hunting, gleaning and fishing. They strategically maintain a cover of mysticism around themselves, which gives them a distinct socio-cultural identity.

The Birhor and the Hill Kharia in east-central India, the Jenu Kuruba, the Soliga and the Cholanaickan in southern India are, in fact, secondary hunters. In the past they practised shifting cultivation combined with hunting and gathering on the forest-clad hill-slopes. Many of these contemporary hunting and gathering tribes are also offshoots of larger ethnic groups. What is intended to be conveyed here is that the adoption of the hunting and gathering mode of subsistence by these groups is not a recent phenomenon. The mode of production that was once subsidiary has now become the principal one. In the context of changing life-situations they have only shifted the emphasis from one technology to another. There has been no perceptible change in their total worldview (Adhikary: 1989).

The forest dwelling and the coast-dwelling hunter-gatherer groups of the Andaman and Nicobar Islands have also come in contact with the outside world. Even the Great Andamanese and the Onge who live in settlements constructed by the government endeavour to keep to their traditional life-style by carefully combining the newly introduced subsistence programme with hunting, gathering and fishing. The Jarawa and the Sentinelese adopt a stance of hostility as a survival strategy. It should be noted here that while the Jarawa have had encounters with outsiders with whom they live in close proximity, the Sentinelese live in an isolated island with little interference from outside. They do not permit outsiders into their territory primarily for fear of losing their resource base (Sarkar 1989,1990). The Shompen who have long had a symbiotic relationship with other ethnic groups in the region, carefully preserve a morally-ordered world of their own in close association with their traditional survival strategy of hunting and gathering.

In the course of this description of the survival strategies of hunter-gatherer groups of India, the emphasis has been on their subsistence technology in the broader context of their worldview. It has not been possible to study in detail the manner in which they organize their societies in changing life-situations. With very few exceptions, however, they adopt a nomadic or semi-nomadic way of life. The nuclear family is the norm among all these groups. The band is no longer patrilineal in the strict sense of the term. It is flexible and often comprises families from paternal as well as maternal sides. Families freely move from one band to another. Among the Birhor several bands agglomerate during marriage ceremonies and at other festive occasions, when gatherings of about 125 individuals may be formed. Individuals see themselves as being bound together by kinship ties but there is no centralized political authority.

The worldview of a people is not simply 'a stable and abstract picture of the universe and its meanings'. It may also be seen as 'something constantly in process: a fluctuating assemblage of more or less connected ideas that change as to focus, affective colouring perhaps, the content and choice of connections and emphasis' (Redfield: 1962:281). While hunting and gathering has become less significant in terms of material return, the people adhere to them as a cultural idiom. Despite gradual individualization of units of production and consumption as well as the diversification of economic pursuits, the members of a group feel themselves bound together in communion with nature.

The collective appropriation of resource, a characteristic feature of hunting societies still constitutes the common purpose of the contemporary hunter-gatherer groups in India. Sharing as a cultural norm is deeply ingrained and is not merely distribution at the end of production; it involves the people into the very process of their productive activities (Ingold: 1988). This goes toward forming a worldview that helps a group survive as a distinct socio-cultural entity in changing contexts.

Hunter-Gatherers in the Context of Modernization: Some Observations

It is obvious from foregoing descriptions that despite changes in their traditional habitat and natural resource base in jungles the contemporary hunter-gatherer tribes of India do show considerable skill and power to construct and sustain a distinct and meaningful world of socio-cultural existence. We have, however, noticed that in the course of their essential economic symbiosis with the caste-peasants and market economy of the regional society many of these groups have been directly pushed into the threshold of our national policy of economic development and social welfare. The Onges and the Great Andamanese of Andaman and Nicobar Islands, for instance, are encysted on all sides by the immigrant population groups and development officials and administrators. Their life is now at stake both demographically and economically. It is difficult to predict as to how long they would be able to manage to survive in the context of our ongoing efforts of development. In the mainland of India the forest-dwelling groups like the Chenchu, the Kadar, the Cholanaickan and the Jenu Kuruba are also not in a favourable situation.

Despite the various statutory efforts on the part of our government to rapidly push these economically backward groups into the 'mainstream' of our market-based modern economy and society the conditions of the people are least improved. The forest reservation rules do not allow them to collect forest products as normal right and sell them in the market. Though various co-operative societies and welfare departments are trying to procure the minor forest products through these groups, there has entered into the scene a number of middlemen and private contractors to usurp the resources for trade in the wider market. Subsequently, the people are pushed into a situation of exploitation and deprivation. Bhanu (1989) reports that the traditional resource base in the jungles of the Cholanaickans has already been encroached upon by another community, the Pathynaickan who regularly collect minor forest products from their territory for sale outside in the market. As a result Cholanaickans have to simply retreat into the interior of forests and try to save themselves from the numerically dominant and hostile Pathynaickan. Anand Bhanu also notes that even the local Girijan Cooperative Society fails to appreciate and utilize the Cholanaickan's skilled knowledge of their forest habitat. Similar situations also prevail among the Jenu Kuruba, the Kadar and the Chenchu of southern India. Misra (1977) reports that Jenu Kurubas have a fair knowledge of jungle resources. They can classify honey into multiple categories based on its taste, weight and effect on the body. But while the government fails to appreciate this ability of the people, the forest contractors make huge profits by careful manipulation of the traditional skills of the Jenu Kuruba. Misra also notes, there are about fifteen items that are considered MFP (Minor Forest Products) but the rights of extraction of the products are leased out every year by the Forest Department to outside contractors. No programme has yet been worked out to make proper utilization of these human resources in the forest. In a recent monograph on the Chenchu, Bhowmick (1989) has tried to make a critical evaluation of the various development programmes that have so far been directed to the area in general, and to the people in particular. He notes, the development oriented planners and workers, despite their statutory ambitions, failed to understand the people's creative potentiality and outlook towards life. They only tried to push the people fast into the modern sectors of productive activities in the 'mainstream' of India. Bhowmick says, 'mere goodwill, however, does not suffice. To translate the goodwill into positive action in favour of the target group, it is equally necessary to understand the society and culture of the same, to follow the meaning of their hopes and aspiration, to learn reasons behind their fear and apprehension' (*ibid:* 375).

Attempts have also been made to induce these habitual nomads to a sedentary life and to adopt agriculture. But from the available records on the Birhor of Bihar and the Jenu Kuruba of Mysore we learn that the planned settlements by the governments could not attract these people substantially. The people were found either to oscillate between a sedentary and a nomadic life or to leave it completely. During the second Five-Year Plan a programme for settling the Birhor was taken up at the state level of Bihar. As many as four colonies were set up in four blocks in Bihar where sixty families were induced to settle as agriculturalists. Houses were constructed for them to live in, and land, plough, cattle and cash were provided for their pursuit of agriculture. But it was found that most of them left the colony. Those who remained in the camp did not, however, adopt agriculture; they simply oscillated between two modes of life, the sedentary and the nomadic. It was also reported that the Birhor who had, in fact, no expertise in agriculture were allotted mostly the unfertile and disputed lands in the area. Moreover, the neighbouring villagers became envious of their fortune and threatened the Birhor (Malhotra: 1960). We have, however, seen how carefully and strategically these Birhor in Orissa manipulate their traditional skilled knowledge of the forest ecology and maintain a meaningful socio-cultural existence. Therefore any induced development programme is likely to fail if it is not implemented in consonance with the knowledge and potentiality of the groups concerned.

It is evident from the available reports that proper attention has not been given by the development oriented planners and workers to make an appropriate utilization of the traditional skills and knowledge of the hunting and gathering tribes in India. Instead, economic and development programmes have been fast thrown upon the area with almost no consideration of the human resources therein. In the midst of the new technoeconomic environment the people, therefore, lack a meaningful world of sociocultural communication and show an adaptive resilience. The worldview of the Birhor clearly reflects the picture of such an adaptive relevance of a view of the world where the meaning of their special relation with forest ecology in the contemporary life situation is reinforced. Questions may, however, be raised if the present-day hunter-gatherer's survival strategies are economically viable specifically in the context of the rapid modernization of our national economy and society. It is true that there has already been erosion in their customary resource base in jungles as well as a perceptible attenuation in the effective scale of their society and culture. But the cognition of this is not always reflected in their worldview and outlook towards life. Moreover, their desires and expectations in life are also limited and the concept of good life in economic spheres involves a perceptible this-worldly orientation. In this context I would, therefore suggest that we should adopt the policy of 'development' in such a manner that the skills, knowledge and the creative potentiality of these 'human' groups be meaningfully articulated to the 'composite' technoeconomic culture of the neighbouring peoples in the region. It may be noted here that in the past, specifically, in the pre-colonial and pre-industrial period of India, many of these tribal groups used to maintain economic articulation to the stratified social system of the regional polity from a secure homebase in jungles. For instance, the Kadar and the Jenu Kuruba of southern India, who now seem to suffer from a spirit of despondency, could meaningfully utilize in the past their traditional experience of capturing, taming and driving elephants in the forest for regional polity. Sinha (1983), based on his empirical observation on tribes and Indian civilization, points out that 'Indian sub-continent had worked out over the millennia the experiment of conservation of culture in the pre-colonial and pre-industrial period with extra-ordinary skill and imagination within an unambiguous framework of inter-ethnic interdependence in hierarchic order' (*ibid*: 25). It must be made clear that my plea is not to preserve these people just as a fossilized archaic specimen of Homo sapiens. What I plea here is that the genuine human potentialities of the contemporary hunting and gathering tribes in India be carefully conserved and developed so as to enable them to participate in our national mainstreams under modern conditions.

3

Hunting and Gathering Societies in India: Structure and Transformation

Introduction

Hunter-gatherers are normally considered as an archaic base of human development and their technology—hunting and gathering—is often referred to denote a 'primitive' mode of subsistence (Childe 1951; Morgan 1910; White 1949). Following this broad trend most of the earlier ethnographers were inclined to reconstruct an ideal type of 'primitive society' from and among the contemporary hunters and gatherers (Boas 1888; Furer-Haimendorf 1943; Kroeber 1925; Roy 1925; Seligmann and Seligmann 1911). Later on, prevalence of the communities persisting the hunting and gathering mode of subsistence over a wider range of ecological diversities induced the ethnographers to study particular cultures and their adaptation to the natural ecology (Bichhieri 1972; Lee and DeVore 1972; Steward 1955; Sahlins and Service 1960). Steward *(ibid)* and following him Sahlins and Service *(ibid)* gave attention to the specific adaptation of the subsistence technology of a particular culture to its immediate natural ecology, and subsequently, tried to delineate the structure of that society. Unlike the earlier ethnographers who tried to give an all-round descriptive account of the various items of culture and practices of hunters and gatherers these latter scholars became interested in the organizational aspect of their techno-economic activities in the context of natural ecology. The emphasis of these studies was, however, on the delineation of their society as a structural-functional whole.

Important as these statistical accounts are almost in all the cases the hunters and gatherers are treated mostly as 'primitive' isolates adapted to an undifferentiated natural environment. The ethnographic reports of many different hunting and gathering societies, however, reveal that they cannot be treated in complete isolation. Almost all the hunting and gathering tribes were or even now are in symbiotic relation with communities having different levels of techno-economy. In many contexts the hunting and gathering mode of subsistence has been a secondary adaptation.

Mention may be made here of an instance of regular economic symbiosis between the Pygmy hunters of Ituri forest and their neighbouring Negro planters in Africa (Putnam 1950). The Pygmy gives honey and meat to Negroes in exchange of plantains. Putnam, however, observes that the relationship between the Negroes and the Pygmies is based on an "ethnic division of labour", and 'there is no strict process of barter involved'. There are hunters who are 'failed agriculturalists' or 'devolved' from a higher level of techno-economic culture (Lathrap 1968; Sinha 1969). Sinha observes that the adoption of hunting and gathering mode of subsistence by the tribal groups in the Indian mainland is a case of 'secondary primitivization' or 'devolution'. He pointed out that the encroachment of the caste-based economy and extensive deforestation forced many of the tribal groups who were shifting cultivators on the hill slops in central-east India to specialize in 'hunting and gathering' (*ibid*:164). Through a careful probe into the historical situation of the people in the tropical zones of South America Lathrap points out that 'many, perhaps, all of these simple and less sedentary groups degraded descendants of people who at one time maintained an advanced form of tropical culture' (*ibid* : 25).

It now becomes evident that the hunting and gathering mode of subsistence in the contemporary situation cannot be treated in isolation as a simple adaptation to the natural ecology. Along with natural ecology the aspect of their adaptation to the techno-cultural environment of their neighbouring societies should also be taken into account for a proper understanding of the nature of their present hunting and gathering mode livelihood. Unlike an ideal-typical setting of their natural ecology this new environmental situation provides the hunters with scope for technological alternatives. For the persistence of hunting and gathering mode of subsistence in this context the hunters would, therefore, require a more rational and calculative exploitation of the natural resources.

Techno-Economic Situation

Hunters and gatherers in India do not constitute even one percent of her total tribal population. There are, however, 20-22 distinct tribal groups who still pursue hunting and gathering for their livelihood. The numerical strength of these groups ranges from a few individuals to a few thousand only, and their distribution is mostly along the forest-clad regions of northeastern and southern India. They are also found in the central-east regions of India, and beyond the mainland, in the Andaman and Nicobar Islands. These communities are spread over a wider region but they appear to be more concentrated in the southern part of India.

Though all of these hunting and gathering tribes in India have some experience of contact they do not have the similar exposures to the outside world, and there are differences in the extent and nature of contact and articulation with the larger society. While explicating the 'multiple scales and networks' of Indian civilization Sinha (1978) observes that there two levels of scales among the hunters and gatherers in India. He includes the hunters of the Andaman Islands at the level of 'primitive' while those in the mainland of India at the 'symbiotic' level. He notes that the hunters of the Andaman Islands are or until recently were more or less isolated and self-sufficient in their economy while those in the Indian mainland maintain a regular economic symbiosis with the settled peasantry in their neighbourhood (*ibid*:125).

Nature of Symbiosis

Of the hunters and gatherers in the Andaman Islands mention may be made of the Jarwas, the Sentinelese and the Onges. Very few ethnographic studies are available on these tribes except the Onges. The number of population of these tribes seems very small. In a recent estimation the total population of the Onges has been recorded as 108 while that of the Jarawas, as 250 (Pandit 1982:183-84). The Jarwas live in western part of the south and middle Andaman. They have experienced several odd encounters in the past and in the course of time developed an attitude of hostility towards any outside people. The Sentinelese who live in the north Sentinel Island are 'yet in a condition when they have absolutely no contact with others' (Bose 1971:269). No information is available about the number of their population. 'Only once, forty-eight adult men were counted when an attempt was made to land there' (ibid: 269). Compared to the Jarawas and the Sentinelese the Onges of little Andaman are more exposed to the larger society. Their forest ecology has also been disturbed to some extent. The exposures of the Onge are, in fact, due to the measures introduced by the Government of India. In spite of the contact 'the Onges live by hunting, fishing and the collection of wild produce, like berries or honey, from the forest. Formerly, and even now, they have no trade with any other people' (*ibid:* 268).

As regards the extent and nature of contact of the hunters and gatherers with the larger society in the mainland of India some instance may also be cited here. Bose (1956) points out that 'the Birhor (literally, 'men of the forest') of southern Orissa have now practically become an appendage of the rural economic system of the caste villages'. He observes that the Birhor, having come in contact with the peasants of the neighbouring villages, have now specialized themselves 'in some industries based on jungle produce'. Since they do not get permanent patronage in any one village they are converted into a 'nomadic caste' and form a complement to the 'non-competitive productive system' of the caste-based Hindu society. A similar observation was also made by Sinha (1968). Based on some secondary source of ethnographic information Fox (1968) also points out caste-like occupational specializations among five hunting and gathering tribes of India, namely, Birhor, Chenchu, Kadar, Nayadi and Vedda.

A close probe into the nature of their articulation would, however, reveal that despite their essential economic interaction with the settled peasantry many of the hunting and gathering tribes in the Indian mainland are found to carefully maintain a distinct social and cultural boundary and retreat into their traditional jungle environment. This must have been possible in situations where the people have a suitable ecological base of jungle resources to fall back upon. Along with a viable ecological base in forests may be mentioned the lack of a meaningful world of social interaction and cultural communication in the local social milieu that helps them perpetuate a distinct social and cultural entity. For instance, mention may be made of the Birhor in the district of Sundargarh, Orissa, where the author made an intensive field investigation during the period between 1971 and 1976. In the course of field study the author finds that the Birhor broadly operate between two ecological terrains, one a natural ecology comprising the jungles and the other a social ecology comprising the settled peasantry. The whole range of their economy is centred around the collection of jungle produces and the perpetuation of a regular economic interaction with the neighbouring village society. The Birhor collect jungle produces and exchange them for cash and paddy. But the forest ecology on which they have to depend for most of their resources is also exploited by the members of the neighbouring village communities. In order to avoid any direct conflict and maintain their essential economic interaction with the people of the larger society the Birhor, therefore, exploit forest resources in a selective and calculative manner and engage themselves mostly in collection of the jungle creeper, Bauhinia, and the hunting of wild monkeys that the local people normally avoid. It may be mentioned here that all the occupations of the Birhor are based on forest resources and the traditional knowledge of these resources with which they seem to have a close and intimate association (Adhikary 1974).

The Birhor prepare different kinds of ropes and rope-made products from the barks of Bauhinia creepers and are specialized in this profession. They exchange the products with villagers for their necessary articles. Hunting of monkeys and other wild games is pursued occasionally and that too primarily for consumption of meat. They, however, sell live monkeys and skins of langur if they find such an opportunity. Hunting, in fact, does not contribute much to their total economy. But the Birhor still keep up the spirit of hunting, and continue this mode of production as a cultural norm (Adhikary 1984:85). In order to perpetuate their day-to-day subsistence activities they have adopted a nomadic way of life and always live in temporary leaf huts at the outskirts of some jungle-infested hills and mountains. While encamping at a place the Birhor also keep in their view some peasant villages and market centres.

In the course of their day-to-day interaction with the Hindu peasantry the Birhor experience some odd encounters that insulate them from the neighbouring caste-peasants and keep them perpetually marginal to the village society. They have come to learn that they are looked down upon by the so-called high caste people of the region, and placed low in the local social hierarchy. The caste people often ridicule the Birhor for their habit ot eating the meat of monkeys and treat them as 'nasty', 'dirty' and 'unclean' people.

The Birhor carefully manage the impressions of the local people and try to pose themselves physically as well as ritually clean and pure when they visit Hindu caste peasants. They say that they maintain occupational and social distances from the low caste people and avoid the eating of beef that are considered polluting by high caste Hindus.

The local people, however, have strong belief in supernaturalism and magico-religious rites, and look upon the Birhor as 'mystic' and jungle life-style with occult powers. The Birhor carefully wear a mystic cover on appearance, stick a close linkage to jungles and make a rational use of the ideas and notions of the local people by working as magico-religious specialists. This strategy of the Birhor helps them not only to widen their economic resource base in the neighbouring Hindu peasant villages but also to make their identity with forest more meaningful.

A deep probe into aspects of their worldview also reveals that the Birhor of Orissa clearly distinguish a world, disum, their own territory in jungles from muluk, the world of the larger society. Subsequently, they have developed 'adaptive strategies of social interaction in the context of two sets of environment: a morally ordered gemeinschaft in *disum,* their own territory in forest, and a rationalist-utilitarian gesellschaft orientation in muluk, the territory dominated by the caste-peasants and market economy' (Sinha 1984 :vi).

The Cholanickans of Kerala exhibit another case of economic symbiosis. In a recent article Bhanu (1982) points out two distinct spheres of subsistence activity among the Cholanaickans living in the Nilambur forest of Malappuram district in Kerala: one, geared to their self-consumption and the other, to barter and exchange for cash and paddy. 'They gather tubers, roots, fruits, berries, leaves and also fish and hunt small games for self-consumption. For exchange they collect minor forest produce like dammer, honey, ginger, soap-seed, tree-bark, cardamom, astringent fruit, etc.' (*ibid* :219). Many external agencies are also found to make regular collection of these minor forest produces for sale in the larger market. The Cholanaickans having fair knowledge of forest ecology and habitual skill in hunting and gathering carefully adapt themselves to this situation of confrontation. They retreat further deep into the forest and dwell in the natural caves on the bank of the small tributaries for their subsistence.

Unlike the Birhor of Orissa or the Cholanaickans of Kerala who still have some effective hold over jungle resources and scope to retreat in the forest the Hill Kharia of Purulia district in West Bengal live 'in a situation where their anchorage to the forest economic base has been rudely uprooted' and are 'thrown at the door-step of the peasant societies as landless dependent communities' (Sinha, D. 1984:85-86). The Hill Kharia of this area have experienced, over the years, a gradual decrease of resources in forests, and subsequently, there has occurred, among them, an 'erosion of technology and knowledge of ecology'.

Unlike the nomadic Birhor the Hill Kharia of Purulia now lead a sedentary life along with various peasant castes and communities, and are very much tagged to the socio-econoic and political networks of the larger village society. In order to cope with the depleted condition of the forest as well as the present situation of contact they have, therefore, adopted various occupational strategies. They often work as casual and contract agricultural labourers to the villagers and prepare handicrafts like broomsticks and fish traps for sale and barter. They are also found to resort to hunting, fishing and gathering in the natural ecology. Mention may be made here of their specific adaptation to the collection of paddy grains from the rat-holes in the harvested fields of the peasants. A careful probe into the annual calendar of the subsistence activities of the Hill Kharia in this region, as given by Dikshit Sinha reveals that much of their time and energy are spent in hunting, fishing and gathering in the surrounding natural ecology with which they still seem to have an intimate and moral relation. Sinha observes, 'although the Hill Kharia realize that the forest resources are more or less exhausted, ...emotionally they find the forest more easier to adjust with because the supernatural power which reigns over the domain of availability of food can easily be comprehended with the help of their cultural idioms' (ibid :52).

In spite of their sedentary village life and perpetual economic interaction the Hill Kharia seem to suffer from a low social position in the local social hierarchy as well as from being stigmatized as a 'criminal people' by the larger society. They, however, try to make their existence meaningful in the social and cultural milieu of the large village society through their participation in the regional festivals of *badhna parab* (cattle festival) and *gajan* (festival of hook-swinging).

Discussion and Conclusion

In the foregoing pages I have described primarily the techno-economic situation of the hunting and gathering tribes in India. For this purpose I have drawn evidence largely from the Birhor of Sundargarh district in Orissa and by way of comparison have brought in the observations and studies made by others on these people and other hunter-gatherer groups. I have purposely tried to bring into relief the situation of their contact, and dealt with the extent and nature of their symbiotic relation with the people of the larger society. The internal social organization of the individual tribes has not been dealt with, and the emphasis is given on the aspect of economic interaction at their community level with the village castes and communities It is observed that even the hunters and gatherers of the Andaman Islands, who still retain a self-sufficient economy in comparative isolation have also experienced or are still experiencing occasional odd encounters from outside. Subsequently, there has developed, among these people, especially the Jarawas and the Sentinelese, an attitude of hostility towards the larger society.

As regards the hunting and gathering tribes of mainland India the situation is somewhat different. Here the hunters and gatherers whose natural ecology has been largely encroached upon by the people of the larger society have virtually been thrown into the threshold of the techno-economic culture of the neighbouring market-based village society. Some of them have also adopted caste-like occupational specializations and form a complement to the agrarian economic structure of the Hindu caste society. In connection with the economic interaction of the tribal groups with various agricultural castes and communities in the Indian mainland Bose (1941) makes an observation. He points out that many of the tribal groups having found a suitable alternative for their techno-economy within the regional 'non-competitive productive systems' of the Hindu caste society have either adopted settled cultivation in the plains or taken up caste-like occupational specializations. The adoption of hunting and gathering and jungle-based crafts by the Birhor has been cited as an instance for the latter. From our above description of the day to day interactions of the Birhor with their neighbouring caste-based Hindu settled peasantry we, however, learn that in spite of their regular economic transaction they do not get any suitable position in the social and cultural system of the local society. They are often ridiculed and looked down upon by the local caste people. Consequently, they have been found to retreat into the terrain of forest ecology and adopt a wandering life covering a wider territorial area. The Hill Kharia of Purulia who lead a sedentary village life and are very much tagged to the larger village society also seem to lack a meaningful world of social interaction and cultural communication in the local society. In spite of their intense endeavour to articulate themselves with the village society the Hill Kharia are only a stigmatized 'criminal people'. They do not even get the service of the Brahmins or other servicing caste groups, and are perpetually kept at the periphery of the village.

With the specific reference to the hunting and gathering mode of production among the tribes in the mainland of India Sinha *(ibid)* makes another germane observation. He contends that many of these tribes, especially the Birhor and the Hill Kharia in the central-east India and the Cholanaickans of Kerala are secondary hunters. He observed that these groups, in the past, practiced shifting cultivation combined with hunting and gathering on the hill slopes in the forests. With the encroachment of the settled Hindu peasantry they find their traditional mode of shifting cultivation untenable and adopt hunting and gathering mode of subsistence.

It may be mentioned in this connection that many of these hunting and groups are, in fact, offshoots of larger ethnic groups. What I want to bring into relief here is that the hunting and gathering technology among these groups is not a recent phenomenon. The mode of production that was once a subsidiary one has now become the principal among some of them. Keeping in consonance with their knowledge and skill they have only shifted their emphasis from one technology of the other still adhering to their traditional domain of jungle ecology. From our description on the Birhor of Sundargarh district in Orissa we have already seen how selectively and calculatively they exploit forest resources through their hunting and gathering technology and strategically perpetuate their linkage to the jungle. In the contemporary life situations they are only found to reinforce 'the meaning of their special relation with the forest ecology'. Even the Hill Kharia of Purulia who have almost no ecological base in forest for withdrawal spend much of their and energy in hunting, gathering and fishing in the surrounding natural ecology, and still retain an emotional and moral relation with forests.

It is evident from the above discussion that the perpetuation of hunting and gathering mode of production among the hunters in the mainland of India has been possible not only for their economic base in forest ecology and the smallness of population size but also for the lack of a meaningful world of social interaction and cultural communication in the midst of the caste-based village society. It may be noted in this connection that the contemporary hunters and gatherers strategically combine their hunting and gathering in jungles with occupations based on the knowledge of the techno-cultural environment in the larger society, thereby extending their operative area of environmental ecology.

4

The Nomadic Mankria: Aspects of Their Articulation with the Settled Peasantry

Introduction

The Mankria is hunting and gathering community of Orissa. They are, in fact, an off-shoot of the Birhor, a jungle tribe of Chotanagpur area of Bihar. In the regions of Orissa, they are known by various names such as Mankidi, Mankria, or Mankar-khia kol. In Orya dialect, *Mankar* means monkey, and *khia,* to eat. In the official census records of Orissa the have also been recorded as such. Thus Mankria or Mankar-khia means the people who eat and share monkeys. In the official census records of Orissa they have also been recorded as such. However, the self-ascription of the people is Birhor, i.e., 'man of the jungle'. Following the self-ascription of the people I shall use the term Birhor in my discussion.

In the earlier studies the Birhor were described as an isolated self-sufficient community primarily dependent on the forest resources (Dalton 1879:158; Driver, 1888:14;

Risley, 1911: 33; Ray, 1925: 41; Sinha, 1968). But in all the writings some contact of the people with outsiders was hinted at, though it was often explained as a casual one, and that too through their occasional visits to markets. It was Nirmal Kumar Bose who, for the first time, pointed out that the interaction of the Birhor with outsiders was a regular one, and was essentially of symbiotic nature. According to him the people, specializing on jungle-based crafts are functionally articulated with the surrounding settled villagers within the framework of the rural agrarian economic structure. He also observed among the people adoption of a few magico-religious elements from the regional Hindu peasantry, as a sign of cultural development, and therefore, described them as an emerging caste (Bose 1956). However, from my own field experience among the people in Sundargarh district of Orissa it becomes apparent that the Mankria not only seek a genuine world of self-expression in the forest but also show a reluctance towards being absorbed in the surrounding Hindu peasantry. Subsequently, my attention was drawn to the problem of their articulation with the settled peasantry, and an attempt has thus been made to study the extent and nature of their articulation, with a special emphasis on the mental state of the people behind it. To explore the mind I have tried to study not only the cognitive organization of objective phenomena but also the unstated assumptions behind each behaviour and activity. Throughout the thesis I have been guided by the assumption that the people have to exploit both the forest ecology and the neighbouring settled peasantry for their vital necessity of survival. From this point of view I would look at the problem and try to study the phenomenon of interaction with the settled people.

Ecological Background

Before describing their essential facets of interaction and the extent of articulation with outsiders let us first see the people in situ. In Orissa, the people are found to move around the districts of Sundargarh, Sambalpur, Keonjhar, Dhenkanal, and Mayurbhanj. All the districts are characterized by dense forest and hills rich in plants and trees of northern deciduous type mainly *sal (Shorea robusta), assan (Terminalia tomentosa)* and *kusum (Adina cordiajolia)*. Monkeys (specially, *Macacus rhesus* and *Presbytes entellus* varieties), hares, snakes and bears are found plentifully. Elephants and tigers are not very rare. The distribution of the Mankria in these regions of Orissa is, in fact, along the forest extension of Chotanagpur plateau, having little variation in rainfall, flora and fauna. In the north of Sundargarh where I studied the people, there is a gradual rise to the table land of Chotanagpur in the north and east of which the main concentration of the Birhor was located by S.C. Roy (1925).

The forest provides the people with certain quantity of animal as well as vegetable food. They take about twenty varieties of animal food, available almost in all seasons. They also take larvae of different ants, honey, roots, tubers, various kinds of fruits, different algae, bamboo shoots and other vegetables. The techniques they use in order to exploit the resources are mainly hunting and gathering, with the aid of a few implements such as nets and axes.

In spite of all these resources in the forest the people have to depend on the neighbouring peasant and artisan castes for subsistence to a considerable extent. They are found to depend on the agriculturalists for rice and paddy, on the blacksmiths for axe and knife, on potters for earthen vessels and on weavers for clothes. The people, therefore, have to exploit two ecological terrains for their livelihood: one, a natural ecology comprising the forest, and the other, a social ecology comprising the settled Hindu peasantry.

Extent of Articulation and Media of Contact

Not only Bose (1956) but also many other scholars have maintained that the Birhor are well articulated with neighbouring peasantry, thus emerging like a caste (Sen, 1965; Sinha, 1968; Fox, 1969). Since their writings lack detailed description, let me present here, in some detail, the extent they are articulated with the settled people. Although the people are expert hunters and gatherers, they are specialized, to a great extent, in the art of making ropes and rope products from forest resources. Barks of bauhinia creepers provide the necessary raw materials for their rope-craft. Rope making is an elaborate process, and almost all of them can accomplish it with great skill. They prepare four different types of ropes, a small kind of basket-pot made of barks for the use of pressing oil seeds, about three varieties of *shika,* etc. They have detailed knowledge of manufacturing techniques, resources and markets or areas of demand of their products. They appear to be highly specialized in this profession and no other ethnic group in the area is found to have ropemaking as a profession.

Hunting is pursued mainly for subsistence, and flesh of monkeys (*Macacus rhesus*) and langurs (*Presbytes entellus*) is a favourite food item of them. Live *Macacus rhesus* and *Presbytes entellus* are also sold to outsiders. Monkey-traders (locally called *gari-sau*) occasionally come to their settlement or contact them in the market for live monkeys. These traders (usually belonging to the Pathan community) often give them cash advance, and stay with them for days together, if necessary. Monkeys (only *Macacus rhesus* variety) ranging from 4lb to 8lb in weight are purchased by the traders at the rate of Rs. 2.00 to Rs. 4.00. The people can tan skins of langur (*Presbytes entellus*) very skilfully. Sometimes the neighbouring Doms and Mahatos purchase these skins for covering their musical drums. The Birhor are found also to work as agricultural labourer in the fields of the settled villagers such as the Mundari, Munda, Kurmi Mahato, Bhumij, Keota, etc.

For the above economic pursuits the Birhor have to extend their traditional barter system to the market mode of exchange in terms of cash. Subsequently, they are exposed to many other ethnic groups than a few artisan castes in the village. Although they usually lump up, at first attempt, almost all the ethnic groups within the single category *diku,* they can identify about 20-22 ethnic groups, specifying their occupations as well as places of concentration. All the ethnic groups known to them are mostly tribal and low Hindu castes. Some of the Birhor are also acquainted with the names of the priestly castes, Brahmin and Vaisnab.

People from the various ethnic groups mentioned above come to the Birhor to learn magical rites and also to purchase medicinal herbs. Many of the peasants are thus found to become disciple *(chela)* of these nomads. The Birhor occasionally make ritual bonds of friendship (*phul* and *saya)* with the villagers. Out of 59 households comprising 228 individuals 5 cases of *phul* friendship and 2 cases of *saya* relationship were recorded. Outsiders involved in such relationship were: Kurmi Mahato-2, Mundari –3, Pauri Bhuiya –1 and Karmakar- 1. Between the persons entered into such relationship new clothes, meals and flowers are exchanged thus binding both the families. *Phul* friendship is established between males of about the same age and sometimes of similar names, while *saya* (also known as *makar*) relationship is developed between females of the same age.

The Birhor are aware of the notion of pollution, a characteristic feature of the Hindu caste society, and often maintain social distance from the Hindu caste groups like the Dom, the drum beaters, the Dhoba, the washermen, the Napit, the barber. The Birhor say that they do not take cooked food and water from those people as they are engaged in unclean occupations, eat polluting food and placed low in local social hierarchy. They are found to participate in the regional Hindu festivals like *gumha purnima, maghi purnima,* etc. and worship *devi mai, dharti mai, mahadeo,* etc. They use vermilion, *tulsi* (sacred basil) plants and flowers in different ritual contexts.

The Birhor take rice as their principal diet. They are also in the habit of partaking a number of other regional food items such as *gangei, gandhli* (a kind of flower which is dried and powdered and then cooked), *khai* (perched paddy), *murhi* (perched rice), *chura* (flattened rice), *gohm* (wheat), etc.

The Birhor have, therefore, through their essential economic transactions with the rural Hindu peasantry, been exposed to a wider socio-cultural world both by interaction and by implication. They have, however, least political contact with outsiders, and as such their social control is entirely maintained by their own ethnic institutions.

Nature of Articulation

From the above description it appears that the Birhor are articulated with the settled peasantry through various channels of interaction. In order to understand the nature of their articulation from such interaction it is necessary to probe the meaning and sentiments of the people and also the conditions that led them to interact with outsiders.

Due to the encroachment of the settled peasantry and the setting up of various mines and factories in these areas the resources of the forests have dwindled and been disturbed to a great extent. The people are well aware of the situation, and often state the games like monkeys (*Macacus rhesus*) and Hanuman (*Presbytes entellus*) have run away into deeper jungles due to frequent sounds generated from the quarries. Besides these, the vegetables as well as small animal games in the jungle which the Birhor are used to exploit for subsistence are now shared by other communities living in the region. The people, however, do not believe in the scarcity of resource as a normal state in the jungle. But for inevitable reasons their sole dependence on the forest resource has been hindered. They thus have to organize their community forming wandering bands of small size and to widen their areas of operation for food and cloth even to the surrounding settled communities beyond the forests. They cannot grow paddy or any other cereals they have to take, nor can they prepare clothes to wear. They have either to barter or trade these things from outsiders. From this point of view, the interaction of the settled peasantry with the Birhor is not as essential as that of the Birhor themselves who have to interact essentially for subsistence. Thus the adaptations in interaction they have are somewhat motivated and well calculated by considerations for survival. They not only specialize themselves in rope-making and turn to markets but also resort to many other occupations and adoptive strategies to cope with the scarcity of material resources.

The barks by means of which the Birhor prepare ropes are also accessible to some of the villagers who frequently utilize them for their own use. Other kinds of ropes such as jute ropes and cocoanut ropes are also available in the markets at moderate price. Thus the people do not have the monopoly over this rope-making business though their ropes are considered by the local people harder and cheaper. The people have, therefore, to wander about a large number of villages or locate a market where their products would have a suitable demand. I have seen a man or woman to wander, in a day, about 5-6 villages covering distances of 20 kms to 24 kms or to traverse about 40-45 kms up-down to attend a big weekly market.

From my observation I also get the impression that the people are neither good agricultural labourers nor do they want to be so. To a Birhor the return he gets from agricultural labour work is much less than what he gets from ropemaking in that time. The people work as agricultural labourer only when the situation arises. For instance, if any villager happens to ask a Birhor if he wants to do the job, he cannot directly refuse for fear of being marked as lazy and 'worthless' people. They also do not feel at ease while working with others in the fields. During my stay with a group from January 1973 to April 1973 I found only three ladies to work as agricultural labourer, and that too on persuasion.

The medicinal herbs the Birhor gather and the diseases they treat are also known to many of the villagers. Sometimes the villagers themselves mention about certain specific medicinal herbs and ask them to collect those. Here too, the Birhor cannot claim to have all mastery over this. But the rarity of the herbs in jungles and their 'acquaintance' or familiarity with those (instead of merely knowing) give them some advantage over others to eke economic gains out of it. The Birhor, however, can claim overall mastery in hunting games like monkeys and hanuman and feel very much at ease if they find an opportunity in trading with such games.

Although the Birhor pursue a number of occupations, they do not always get enough patronization in villages. In majority of cases, the villagers do not make cash payment for services they get from the people who, however, often need cash payment to fulfill many material needs (i.e., clothes, metal utensils, axes, tobacco, etc.) that are not easily available in exchange or barter in the villages. They, therefore, attend markets to earn cash for the purchase of their essential commodities. By attending a market they also get the advantage of covering a number of villages at a time and space. Due to the exposure to a wider area they are also conscious of the comparative picture of demands and prices of their commodities. Thus when a market is found to be attended by too many people from more than one or two camps, the demand of their ropes diminishes. Calculating the decreasing demands some of the people then simply withdraw from the particular market and shift to other places.

In course of their day-to-day contacts with outsiders the Birhor have to face many odd encounters. Villagers usually keep off these people, and nourish frightful impressions about them. They also ridicule and look down upon them by saying that they are 'dirty', 'nasty', and 'eat' unclean food (usually referring to their habit of taking the flesh of monkeys, and ridiculing them as *mankria* or *mankar khia*). They are aware of the fact, and thus try not only to be clean and ritually pure to the eyes of outsiders but also try to minimize the tensions and constraints generated in such encounters by developing ceremonial friendship (*phul-saya*) with the villagers or through a 'silent trade' of mendicancy in the institutional form of *guru-shishya* relationship. There is also a calculated attempt on their part to present a 'conscious model' of their own community keeping in mind the perspective of the neighbouring settled Hindu peasantry. They do it mainly with a view to maintaining their essential economic transactions with the villagers in a peaceful as well as prestigious way. Thus when a Birhor goes out in the villages for begging during regional festivals like *gumha purnima,* etc. in the guise of a 'sadhu' (a wandering mendicant), he not only appears relaxed from social constraints in his transactions with the villagers but also finds some peaceful and easy way of economic transaction with them by performing various sorts of magical work such as prediction, divination, etc. In such encounters they usually create the impression among villagers that if they do not pay, the prediction will not be fruitful. The Birhor keep socio-ritual distance from the low Hindu castes like the Dom, Dhoba, Napit, etc., by saying that the latter are attached to 'unclean' jobs and eat 'nuisances' (i.e. flesh of dead cows and buffalos, etc.). They themselves claim to have given up eating beef, and try to be as clean and pure as possible by wearing moderate clothes and anointing oil while attending villages/markets.

Although the Birhor claim to have abstained from taking beef, they are nevertheless found to take it. When it is pointed out to them, they still try to stick to the idea by saying that those who like may take it but they (Birhor) should not take beef. However, if anybody asks if they take beef or not, they would put counter-question whether the questioner takes it or not. If he replies 'no', they would instantly say 'no'. If he says 'yes', they would pause for a while to measure the answer and reply 'where would we get it?'

Guru-Shishya relationship is essentially an economic or trade relationship with a ritual cover. Status of *guru* here is somewhat self-imposed, and this image is drawn from the outside world mainly from the *sadhus* who wander about in the villages and markets, begging and predicting. Such a relationship is, in fact, a transitional phase towards the institutionalization of *phul-saya* relationship, and is primarily initiated by a villager. Although a villager takes the initiative in developing such relationship with a Birhor, it is the latter who really alludes/induces the villager by posing himself as an expert in magical rites. He behaves reflexively, and his identity as 'jungle man' gives him an advantage in this interaction. The rich contents of supernatural beliefs in the region, in fact, help them to a great extent. When an outsider approaches a Birhor to learn magical spells or rites, he speaks as fluently and stutteringly as possible in order to create an impression of mysticism. This puts the learner to a hard situation to commit the spells to memory thus compelling him come to the Birhor specialist for a considerable period of time. This long process of magical training often promotes intimacy and reduces the socio-ritual distance between them, ultimately leading to the development of a ritual kinship bond between their families. In such cases the initiative may come from any side, but usually it comes from the side of the Birhor. In making ceremonial friendship with the villagers the main intention of the Birhor is to gain certain advantage out of it, such as to live closer to the villages in safety, to keep their hunting nets in the villagers' houses during rains, to get an opportunity for husking paddy in their husking lever, and so on. It is a kind of 'social insurance'. By having such an articulation with the villagers they also try to get relieved of the occasional tensions they suffer from the villagers' ridicule.

Summary and Discussion

It is obvious from the foregoing description that in order to maintain their essential economic linkage with the larger society the Birhor have devised not only various channels of communication but also have developed certain adoptive strategies to tackle the situation like enhancing their areas of operation, making certain social relationship with the villagers, managing the impressions of the surrounding neighbours by adopting a few cultural elements of the region, and so on. The kind of relationship that has been developed with the outsiders is, indeed, instrumental, and primarily intended to earn economic or material gains. Even the ceremonial friendship (*phul-saya*) of the Birhor with the settled peasantry is well calculated and motivated, and its social aspect hinges on economic or material aspects. Though the relationship looks like one of mutual obligation, there is an unstated assumption/endeavour on behalf of the Birhor to maximize benefit out of it. To a *phul* or a *saya*, he may present a rope but primarily with an expectation of having some material gain in return. Thus he is often found to pose, in such transactions, his poverty or needs, as if he would starve if he does not get anything from the village.

The Birhor term as diku almost all the culturally and linguistically different ethnic groups. They may not be quite stranger or enemy. They simply know them but may not have 'acquaintance' with them. Briefly speaking, the distance of a group and the consequent pattern of interaction are measured by the frequency of contact and the degree of acquaintance with it. Thus when a group becomes acquainted more and more, it is usually specified either by its occupation or the place of its concentration or the typical nature or any combination of these. Nevertheless, their interaction with any outside group may, in fact, be characterized by 'balanced' reciprocity and there is hardly any moral disapproval for exploiting or deceiving any such people.

In conclusion, we may say that while interacting with the outside people, the Birhor not only find their ethnic identity at stake but also lack a meaningful world of communication. The 'moral community' formed by the Birhor in their intimate meaningful interaction with their forest ecology, is not seriously disturbed by the segmental and peripheral and strategically adaptive interactions with the outside world.

5

Nomadism, Economy and World View of the Birhors of Orissa

Introduction

The Birhors, in contrast to the sedentary village population of rural India, can be identified as nomadic hunters and gatherers who operate between the forests and the settled peasantry. They move along forest-clad areas and are distributed in Bihar, Orissa and Madhya Pradesh (Census of India: 1971). In Orissa they are found in the districts of Sundargarh, Sambalpur, Keonjhar, Dhenkanal and Mayurbhanj. Besides being known as the Birhor these people in Orissa are often identified as Mankidi, Mankirdia and Mankar-khia-kol all referring to the people who share and eat monkeys (*mankar*). The self ascription of the people is, however, Birhor, meaning man of jungle (*bir* means jungle and *hor,* man).

The phenomenon of nomadism among the Birhor was explained by different authors though it did not draw their serious attention as a subject of enquiry. Roy (1925) who studied the people primarily as a primitive hunting and gathering isolate observed that the Birhor were nomads because of the very nature of the forest resources they used to exploit. When the roots, the tubers and the wild games were found to be exhausted in a forest they left for another. Bose (1956) explained the phenomenon of nomadism among the Birhor as a consequence of the lack of permanent patronage of their products in any one village. He observed that the Birhor having specialized in hunting, gathering and jungle-based crafts operated within the broad framework of the agrarian economic structure of the rural peasantry. Since they did not get permanent patronage in any one village they took to a wandering life, thus forming a complement to the 'non-competitive productive system' of the caste-based Hindu society in rural India. Sinha (1969) observed that the adoption of nomadic hunting and gathering mode of subsistence by the Birhor was a case of 'secondary primitivization' or 'devolution'. He noted that the Birhor like many other Mundari groups of tribes in Chotanagpur were, in fact, shifting cultivators on hill slopes. Later on, 'penetration of the caste-based economy into these areas and extensive deforestation' forced the people to specialize themselves in 'hunting and gathering'. While Roy described the nomadism of the Birhor as their subsistence adaptation to the natural environment (specifically, the scarcity of forest resources), Bose and Sinha broadly emphasized that their nomadism was an adaptation to the demands of their jungle products to the neighbouring settled peasantry.

Bose's observation was that the Birhor like many other tribal groups in India found a suitable alternative of their techno-economy within the non-competitive productive system of the Hindu peasantry and were gradually being absorbed into the folds of the Hindu caste system by slowly emulating cultural features of the dominant Hindu upper castes. Sinha, however, noticed among some of the tribal groups who were in close interaction with the Hindu caste system a level of awareness that they were looked down upon by the caste people and subsequently, a sense of discontent for their low social position (Sinha 1972:413). Sinha pointed out a phenomenon of 'oscillation' among the Birhor who operated between a settled (*jagghi*) and a nomadic (*uthulu*) life (Sinha 1973 :99-108). In fact, while Bose was talking of a mechanism of tribal absorption into the non-competitive productive systems of the Hindu peasantry in villages Sinha was endeavouring to note the social-cultural organization of the Hindus that accorded low and marginal social positions to many of the tribal groups and kept them at the periphery of the Hindu society.

In the course of my study among the Birhor of Orissa I, however, observe that the Birhor are not only aware that they are looked down upon by the caste-peasants but also find themselves in a competitive economic situation where many other communities equally exploit the forest resources which the Birhor exploit. In order to avoid direct conflict with the villages as well as to perpetuate their essential economic interaction with them they, therefore, have to adopt several adaptive strategies and pursue a number of occupations. All the occupational are however centred around forests. Subsequently, I get the feeling that nomadism of the Birhor cannot be explained as a simple economic adaptation either to the forest ecology or to the settled peasantry. Forces from both the forest ecology and the surrounding settled peasantry equally influence their adaptation, and it cannot be understood well without a deep probe into how the people look at these forces. In the following pages I will try to broadly describe the various economic pursuits of the people, their nature of movement as well as aspects of their worldview in order to facilitate a comprehensive understanding of the perpetuation of nomadism among the Birhor.

Economy

Though broadly classified as hunters and gatherers the economy of the Birhor can no longer be described as a simple primitive one. The people, unlike other primitive hunting and gathering isolates, are exposed to the complex market system. The whole rubric of Birhor economy, indeed, involves the exploitation of the forest resource on the one hand and the maintenance of an essential contact with the larger society on the other. For their day-to-day subsistence activities the Birhor have to collect forest products and convert them into necessary consumable articles through markets and peasant villages.

From forests the Birhor exploit about 20 varieties of games and about 17 varieties of vegetable products. These forest products are also exploited by the village caste-peasants and tribes. They, therefore, exploit these products primarily as they come on their way and do not spend much time or make any special effort to collect them. The Birhor, however, spend most of their time and energy in collecting the barks of bauhinia creepers and hunting wild monkeys. The neighbouring villagers hardly exploit these forest resources.

For survival, the Birhor have to pursue, indeed, a number of occupations and utilize resources from the forest as well as the peasant villages and the markets of the larger society. Of all the occupations the manufacture of ropes and rope-products from the fibres of bauhinia creepers is the primary one. They have specialized themselves in this craft. They prepare about four varieties of ropes namely, collar ropes for tying the cattle, draw ropes for pulling water from wells, *dhauri* (a variety of collar rope with a chain of loops) used for tying a number of bullocks together at the time of treading them over paddy plants for threshing grains, and *joti*, a narrow rope for domestic use by the villagers. Besides these the Birhor also weave a variety of small basket with the barks of bauhinia. These baskets are locally known as topa, and used by the local peasants for extracting oil from oil seeds. They prepare a few varieties of rope-net hangers, locally called *sikha*. These are used by the potters and the hawkers to carry their luggage on shoulders from one place to another; they are also used by the householders for hanging food and other articles from the ceiling of their houses. The ropes and rope-products are exchanged for cash as well as kind.

The hunting of monkeys and other wild games like hares, porcupines etc., is another occupational pursuit of the Birhor. Though the wild game is hunted primarily for direct consumption it is also used for barter and sale. Small games like hares and porcupines are sometimes disposed of, if the villagers insist on. Some monkey traders *(gari sau)* move around the region. They often come to the Birhor, live in their camps and insist on hunting monkeys for them. They also advance cash for the purpose. The skins of monkeys (only of *Presbytes entellus* variety) are also sold to the villagers who use them for covering their musical drums.

Some of the Birhor deal with jungle herbs of medicinal value. Horns, bones, skins, and many other parts of rare and wild animals that are left in deep jungles and are considered by the villagers to have much supernatural power and magical value are also collected and exchanged by the people. Some of the Birhor also act as magico-religious experts to the villagers. Because of their close association with jungles as well as unusual halfclad appearance the villagers normally consider them mystic and experts in magico-religious activities. In order to learn the expertise of such activities the villagers often approach the Birhor to be initiated as their disciples (*chela* or *shishya*) and enter into a kind of *guru-shishya* relationship. This *guru-shishya* is essentially a trade relationship though ultimately it may lead to the establishment of a kind of bond friendship (*phul-saya*) between the families concerned. Some of the Birhor also move about the villages and markets as itinerant mendicant and resort to religious begging. In this pursuit they draw heavily on the image of the *Vaishnab sadhus* who move and beg around the region.

Nomadism

The basic production and consumption unit of the Birhor is the household that is built around the nuclear family of husband, wife and unmarried children, or variants of it. Though the Birhor usually move and camp in small bands of related households, every household has got the economic freedom to move from one band to another. In course of their movement the Birhor encamp near some peasant village located by the side of a road. While selecting site for their temporary camps they also keep in view forests, markets and water sources. They do not camp near every village. The villages must be previously known to some of them. It may be mentioned here that the Birhor often use these villages as reference points for their temporary camps. For instance, if a camp is located near the village Birtolla they refer it as Birtolla tola.

The Birhor do not possess many material belongings, and usually move on foot. Every household possesses one or two baskets made of bamboo splits, a few rope-net bags, one axe, one or two hunting nets, a few sticks and earthen pots, and one or two small clothes. At the time of movement the adult male of the household carries the major portion of the load which is kept hanging by two *shika* from a long stick (locally known as *bahinga*) across his shoulder. Other members, even the small children, may also carry whatever they can.

The movement of the Birhor is determined by several factors. They collect resources not only in terms of their availability in the jungles but also in terms of their demands in the larger society. When they feel a shortage of resources in a jungle or find demands of their products diminishing in the neighbouring villages and markets they move to another area.

The usual stay of the Birhor at a place varies from 15 to 30 days or sometimes more. During rainy season when the roads in these areas of Orissa are often submerged under water, they, however, have to stay at one place for more than a month. During these days it becomes difficult for them to mount the trees and collect the bauhinia creepers. Their ropes and rope products also do not get adequate market in the locality. The season appears very dull to them. The Birhor seem to lack pleasures of their usual free movement during this time. In rainy days they depend heavily on the villages in various matters and make use of their ceremonial relationships with the villagers. Sometimes they give some ropes or rope products to their ritual friends or disciples as gifts who, out of obligation, offer them some rice or paddy in return. The quantity of rice or paddy in such a context is more than usual. Some of them also work as agricultural labourers or beg about in the nearby villages as itinerant mendicants.

The winter is considered the best of all seasons; they feel free to move about, have easy access to the jungle resources as well as good market for their products in the locality. Almost all the varieties of their ropes and rope products are in good demand in the neighbouring markets and villages. The hunting of wild games by nets, difficult during rainy season, becomes easier at this time. Summer months are also favourable to the Birhor.

When the Birhor feel that there will be no more collection of bauhinia creepers in the proximal jungles they either extend their area of exploitation still staying at the place or shift their camps to another area. If there are good markets and big peasant villages around, the Birhor try to extend their area of exploitation in forests or, they may shift to a nearby convenient place but never far away from the markets and villages. When a market is found crowded by the Birhor of more than one or two bands living in proximal distance or together at one place, the demands of the goods diminish. In such a situation some of them either visit other markets or simply withdraw from the site and move to a far-off place. Sometimes overcrowding at a place is solved by splitting a band into 2 or 3 smaller units and dispersing in different directions.

Besides these external environmental factors there are also some internal factors that influence the movement of the Birhor. For their day-to-day subsistence activities the Birhor have to divide their community into independent production and consumption units and move around a wider area. This not only stands in their way of perpetuating large corporate kin group but also in finding marriageable spouses. For meeting relatives as well as for seeking spouses the Birhor are often found to leave one band and move to another.

The Birhor usually move in a circular manner, and there is no fixed territory for any band or household. They move along known routes. The area the people of a band would like to move about is ascertained primarily on mutual understanding of the people and there is no central authority in any band guiding their movement. If a band moves in a particular area it does not come back to the place immediately. Instead, it passes through another area. During their occasional encounters in villages and markets information is exchanged between the individuals, and subsequently, the Birhor band come to know which area is worth moving and which is not.

The places a Birhor band moves in a year are not confined to any particular administrative zone. A cycle of movement of a Birhor band may cover areas of different police stations, or of different subdivisions and districts, or even of different states. However, they always move along forest-clad areas intersected by peasant villages and markets.

World View

There is a story common among the Birhor of Orissa that gives some as to how they took up the forest life. The story runs as follows:

> Once upon a time there was a Kherwar king who had two sons. After the death of the king there was a dispute, between the sons, over the throne. The elders of the State came up and suggested that the princes would run a race on horseback, and the one who would win the race might sit on the throne. Subsequently, the race was held and the younger prince won. The elder one was delayed because his turban was stuck to a bush in the jungle. The younger prince became the king of Padma (Ramgarh State) in Hazaribagh district while the elder took to a wandering life in the jungle cutting wood and hunting games. This prince and his descendants were afterwards known as 'men of jungle', i.e., Birhor.

Whatever may be the authenticity of the story there is an indication that the people used to lead settled life and had a well-defined territory of their own. The adoption of nomadic hunting and gathering way of life is a later phenomenon. Though the people normally identify themselves as 'Man of Jungle', they seem to have a strong nostalgic feeling for their past life as Nagbansi Kherwar i.e., the Kherwar originally inhabiting the region of Chota nagpur. The contemporary Birhor are, however, dispersed over a wider region but the people still find pleasures in refreshing memory of their traditional clan homes located on the hills and mountains of Chotanagpur. Most of them do not know the exact location of their traditional home sites. They, however, worship and regard them as sacred seats of their ancestors.

Besides the occupations the Birhor pursue they also know of a few other professional work. The people, however, consider all of these activities linked with settled life which the Birhor do not like to adopt. To them these jobs require hard manual labour and are also not rewarding. They know occupations like agriculture, basketry, pottery, blacksmithy, leatherwork, weaving and 3-4 types of labour work. Of all these occupational strategies they consider cultivation is more rewarding than others. But to the Birhor in Sundargarh areas of Orissa there were no good cultivators. The Agarya in Bamda areas of Sambalpur district and the Chasa of Talcher district (both in Orissa) are good and rich cultivators to them. The observation of the Birhor, in this regard, coincided with ours. Other occupations are economically less rewarding as well as insecure. Labour work in road construction and agriculture, and artisan work like basketry, pottery, blacksmithy, leatherwork and weaving—cannot be run equally throughout the year and hence, are considered temporary as well as insecure jobs. The Birhor contend that in such work the people have to depend solely on other people while they can pull on independently by virtue of their close relation with forests even if they lack patronizaton from the villagers. From their knowledge of, and attitude towards the different occupations it is found that the people suffer not only from a technological constraint but also from a social constraint of losing their social distinctiveness and freedom as well as being placed at a low rung in the local social hierarchy.

The Birhor possess an unfavourable image about life in a village. They feel a sort of insecurity of their women in villages, and a lack of their habitual freedom of movement. Besides, in the course of their day-to-day encounters with the villagers they have come to learn that the people following different occupations are mostly marked with low social status in the neighbouring socio-cultural ambience.

However, while acting as magico-religious experts to the villagers and moving around the villages as mendicants like the Vaishnab sadhus the people seem free from the usual social and technological constraints. In perpetuating such a profession (though only a few) the Birhor make a careful and rational use of the widely prevalent belief in supernaturalism in the locality as well as the image of the itinerant sadhus. The strategic exploitation of ideological contents of the Hindu society is also found among various other nomads (cf. Misra 1969). The settled people possess an awe-stricken attitude towards the Birhor who are thought of to be very close to jungles and the supernatural. This association of mysticism by the settled people is carefully manipulated by the Birhor. A close probe into the activities and the notions of the people reveals that many of the spells and incantations, and even the jungle produces that are used in magico-religious performances are learnt by them from the villagers of the larger society in different areas. By assuming a half-clad appearance and performing the rituals in a mystic manner they often pose themselves to be experts in magico-religious activities.

The Birhor not only face repulsive forces from the neighbouring socio-cultural environment and interact instrumentally but also show a very close and intimate relations with and humble dependence on forests. The Birhor make little effort in exploring forest resources while in case of their interaction with the larger society they have to work hard and carefully.

Almost every Birhor, male or female, young or old, has some knowledge of forests while all are not equally acquainted with the larger society. In fact, forests are manifest in various aspects of their life and activity. Manifestation of forests can be observed in their settlement pattern, day to day activities and important socio-cultural performances. Briefly speaking the Birhor live in a world where the supernatural and the natural are bound together and their life operates in a cyclic order within this broad universe.

The worldview of the Birhor is, however, not static, and it is a dynamic construction of a whole in which two opposite forces, one, centripetal and the other, centrifugal are in operation. Their subsistence strategies, economic values and non-sedentary nomadic life-style with spiritual ties to the forest point to a centripetal force while the practical and existential relations to the caste-based peasant villages and the political economy of the larger society exhibit a force of alienation from the forest. The people meaningfully combine the forces to form a meaningful cosmos of their own.

6

Status and Role of Women in Birhor Society

Division of labour in terms of sex is almost a universal feature in human societies, and it is usually assumed that this distinction between men and women is due to their natural biological and psychological make-up. The comparatively subordinate position of women as reflected from their differential 'activity worlds' is, therefore, thought primarily as a consequence of their innate biological and psychological weakness not a sociological phenomenon.

Anthropologists have traditionally viewed the overall position of men and women in terms of their respective rights and duties as reflected in customs and norms of the society. Considering the comparative dominance of male and female in these aspects a particular society is ascribed as Father-right or Mother-right, or more popularly as Patrilineal or Matrilineal. In fact, positions of men and women in a society have usually been ascertained in terms of their mode of descent, inheritance, and succession within the broad structural framework of patriliny or matriliny.

The Birhor of eastern India with whom we are concerned here are usually identified as patrilineal/ patrilocal people. They are broadly branded as hunters and gatherers. It is assumed that hunting needs dominance of male over female (Service 1966) and hence these people are patrilineal. This evaluation was made primarily in terms of the ideal structural norms instead of organization of practical activities of material exploitation in particular environmental contexts. Social organization of the Birhor, however, reveals a bilateral mode of grouping instead of a unilineal one.

The Birhor, at present, have to procure their principal food item, rice from the neighbouring settled peasantry instead of subsisting directly on forest resources. They collect barks of certain wild creepers and make ropes and rope-made products, and subsequently convert them into food-grains or cash from peasant villages and local markets. They also hunt monkeys and other wild games. But they do it primarily for their own consumption. Sometimes they sell live monkeys (only *Maccacus rhesus* variety) and skins of langurs (*Presbytes entellus*) to the monkey traders (*gari sau*) and other interested villagers. It may be mentioned here that the making of ropes and rope-products has now become the primary occupation of the Birhor. This occupation can be run almost throughout the year while the hunting of wild games is not always very certain and contributes somewhat marginally to the total economy of the Birhor.

In all those spheres of economy the Birhor have to convert forest produce (raw and/or finished) into cash or food. In brief, the whole rubric of Birhor economy involves the extraction of forest resources on one hand and an essential economic interaction with the settled peasantry and the local market on the other.

With these aspects in mind the Birhor have to organize their society. The basic production and consumption unit of them is built around a nuclear family of husband, wife and unmarried children or a variant of it. This unit is locally known as *orha* or household. The most conspicuous economic activity of it is to collect barks from forests and process them into ropes and rope-products so as to make them saleable and/or exchangeable. In a normal set up the husband goes to the forest for collection while the wife keeps the house. Besides the normal duties of cooking and rearing up the children the wife has also to visit the gaoli bazaar or village markets with ropes and rope-products. Boys and girls on their attainment of 7 or 8 years of age, are given due economic importance. Boys go to the forest with their father or elderly brothers. Girls either accompany their mother to villages or look after younger brothers and sisters in the camp thus helping their mother working outside in the village. The children who have not weaned are usually carried on by their mothers.

In the early morning the men of every household leave their camp for the forest. Immediately after their departure the women hurriedly collect some firewoods, drinking water, and arrange them by the side of their huts. After these preliminary works they leave for the villages.

The women hawk ropes and rope-products from village to village. Usually, the women of two to three households move together. In one day a woman can, in this way, cover seven to eight villages traversing a distance of eighteen to twenty miles in both ways. In the villages the women have to decide the price of their commodities. They also have to decide which villages they would visit. Whether a particular commodity is to be exchanged for cash or kind is also ascertained by them. Though these considerations depend, to a great extent, on the domestic requirement of the family, it is, indeed the women who have to take the decision on the spot.

At dusk the men leave the forest for their camps, with a load of barks and other jungle products hanging at the back from a stick across their shoulders. Almost at the same time the ladies start returning from the villages, along with their daily earnings in the form of rice/paddy and sometimes vegetables and cash. Indeed, every day just before dusk one would often notice some dark shadows coming from jungle sides, with loads hanging at the back and some from the village sides, with loads on heads silently approaching a Birhor camp. On reaching the camp the men sit with the barks. For dehydrating the raw barks they display them beside the fireplace either by hanging them from the lower branches of trees or by keeping them on the slope of their leaf-huts. They also cut the already dehydrated barks into small pieces, and start preparing coarse ropes. After making arrangements for cooking the women too join their husbands and exchange one another's information.

Besides the household the Birhor economy also involves social organization of another group namely, the band *(tola)*. A band is group of interrelated households moving and camping together. The major economic activity at the level of band is the pursuit of hunting monkeys and other wild games. For the purpose of hunting monkeys an average man power of 8-10 is necessary and hence the agglomeration of a few households at a place. The band among the Birhor comprises bilateral kin i.e., both affines and agnates. It consists of marriageable spouses, and invariably involves members of their women's lineages.

For essential economic adaptation the Birhor have not only to move from place to place but also maintain an optimum size of human personnel in such a way that scarcity of spouses be solved. Therefore, the people, instead of operating a lineage as a band divide it into small family-centred household units, and then allow them to unite with households of other lineages with which spouses can be exchanged. When a boy or a girl matures, one household seeks another household where exchangeable boys and girls are found. When a girl of one household is married to a boy of another, the former expects one girl from the latter. But if the latter cannot afford the same or do not have any at disposal at that time, it moves along with the former thereby cooperating in day to day economic spheres. In fact, households align together to form a band through a guild of exchange marriage. It may be mentioned here that unmarried boys and girls are of such economic importance to a household that when they grow up the parents feel somewhat insecure, and exclaim:

The children have grown up

There is no more children

It is not good

The tree shade is no more

Above our heads.

It is obvious from the preceding pages that though there are two different domains of activity, 'private' and 'public', the women play an important role in both the domains. The women have, in fact, a pivotal position in the social organization of the total economy of the Birhor. The extraction of forest resources seem to be the job of the men while that of the settled peasantry is the domain of the women. This division of work between men and women is not merely a physical adaptation; it has also some cultural prop. The hunting of wild games, and the entry to the deep forests are normally tabooed to the women. The women have also to observe strict sexual chastity when their husbands go out on hunting. A menstruating woman must not touch hunting nets and other implements.

However, in the management of household organization the Birhor women have to directly play an important role, and here without their participation the rope-making activity could have hardly been perpetuated. In case of band organization also inclusion of wife's lineages is necessary not merely for maintaining an optimum manpower in hunting but also for the vital necessity of perpetuating their very biological existence.

We have seen that the Birhor have to remain in constant contact with the settled peasantry for their day-to-day economic activities. For this they have to interact in such a way as not to arouse any dissent among the villagers. Therefore, the Birhor men often develop ceremonial friendship with the villagers for social security in the context of their essential economic interaction (Adhikary 1974) and in the process their women play an important role. Indeed, the women's frequent visits to the villages and exchange of talks with the villagers create a friendly social ambience that helps keep up the relationship alive. Moreover, the villagers do not appreciate frequent visits of Birhor men to their hamlets. The Birhor men are considered to have magical power to bewitch village women.

It seems apparent from above that the Birhor can no longer maintain the patrilineal type of social structure. However, there is an agnatic core in their social organization. A woman at birth, like a man, inherits the clan name of her father, and it lasts throughout her life. Though a descent group can hardly operate as a property holding corporate unit, it operates as an exogamous unit. Authority lies usually in the hand of father, husband or the older male member according to the composition of the household though the superiority of male power is not expressed in any formal manner.

In spite of their increasing workload the women, however, do not think that they are more competent than their men in handling the major socio-cultural problems. The men also do not make any conscious effort to keep their women in subordinate position. Both men and women contend that if allocation of work is not done in the manner they do, there would be difficulty in procuring food. In case of bark collection the women, therefore, do not hesitate to admit their physical incapability in climbing tall trees. In case of hunting, the notion of the women is that if they do it their gods (*bongas*) would be angry. The women would, however, say that their work in the camp, in villages and markets, is as important as that in the forests for the maintenance of their households. The men also admit it. It, therefore, becomes apparent that there is a mutual endeavour to adjust with the external forces. Indeed, both men and women among the Birhor organize their division of labour keeping in view mainly the perspective of the whole society instead of individual interests in terms of sexual difference.

7

Social Structure of a Dongria Kondh Village (Khambesi)

Introduction

The village Khambesi is located in the district of Koraput in Orissa. It stands on the Niyamgiri hills at a height 4030 ft. from the sea-level. Its nearest railway station is at Chatikona in the plains which is 9 miles away from the village. There was no well arrangement of transport and communication between these two places in 1968 when the author worked.

The village was inhabited by two different ethnic groups—one was the Dongria Kondh, a section of the Scheduled Tribe Kondh and the other, the Dombo, a Scheduled Caste group. The total population of the village was 414 of which the Dongria comprised 256 and the Dombo, 154. The rest four people who were temporarily posted there as social workers belonged to other Hindu caste groups. The entire population of the Dongria was distributed into 44 households while that of the Dombo into 25. A table is furnished below showing the number of households and sex-wise population of the village:

Table 1: Showing the Number of Households and Sex-Wise Population

Name of Ethnic Groups	*No. of Households*	*No. of Persons*				*Total*
		Males	*%*	*Females*	*%*	
Kondh	44	111	43.3	145	56.7	256
Dombo	25	67	43.5	87	56.5	154
Other Castes	02	02	50.00	02	50.00	04
Total	71	180		234		414

The Village

The village Khambesi, as in most other cases in India, is a cluster of houses *(modenilu)*. The houses is arranged in two rows *(ri-sahad)*, and in each row *(sahad)* the houses are continuous in a fashion. Between the two rows is the main street of the village.

Both the Dombo and the Dongria live in two distinct wards known respectively as Dombo *sahadade* and Kuan *sahadade*. Each of these wards is again composed of two rows of houses with a common courtyard at the centre and is a unity on some occasions. For instance, all the households of the Dombo ward together unite together and perform the Diwali festival. The Dongria neither subscribe nor actively participate in its organization. They have, however, separate rituals of their own.

In the case of any death or birth also only the ward in which it occurs is ritually polluted, not the other. If there is any death in Dombo ward, the inhabitants of that ward only join the funeral party not the other. The corpse is burnt or buried as per social norms of the concerned ethnic group. Both the Dombo and the Dongria have their separate cremation grounds located on the bank of the village stream.

As regards occupation the Dongria Kondh practise shifting cultivation on the hill-slopes while most of the

Dombo households have no land for cultivation. They maintain themselves either by weaving clothes, working as daily labourers or making some sorts of pretty business.

In dress and hairstyle also the two ethnic groups maintain perceptible distinctiveness. The Dongria are used to put on a long narrow piece of cloth *(drili)* round the waist in such a way that the two embroidered ends remain hanging, one, in the front and the other, at the back. The cloth round the waist is so tightened and narrowed that it hardly comes downward. The Dombo, on the other hand, wear a broader piece of cloth. In their case the ends of the cloth are not kept hanging but the lower margin comes more downward and remains just above the knee. The Dongria men keep long hair like their women, and dress them either at the back or at the top of the head.

However, in spite of diverse origins, occupations and cultural constellations, the ethnic groups of the village show unity in several contexts. But before describing the contexts of their unity, I would like to give here a few points about the Dombo's social position in the village. The Dombo are present almost in all villages of the Kondh. They are considered low in the local social hierarchy, and thus are not allowed to enter into any Kondh house. In social interaction the Kondh never take any raw *(kachha)* or cooked food from a Dombo's hand. The Dombo also concede their low social position in the locality and show no outward discontent.

But there are some Dombo families who have been living there for a few generations and thus have adapted themselves to many of the Dongria habits and customary behaviour. They have also been able to draw the confidence of the Kondh through their long service to them. The mother tongue of these people is Oriya, but they have, in the course of their proximal living and close interaction with the Kondh, also learnt well Kui and Kuvi, the dialects of the Kondh. These people have since long been acting as intermediaries between the Kondh of the hills and the markets of the plains. They take the products of the Kondh to the markets for sale and barter and fetch them their necessaries. Some of these Dombo families have also acquired cultivable land on the hills. These families are considered members of the village community and allowed to participate in all community rituals and festivals.

This village, possibly like any other Kondh village can function as a unity at four possible levels:

(i) the occasions when all the Dombo and all the Kondh unite together,

(ii) the occasions when all the Kondh and some of the Dombo unite,

(iii) the occasions when some of the Kondh and some of the Dombo unite, and ultimately,

(iv) the occasions when only the Kondh unite together.

When there is an attack of cholera or small pox or such other infectious and fatal diseases, the entire village acts as one and move away to a different village. It really happened so in the case of the village Priscouri, which is now deserted and lying defunct.

Priscouri was a village under the Mutha Wadaka where the village Khambeshi is located. A few years back when there was an attack of epidemic, all the villagers, irrespective their ethnic affiliations, together fled to the villages Khambeshi and Kohrjuri. They also propitiate together the deities presiding over these diseases.

The village boundary has ritual significance. I have seen in Puibhata, another village of the Mutha Wadaka, that at the time of *'jatra gudi' puja*. Wadaka Davoda kept a handful of rice on the border of the village and then uttering some spells killed a chicken whose head was put on the mound of rice. On enquiry I came to learn that some evil deity from Bissum Cuttack tried to come into the village and one of the *'pejenis'* (female shaman) on being possessed by her deity, came to know that. That is why Davoda propitiated the evil deity by some offering on the border and requested not to enter the village.

For good crops the villagers occasionally unite together and hold the *'jatra gudi' puja.* In Khambeshi I have seen a few families unitedly performing such *puja.* On that occasion only dombo who are having land and cultivating it, joined and subscribed to the cost of the rituals. It is to be mentioned here that there is no separate group existence of those Dombo who are not having land. They are like the floating members of the village and are being represented by a few of them who have been living there for generations and have the privilege of owning and cultivating land.

In some ritual and economic activities I found a very interesting extension of the unity of the villagers of Khamesi to those of Kohrjuri and Puibhata. Both these two villages are under the same political head of Khambesi. There was a striking demonstration of the unity among these three villages during my stay at Khambesi. When our party first reached the village we all felt the lack of firewoods and leaves. We, therefore, requested the local Rural Welfare Inspector (R.W.I.) Mr. N. Dhora to help us. He called the headman of the village and told him about our problems. The Headman then raised the matter before their daily village assembly, and from the next day we had been getting our fuels and leaves regularly. Every family of the aforesaid three villages in turn went on supplying fuels and leaves to us. I later on came to learn from Wadaka Davoda, the village headman, that the money paid by us was deposited in the village communal fund of Khambeshi to be spent at the time of any village festival.

In some ritual also these villages function as a unity as in the case of phulapingalanaru puja. During this puja each of the 52 families of the three villages brought offerings to the deity in winnowing fans. Each winnow contained cooked rice or *kosla,* one chicken or egg and burning censer, and the winnows were arranged in rows. Then the village priests Jalia and Wadaka Davoda drew a rectangular structure on the ground which was partitioned into 52 small compartments. They then made a small mound of mandia powder in each of the compartments. Along the middle of the entire rectangular figure a fine thread was passed over the mound. The significance lying behind it is that each compartment represented a family and the thread connected them so that the unity among them would be maintained.

Unfortunately, I did not find any other unit of this sort or, to confess frankly, I did hardly get any time to investigate more intensively. It appears as if I could consider it as a sub-mutha of the Mutha Wadaka. But the populations of the villages Puibhata and Kohrjuri are very small. There are only two families (one Dombo and one Kondh) in Puibhata and four families (all Kondh) in Kohrjuri. Naturally, they would find it difficult to hold a ritual separately, which is at times, very costly. Since these two villages have no separate political heads and are always dependent economically and ritually on the village Khambeshi together, they may be called and taken to constitute one village sociologically.

In the *sadar ghar* which is the common meeting place of the village, all the elderly Kondh assemble every early in the morning. The village Bariki, essentially a Dombo, calls the Kond early in the morning. The Kondh then come out and assembly in the sadar ghar round a fire. Here they discuss about the works of the past, the present and also of the future. Judgements regarding any dispute or crime and offence are also made here. If anybody requires labourers for harvesting his crops, he may propose for the same before the assembly. The assembly then decides the matter. The Bariki who remains sitting near the assembly may also propose for the same on behalf of other Dombos or the Dombos who require labourers can personally approach for the same. It is, indeed, a striking demonstration of the village unity when all the villagers irrespective of ethnic and social affiliations participate in one's harvesting or in the first clearing of jungles for cultivation. This sort of unity can also be observed in the construction of one's new house. All these demonstrations are mainly based on the principle of mutual exchange of labour and service which is the characteristic social norm of the Kondh.

Although the Kondh are numerically dominant the dombo are involved in the administrative activities of the village. The village headman is, however, a Kondh and the post is hereditary. Wadaka Davoda was the headman of the village at the time of my field investigation. In the village assembly each of the Kindh households contributes a member. The Bariki who come from the ethnic group, Dombo, acts as a messenger. He also represents the other Dombos of the village. The Bariki in fact by virtue of his constant association with the headman draws some power. He, however, cannot exert any independent political decision on the members of his own ethnic group. He simply acts as a mediator between the two ethnic groups.

Lastly, I would cite a demonstration of the unity of the Kondh that I witnessed at the time of our departure from the village Khambeshi. On the day we were to come down to the plains the Dombo labourers were engaged in other works. Some of them were also out of the village for some business. The Kondh do not usually carry luggage of others. As a result, we were put to difficulties with our luggage and were in a fix as to what to do. The village headman, Wadaka Davoda, was informed of our difficulties. To our surprise within half an hour almost all the Kondhs of all ages gathered in front of our camp, and agreed to carry our luggage to the Dongria Kondh Development (D.K.D.) office in the plains. The boys, the young and even the elderly persons enthusiastically carried our luggage to the plains and showed their last sign of hospitality to us.

The Dongria Kondhs are shifting cultivators. They grow mandia, kosla and sometimes paddy on the hill slopes. They also grow huge plantains, oranges and pineapples. All the land on the hill slopes belong to the Kondh, and consequently, the large number of wild mango and jackfruit trees do belong to them. All the land is under the possession of the village community and no one has the right to dispose of, or sell it to others. It is a communal property of the Kondh. A particular family gets only the right to cultivate it on the approval of the village assembly. The Dombo, on the other hand, have no land. Some of them are, however, given a temporary right to cultivate a piece of land. The Dombo are otherwise mainly weavers and businessmen. Some also work as labourers. The Kondh use mandia, kosla and rice for consumption and ceremonial purposes. They sell or barter oranges, pineapples, jackfruits and mangoes to the Dombo for their essential things like clothes, iron tools, salt, fowls, goats, buffalos, cows and the like. The Dombo regularly visit the markets in the plains, and deal in the commodities purchased or bartered from the Kondh. They also take the commodities essential for the Kondh and sell or barter them with the people with high profit. The Dombo, in fact, operate as intermediaries between the Kondh and the markets of the larger society.

There is, however, a shop at Chatikona at the foothills about two miles away from Khambeshi. It is constructed specifically for the tribals and run by the DKD (Dongria Kondh Development) authority. The Kondh may easily dispose of their products at the shop and procure their necessaries at reasonable price.There is also one charitable hospital for the people. But the Kondh do not like to visit the place in the plains; instead they are found to depend on the Dombo for their essential marketing. The Kondh are well aware that the Dombo often cheat them and make huge profit from the marketing of their goods. But they rationalize it by saying that the Dombo have been with them since long and will also be here in future while the Government people are very temporary and will soon leave them.

No doubt the grouping of people on the basis of their common residence is extremely important and the very fact of living in close touch for a life-time, forces the people to cooperate in work and play, and to adopt some unity of attitude on many of their common problems. But however strong the tie of locality may be in creating and maintaining human groups, it is usually reinforced by other principles such as those of kinship. In every village the population is heterogeneous in the sense that there are both the Kondh, a tribal population and the Dombo, a Scheduled Caste people. Among the Kondh there are members of different descent groups among which a clear sense of hierarchy is prevalent. The different descent groups of the Kondh living in a village are tied together or feel themselves tied to one another through marital relations. The Kondh families in any village are related to one another either consanguineally or affinally. Besides such relationships the families are also bound to one another on ritual kinship. Friendship is initiated between two individuals on mutual liking and subsequently, becomes socially recognized through ritual observances. This type of ritual kinship is found to bind together also the families of the Kondh and the Dombo.

The friendship between the members is sanctified by a ceremonial eating of cooked food on certain festive occasions. The members concerned sit face to face and take the food simultaneously from the same plate. This ceremonial eating is done in front of the villagers. The individuals generally enter into this kind of union at an early age. After this ceremonial friendship the families of the individuals concerned are tied together through a reciprocal exchange of gifts and services. On occasions they also invite each other. When the two families are of two ethnic groups, i.e., one from the Dombo and the other from the Kondh they do not take cooked food from the same plate. In such case the Kondh or girl is invited to the Dombo family concerned. The Dombo family arranges everything and the Kondh boy or girl himself cooks the food. The cooked is then distributed in two separate plates that are kept apart. The concerned boys or girls sit at their plates and take their food simultaneously. Though there is some sense of pollution between the Dombo and the Kondh, this ceremonial friendship deepens the tie between the families and occasional exchange of presentations is made among them. It would not be out of place to mention here that the friendship is confined to the members of the same sex and age only.

The two friends have some duties and obligations towards each other. None of the party would utter each other's name. In the case of married male friends none will talk to, or even see the face of the other's wife. One may talk to his friend's wife keeping a considerable distance and without looking at her face. It is a serious offence to call her by name. The friends call on another as snai. A man calls his friend's wife as *snai*. The girl friends also call each other as *snai*.

These friends through the maintenance of some avoidance of relationship among the members of their families and also through the obligation of mutual give and take at the time of need indirectly bind two families. Sometimes in each generation the members of the families continue to make such friendship. For example, Wadaka

Davoda is the bond friend of Bidika Lachhan, a Dombo. Now they are old and almost inactive. But the relationship between the families is still continued and Wadaka Gundu, son of Davoda has established bond friendship with Bidika Prakash, son of Bidika Lachhan. Thus the institution of ritual kinship, though based on mutual liking and exists between two individuals, survives even after the death of the individuals linking the families over generations.

8

The Juangs of Orissa: An Ethnographic Note

The Juang is a 'primitive' tribal group of Orissa. In the 1961 Census of India the total population of the Juang was recorded as 21,890. They were distributed primarily in the districts of Dhenkanal (11,551) and Keonjhar (9768). They were also found sporadically in the districts of Cuttack (416), Koraput (154) and Mayurbhanj (2). The original habitat of the Juangs was in the district of Keonjhar from where they migrated to Dhenkanal and other districts.

It was said that the Juangs were previously under the rule of the king of the princely State of Mayurbhanj. The then capital of the State was at Khichching near Keonjhar. But later on the king shifted his capital to Baripada which was situated far away from Keonjhar. From Baripada it was somewhat difficult for the king to look after his tribal subjects, like the Juangs who lived in Juangpirh that covered the hilly tract bordering Dhenkanal and Sundargarh districts. In spite of their exposure to the centralized political system the Juangs are found to operate their traditional system of social contract at the village as well as the ethnic level.

The primary economy of the Juang in Keonjhar is shifting cultivation on the hill slopes. In the district Dhenkanal the Juangs, however, practice shifting as well as wet cultivation. In most of the areas of Dhenkanal the Juang have switched over from *taile* (shifting) cultivation in high lands to wet cultivation in low lands. The Juangs of Pallahara, (formerly a princely State, now a sub-division of Dhenkanal district), have almost given up shifting cultivation under the restriction of forest rules and adopted wet cultivation in the plains; but owing to low yield of their lands most of them are now found to take recourse to the manufacturing of baskets and basket-products based on the wild bamboos growing in the surrounding natural environment.

Field investigation was conducted for a period of one and a half months in the districts of Dhenkanal and Keonjhar. The Juangs of Keonjhar live on the hill slopes and have less contact with the neighbouring caste-peasants while those of Dhenkanal district mostly live in the pain areas and perpetuate symbiotic relation with the regional Orya caste-peasants. In Dhenkanal the Juangs live in multicaste villages and in Keonjhar they live mostly in uni-ethnic villages though there are always a few households of the Gond tribe and Patra castes located in separate hamlets.

For intensive field investigation two villages namely, Guptaganga (in Keonjhar) and Aluajharan (in Dhenkanal) were selected. Guptaganga is 10 kms. away from Keonjhar-Pallahara bus route and located on the hill-slopes near the source of the river Baitarani. Aluajharan is about 8 kms. away from Kamakshyanagar sub-divisional town and located about 2 kms away from the Dhenkanal-Kamakshyanagar bus route.

Village Organization

The Juang society is traditionally characterized by clan-lineage based segmentary system. In the following pages the prevailing norms and customs with reference to certain institutions will be described.

Two important levels of territorial organization are found among the Juangs, one, at the level of village *(gram)* and the other, at the level of pir. While the village *(gram)* is a cluster of households arranged together, a pir comprises a number of villages. Every Juang village is traditionally inhabited by a single clan *(bak)* and has the following officials: *(i)* pradhan, *(ii)* dihuri or nagam, *(iii)* nayaka, *(iv)* kaji, and *(v)* dangua.

Pradhan is the secular head of the village and is usually selected hereditarily. Sometimes he may be recruited otherwise. If the *pradhan*'s sons are not grown up and experienced enough, the oldest knowledgeable man of the village is selected for this position. In fact, the most competent and rich men of the village become pradhan.

Dihuri or *nagan* is the priest or the religious head of the village. In every matter of the village he is consulted. In every ritual function of the village community he is assisted by all other village officials.

Nayaka and *kali* assist the *dihuri* in all the ritual activities of the village. In village rituals the pradhan sacrifices the animal while the dangua helps him either by stretching out the legs of the animal or pulling apart the collar rope.

In some Dhenkanal and Pallahara villages all the above officials are not found. *Nagan* is, however, found in every village. Apart from the council of these officials there are certain other informal mechanism for the maintenance of social order.

Any meeting of the village is held at the dormitory *(majang)* of the village. The dormitory is the biggest house in the village. One side of the dormitory is kept open. It is usually built in the heart of the village. Though it primarily functions as the sleeping house of the young unmarried boys of the village, all the informal and formal gatherings are held in the dormitory. The jurisdiction of the village officials does not go beyond their own community people, and is mostly confined within the village. Punishment is given usually in terms of ostracism or fines in cash or kind. No physical punishment is meted out.

The young unmarried boys who sleep in the dormitory operate as an informal group among themselves. They maintain the dormitory house. They bring firewood for the fire place, which is always kept alive, and preserve a basketful of paddy for the village guests. If there is any guest in the village, he is entertained by the unmarried boys of the village with the paddy stored up in the dormitory. Occasionally unmarried boys and girls from one village may visit another village; in such cases the guest boys and girls sleep in the dormitory house and are entertained by agemates of the village.

Boys of about seven to eight years of age are initiated to the dormitory. At the time of initiation the parents of the boys provide them with one *maan* (about ½ kgs) of rice, one chicken, one bottle of liquor, one shirt and one small piece of cloth; and ceremonially send them to sleep in the dormitory along with other boys.

Pir Organization

Apart from the village council of the officials mentioned above the Juangs have an inter-village organization which may be described as pir organization. The Juang territory is locally known as Juangpir. It is divided into six smaller divisions *(pir)* namely, *(i)* Jharkhond *pir* compring seventeen villages, *(ii)* Rebena *pir* compring 16 villages, *(iii)* Kathua *pir* having 12 villages, *(iv)* Satkhond *pir* having 7 villages, *(v)* Charigar *pir* having 6 villages, and *(vi)* Hunda Dandapat *pir* having 11 villages.

Each *pir* had one headman, called *sardar,* who was appointed by the king. The *sardar* collected revenue in the form of cash and goats from the villages under his jurisdiction and presented them to the king. In the month of *pausa* (a month in Orya and Bengali calendars) when the winter crops were harvested the *sardars* collected crops like *rasi,* paddy from the villages under jurisdictions for the king. Each of the *sardars* had to give 25 *pai* of *rasi* and 11 *khondi* of paddy (440 kgs). *Rasi* was offered to the temple and the paddy, directly to the king as revenue. At the time of Car festival in the month of Ashad (a month in Orya and Bengali calendars), the Sardars had to provide coir to the king's palace for pulling the car. The king, in turn, presented red or black turbans *(shiropa), dhoti* and shirts to the *sardars*.

The *sardars* were appointed by the king. At the time of appointment the king took the votes of the *pradhan* (head) of the villages. The man who was elected by the majority of the *pradhan* was selected or appointed by the king as *sardar* of the *pirs*.

The *sardar* had to look after the villages under his jurisdiction. He had not only to collect the revenue for the king but also to settle the disputes or litigations within his jurisdiction. In case of any inter-village dispute all the pradhans of his village were called at the convenient place and a meeting was held under the leadership of the *sardar*, no official could exercise arbitration. Decisions were taken unianimously.

It may be mentioned here that the pir organization is no longer in vogue. Most of the Juangs in Keonjhar, however, still remember the system, and the sardars are respected. The villagers, under his jurisdiction often ask for his mediation in mitigating any litigation among them.

The constituent villages of a pir are related by kinship ties. There is thus a continuity between their traditional mode of social control by kin-based non-centralized social system and the territorial organization introduced by the king of the princely State.

Panchayat System

In Gonasika pachayat 17 *mouzas* or revenue villages were grouped into 12 wards, each having a representative member to the panchayat. Of these 8 were from the Juang community, 1 from the Patra, a scheduled caste community, and 3 from the Bhuiyan, another major tribal community in the area. The Secretary was a Gonda by caste while the *Sarpanch* was a Juang.

Although in the gram panchayat the majority of the members are from the Juang community, they hardly bring any internal problem of their community to the panchayat for trial. Rather, cases involving other non-tribal are brought to the panchayat. If any land or property of any Juang is forcibly occupied and enjoyed by any non-tribal, the case is invariably brought to the panchayat, or even to the police station. Internal problems are handled within the village and among the members of the community.

Jati Panchayat

In Dhenkanal the Juangs, like the low Hindu caste groups of the locality, form councils of their community. They locally refer to such councils as *jati shabha*. A *Juang jati shabha* normally covers a number of villages and consists of three main officials, namely *bade behera, sai behera* and *pai behera*.

Bade behera is the head of the *jati shabha*. He is also called *sabhapati*. He can convene any meeting at any time. No *jati* meeting can be held without his notification. *Sai behera* is the head at the village level. Every village has one *sai behera*. There may be more than one *pai behera* in a village. The function of a *pai behera* is to announce the date of a meeting among the community members of the village and to help sai behera in various other matters.

The cases of divorce and adultery within the community are usually dealt with by this council or *shabha*. There is no venue earmarked for the meeting of the *jati shabha*. It can be held in any village under the jurisdiction of the *Shabha*.

The officers are not hereditary. Experienced and knowledgeable persons are appointed to the offices through election.

Nuclear Family

The Juangs living in the districts of Dhenkanal and Keonjhar organize their society mostly in terms of nuclear family; only a few joint families were found at the time of field investigation. Authority rests on the father or the husband according to the nature of the family. In the district of Keonjhar the sons who, on marriage, form separate families and run independent households, however, hold and cultivate the land jointly with their father. In such cases authority rests on the father.

Age at Marriage

Boys among the Juangs are married usually after 15 or 16 years of age. Girls are married after they attain puberty. The Juangs' belief is that girls attain puberty usually at the of 11 years or above. Though maximum marriages are settled on the mutual consent of the bride and groom, it is hardly found that younger brothers or sisters are married before their elders.

Bride-Price

The Juangs of Keonjhar have the custom of bride-price. At the time of marriage the groom's party gives one rupee to the bride's mother's brother and another to her father. This system of bride-price seems symbolic in nature.

Marriage is performed on auspicious days that are ascertained by the village priests, and involves much preparatory functions. Whether a particular marriage will be a good one or not is also ascertained by the priest through his usual method of divination. Three grains of paddy are kept in such a way that one remains above the two. Then these grains of paddy are covered with a basket, and kept there for one night. After lifting it if the grains are found undisturbed, it is presumed that the prospective marriage will be a good one. There is one major difference between the marriage practices of the Juangs of Dhenkanal and those of Keonjhar. While in Dhenkanal the Juang grooms go to the bride's village for marriage in Keonjhar the bride has to come to the groom's village.

Marriage

The types of marriage followed by the Juangs are as follows:

(i) *Kamandiria kania:* it is a marriage by negotiation. Someone acts as a middleman. After the marriage is settled and the date is fixed a party comprising women, unmarried boys and girls of the bride's village take the bride to the groom's village. The boys accompanying the party carry with them their musical drums *(changu)*; they dance and sing in the groom's village and celebrate the marriage. The groom's father entertains the members of the bride's party with food and drink.

(ii) *Digar kania* is a marriage by capture. If a boy falls in love with a girl he may arrange to capture her by his friends from the dancing ground or from the bathing ghat, or from the jungle and take her to his paternal house. After the capture the boy's father sends information to the girl's father seeking his approval of her daughter's marriage with his son. The approval is invariably accorded. However, after the ritual is over the couple pay a ceremonial visit to the bride's natal house and the groom pay money, clothes, paddy and other things as token of bride price.

(iii) *Mana mani:* It is a love marriage which is widely prevalent among the Juangs of the locality. Juang boys and girls often fall in love during their ceremonial music and dances. They express through symbolic gestures their mutual liking during dances. The Juangs dance in two rows, one of boys and men and the other girls and women, facing one another. A boy may express his liking by touching the foot of a girl in the opposite row. The girl if agrees conveys her consent in the same manner as the boy. Afterwards they visit each other's villages, go on outing in jungle and exchange gifts. The boy later informs his parents of his liking who, in turn requests the girl's parents for consent. Normally, the marriage is approved and ceremonially performed.

(iv) *Surum kania* is essentially a marriage by elopement. If the parents of the girl do not approve of her love to her boyfriend, she flees with him to another village and settle there as married couple After several years when the problems seem to have calmed down the boy comes back, along with wife, to his natal village

(v) *Udung kania* is a marriage between a boy and a pregnant girl. Sometimes unrestrained dating and lovemaking lead to sexual indulgence and subsequently the pregnancy of the girl. In such cases, the boy is forced by the *jati* council to marry the girl. In a public meeting the parents of both the boy and the girl are fined by the *jati* council. Fine is charged in terms of money which is used by the officials for drinking liquor. The father of the boy is asked to offer also a feast to the villagers of the girl. This type of marriage is locally called *udung kania*.

Monogamy is the rule but polygyny is not rare. A man may keep more than one wife at a time. In Keonjhar I found one man who had four wives—all living together with one kitchen but in separate huts. The reason of polygyny as told by my informants, is normally the barrenness of wife. There are certain social and economic reasons too.

The Juang society is divided into a number of exogamous clans *(bok)*. Some clans feel themselves related to another and referred to as *kutum bok*. The members of these clans trace their descent from a common ancestor, and hence marriage among them is considered incestuous. There is another category of clans called *bandhu bok* with whom marriage is socially permissible. Both the *kutum* and the *bandhu boks* are reference terms; the member-clans of each category refer to one another as *kutum* while the clans that are related maritally are referred to as *bandhu boks*.

There is another category of clans known as *surya bok*. Unlike the clans of *kutum bok* who consider themselves related to one another on the assumption that the are descended from a common ancestor the member-clans of this category can trace their common descent from a known ancestor. Marriage among these clans is prohibited.

Since every village is inhabited by the members of a single clan or the clans belonging to a *kutum bok*, marriage within the village is also not permitted and the village exogamy is the rule. There is a tendency towards mother's brother's daughter marriage. The Juangs, however, try to avoid actual mother's brother's daughter, and prefer to marry classificatory mother's brother's daughters.

The Juangs of the locality follow the custom of marrying elder brother's widow. Younger brother's widow is, however, avoided. Junior sororate i.e., marrying wife's younger sister is permissible among the Juangs if the first wife is dead.

Divorce is locally called *chharpatra* and it is effective only with the consents of both the husband and the wife. Normally a man asks for a divorce if his wife fails to bear any children for him and the man is unable to maintain more than one wife at a time. A wife may also ask for divorce if she finds the man no match for her, and has love affairs with another man.

Affairs of divorce are, however, settled in the village council. If it is found that the husband is guilty, he has to give Rs. 20/- to Rs 30/- and one sari to his wife. If the wife has any child in arms, the husband has also to bear the cost for the maintenance of the child until it is grown up. The husband, however, has the right to take away the child after it has weaned.

Pre-marital sex-indulgence is permitted, but within certain limits and privacy. Pre-marital love leading to pregnancy is socially depreceting. In such cases the boy and the girl involved are forced to marry by the village council. Marriage among the prohibited range of kin relations is a serious offence. The boy and the girl are both ostracized from the village community; they may, however, live in some distant village and come back again. The man so punished normally plants a tamarind tree in the village before leaving for another village and returns to it, along with his wife and children, when the tree starts bearing fruits. The man, on his return, has to organize a communal feast in which some curry of the tamarinds of his tree must be a menu.

Property

In Keonjhar land is owned collectively as well as individually. The Juangs of this area practise shifting cultivation on hill slopes. The land on the hills surrounding the settlement belongs to the village. One has just to clear the jungle and prepare the land for one's own cultivation. The man has only the usufractory right on the land he is able to clear. The household normally consists of nuclear family of husband, wife, and unmarried children and acts as the usual production and consumption units of the Juang. Sometimes several agnatically related households of the village jointly perform the productive activities. The products are, however, distributed among the households in terms of their labour-contribution.

In every village there are jackfruit and mango trees. Some of these trees belong to lineage groups and some, to the village community, and some, to individual families. Normally, the ownership of a tree rests on the individual who plants it, and after his death the ownership is transmitted to his descendants. But the trees of the man who dies without any heir become the property of the village community, that is shared equally by the villagers. If a man leaves a village permanently, he may also donate his trees to the village community.

Moveable properties are normally transmitted in the male line. Married girls may sometimes get their share of fruits from the trees of their natal families. Sometimes mothers give their ornaments and clothes to their daughters, though there is no hard and fast rule in this connection.

Conclusion

In the foregoing pages an attempt has been made to delineate the traditional norms and customs of the Juangs of Orissa. At present the Juangs, like most other tribes of India, are exposed to the forces of market-based economy and politics of the larger society, though the exposures are not always uniform.

The Juangs of Dhenkanal and Pallahara districts live in multi-ethnic villages of the plains and combine wet cultivation in low lands with swidden cultivation on the hill slopes for survival. Many of them have also been given lands and other aids in cash and kind by the government and non-government development agencies. As a result there has occurred a perceptible transformation in their pattern of ownership of land and other types of property. The idea of private property and individual ownership seem to be replacing the their traditional spirit of collectivity. The people now resort to the assistance of the regional Block Office and Police Stations for solution of their land problem and inter-ethnic disputes.

In the course of their day-to-day interaction with the larger society the Juangs of Dhenkanal and Pallahara have also emulated certain features of social control mechanism from the Hindu caste-peasants of the locality. The low caste groups of this locality have their own councils (locally called *jati panchayat*) where the problems of their caste people are discussed and settled. The *jati panchayat* among the Juangs seems to be an adoption of the model for the maintenance of social order among the people across villages that are no longer uniethnic. In neighbouring peasant villages marriage is held in the bride's parental house. The practice of *kamardira kania* marriage of the Juangs, in which the bride and her party come to the groom's village for marriage is gradually being given up. The communal dance of men and women and the beating of their traditional musical drum *changu* in connection with the marriage are no longer prevalent. It may be noted in this connection that many of customary practices of the Juangs are looked down upon by Hindu caste-peasants of the locality. Juangs are aware of this notion of their neighbours and try to strategically organize their society to adapt to the surrounding socio-cultural environment. Despite apparent transformations there is a strong in-group sentiment among the people.

The Juangs of Keonjhar are, however, less exposed to the modernizing forces of the larger society. Though in every village of this locality there are some households of the Hindu caste groups: the Gouda and the Patra, the Juangs are dominant in all respects. In the case of any dispute the Goudas and the Patras approach the traditional village council led by the Juangs. The Gouda and the Patra families in any village are tied to some Juang families primarily in terms of economic transaction. It may be noted here there are also in every village one or two blacksmith families. It is reported that during the king's rule the forefathers of these caste families were settled by the Juang into their territory for some essential work and service necessary for their survival. The Gaudas used to herd their cattle, the Patras supplied their liquor and the Blacksmiths manufactured and repaired their iron implements.

The pir level of territorial structure of the Juangs that was developed by the kings of the former princely states of Mayurbhanj and Keonjhar over their traditional clan-lineage based segmentary system of kinship did not, however, lose its social significance. All the families of the villages of a pir reckoned their relationship to one another through common kinship tie. The clans comprising the families traced their descent from a common ancestor and considered themselves as one social entity, kutum bok. The eldest male member of the dominant clan of the kutum bok used to hold the office of the Sardar or the chief of the pir, and it was succeeded hereditarily. Although the institution of centralized authority is no longer in vogue; the people still seek for the intervention of the Sardar in the case of any inter-village dispute in the *pir*.

9

Social Organization and Change: A Study of the Santal in a Village of West Bengal

Introduction

The Santal like most other tribes in India have usually been conceptualized as a self-contained distinct homogeneous community. The earlier ethnographic studies on these people were concerned primarily with the reconstruction of the normative pattern of their life and culture (Sherwill 1851, Dalton 1872, O'Malley 1910, Bodding, Culshaw 1949, Mukherjee 1962, Archer 1974). Later on, the attention of the ethnographers was drawn to the situation of their contacts with the larger society, and subsequently, a few studies were made on the people pointing out aspects of changes in the normative pattern of their social and cultural life (Dutta-Majumdar 1956, Orans 1965, Mahapatra 1977, Gautam 1977). These studies, in fact, broadly dealt with the aspects of their emulative-acculturation, and little or attention was paid to the processual aspect of their social organization in the context of their changing techno-economic situation. In his study on the Santals in Santiniketan, Birbhum, Kochar tried to delineate aspects of their social organization. He, however, studied the social organization of the Santal primarily in relation to their traditional system of kinship and descent within the broad framework of 'social structure' of the British School of Social Anthropology (Kochar 1970). It may be mentioned in this connection that ideal-typically a tribal society is conceptualized as a clan-lineage based segmentary system characterized by mechanical solidarity. Within this broad framework, most of the studies on the formal aspects of social organization of the tribal groups in India were made giving little or no attention to the context of their subsistence technology.

Since long the Santal have been pursuing plough cultivation and operating their subsistence activities within the broad framework of the agrarian economic structure of the caste-based Hindu society. They have also been exposed to the market as well as the political forces of the larger society. From a deep probe into life-situations of the contemporary Santals we, however, get the impression that despite their adaptation to the plough cultivation and exposure the politico-economic forces of the larger society the Santals seem to live in a world of dynamic isolation perpetuating a distinct social and cultural life. This social and cultural distinctiveness has been attributed broadly to the traditional value system of the people (Sinha 1958, Bhattacharya 1968). In order to understand the nature of their society an attempt has been made here to study the manner and the way the Santals adapt their traditional social structure to the present techno-economic situation. The society of the Santals, in fact, is to be studied as if in a state of adaptive process both in terms of their traditional social structure based on kinship and descent and the existent subsistence technology.

For the purpose of our study intensive field investigations were made in a village named Mahisdal in Bolpur-Sriniketan Block, Birbhum, West Bengal. Preliminary census of the households in the village was collected through structured schedules. Genealogical tables were also prepared to understand the nature of relations among the members of the households, as well as to understand the effective and affective range of their descent groups. The members of the village belonging to different age and sex groups were interviewed and their day to day activities especially in connection with their subsistence activities were observed. Observations through participation in many of their productive and cultural activities were made, and respondents were often asked about the meanings of their behaviour in the context.

Mahisdal is a revenue village and is inhabited both by the Santal and the Hindu caste people. But they live in two different hamlets separated by a long stretch of paddy field and operate as two distinct entities. For the purpose of our present study we will, however, concentrate primarily on the Santals and their hamlet.

Techno-Economic Activities

Though the Santals of the village operate within the broad framework of the agrarian economic structure, only a few of them own cultivable lands. Out of 115 households of the village only 9 (7.8%) households own lands. Twelve households (10.43%) are landless; these households have however, their own plough and cattle. These landless householders work as share-croppers *(bhagchasi)* in the lands of their neighbouring Hindu caste-peasants. Sixteen households (13.9%) have neither land nor plough and plough-cattle; they also work as share-croppers in the fields of the caste-peasants of the locality. These category of sharecroppers is, however, locally known as *kirsan*. Both the *bhagchasi* and *kirsan* work on share-contract. While the ratio of the share between a bhagchasi and his landlord is 50:50 that between a kirsan and his landlord is 25: 75.

There are 22 (19.13%) households that have small amount of land. These householders cultivate their own lands and also work as share-croppers *(bhagchasi)* in the lands of the local caste-peasants. There are four (3.4%) households that are tagged to the non-tribal landed peasants as *mahindar.* These people are engaged by the Hindu peasants for the whole year and besides the routine agricultural activities they have perform all sorts of work for the landlord. The *mahindars* are paid in cash and kind. Of the rest of the landless some are attached to the non-tribal peasants as nagare munish. Unlike the *mahindar* these people work for their employers only during the agricultural season at a cheaper rate. During lean periods these labourers take advance from the landlords in cash or kind on the condition that they would pay back the same by working in their lands at the rate at the time of borrowing. Thirty eight households (33%) earn their livelihood primarily as daily wage labourers in agricultural/non-agricultural sectors. In the non-agricultural sector the Santals work mostly as casual labourers in the rice mills, the construction of buildings, the digging of wells and similar other fields. It may be mentioned here that some of their women work as maidservants in the non-tribal households in Santiniketan and Bolpur areas.

The Santals of Mahisdal are also engaged in other occupations. Seven persons (six men and one man) work as regular employees in private and government concerns. Among them two persons work as unskilled labourers at Visva-Bharati, Santiniketan, one as a compounder to a medical practitioner at Bhubandanga, two at the irrigation Department, Govt. of West Bengal, one at a local pipe factory, and one as a teacher in the primary school of the village. There are also three grocery stores run by three Santals of the village. One man has a sewing machine at his house and runs a tailoring shop in the village and another has a rickshaw that he pulls at Bolpur. Shop-keeping is primarily a secondary occupation and those who run shops do not seem to be enterprising. The shops are run mostly by some young members of the land-owning Santal households specifically when the harvesting of the crops is over. One of the intentions behind shop-keeping is to make the domestic necessaries readily available to the villagers through their traditional mode of exchange in cash, kind or both. The village shops also serve as important venue for the gossip of the old.

Despite occupational diversities almost all the Santals irrespective of age, sex and economic status engage themselves in hunting, fishing and gleaning in the natural environment of the region. Though many of the households do not have plough and plough-cattle, almost every one of them possesses one or two sets of bows and arrows, one or two or even more sling-shots *(batu)*, a few bird-traps and quite a good number (9) of fishing implements. Small boys have their own bows and arrows, and are often found to move about with them. They move primarily in a sportive manner and in the course of time get themselves trained in the art of hunting games. Though the Santals do not get much economic returns from their pursuits of hunting, gathering and fishing, they get much pleasures in them and appear to have natural skill in it.

The region where the author studied the people is primarily a mono-crop area. The agricultural season starts with the onset of monsoon rains in June-July and ends in December-January. The Santals manure and plough their fields in June-July. The sowing of seeds starts in July-August while the transplantation of seedlings and the weeding of the fields are over by August-September. Harvesting starts in November and by January it is over.

A close probe into the work situation reveals that the sandals of the village remain engaged in agricultural activities for about five months in year but not in a uniform manner. For the rest of the year most of the landless householders resort to the labour-work in non-agricultural sectors. It may be mentioned here that Santals, irrespective of their land positions prefer to remain engaged in cultivation. But when agricultural activities are over they would like to engage themselves in hunting, fishing, and gleaning the common property resources in the surrounding locality. It may be noted here that the exploitation of common property resources can be done almost uniformly throughout the year.

The Santals of Mahisdal have fair knowledge and expertise not only in the day-to-day activities of agricultural and hunting and gathering but also in the preparation of different implements associated with them. There are five craftsmen in the village who are experts in manufacturing agricultural implements like plough and ladder. They can also manufacture husking lever, wooden doors, windows, beams cots and the barrels of drums. They say that due to the scarcity of jungles in the locality and the non-availability of necessary timbers they can no longer pursue the craft. These people, in fact, used to operate in the past more or less as a specialized occupational group for their proficiency and skill (though every Santal appears to have the preliminary know-how of the crafts). From a deep probe into the techno-economic activities and the knowledge and expertise of the people I get the impression that the Santals have a natural proficiency and skill in hunting and fishing, as well as in the manufacturing of its implements. Even the boys of 6-7 years of age can prepare bow and arrow, and slingshots. Almost all the fishing implements are prepare by themselves though nowadays, a few of these implements are found to be purchased directly from the market or from the professional caste people of the locality. Besides these the Santals also distinguish three distinct types of soil and are well aware of the kinds of crops suitable for each of the types.

Food Habit and Living Standard

The principal food item of the Santal is rice and they normally take two meals a day. Their meals are very simple and consist mostly of cooked rice with a pinch of salt and chili. Those who can afford prepare some curry that consists mostly of some boiled/fried vegetables. Meat or fish is prepared specifically on festive occasions or at the time when some close relatives or guests are to be entertained. Children have no fixed time for meals; they take as and when they need. They are at liberty to consume instantly on the spot the fishes and the games they catch during their itinerary.

The Santal are very fond of rice beer *(handi)*. During summer and festive days many of them are often found to go, without food, on only drinking *handi* and *tadi* (fermented palm juice) for two or three days at a stretch. They say that these drinks not only give them pleasure but also satisfy their appetite. An enquiry into their nature and kind of food items reveals that the range of their food is wider than that of any other people in the locality. Many of their food items involve raw natural products that are often avoided by others. While refreshing their memory some old Santals, however, noted that there were enough food in nature when they young and cereals and pulses like *janhe, jandra, gundli, iri* and *irba* were grown profusely in the hill-slopes.

Though the Santal women are fond of keeping themselves neat and clean and decorating their body with flowers and ornaments, very few of them possess more than one pair of garments. The women normally use *lungis* (a long piece of cloth the ends of which are sewn together) as lower garments and another piece of long cloth as upper garment which they roll over their breast and tie to the lower garment at the waist. Some of them also wear blouse and sari like their Hindu neighbours. The men usually use a small piece of dhoti or lungi as loincloth. In the village, normally they do not use any upper garment. Some people are, however, found to use banyan and shirts as upper garments specially when they are on an outing. Children of 5 or 6 years of age and above use shorts as lower garments; normally they do not use any upper garment.

Most of the villagers live in mud-built houses thatched with straw. One Santal big farmer has, however, two houses with corrugated tin sheds. This man has also a bicycle, and a horse. He uses the horse both for pleasure-rides and cartpulling. There are also five other bicycles and three transistors in the village. However, if we look deep into the day-to-day life-style of the people, it becomes evident that their standard of living is not much incongruous to their economic condition. There is a craving, specifically among the young boys and girls, for luxury goods. The cultivators who are economically better, however, prefer to invest in their children's education as well as in the purchase of land. The culture of consumerism does not seem to have any perceptible impact on their normal concept of good life in the given economic situation. On an average the modern amenities of the larger society have not been able to make any perceptible change in the normal expectations and desires of the people.

Household

The Santals of Mahisdal organize their subsistence activities primarily in terms of the groups: household *(orak)* and village *(ato)*. Of these two, the household is their principal production and consumption unit. A probe into the size and composition of their households reveals that though there is a tendency towards nuclearization of their production and consumption units, the Santals always prefer to form group with some of their agnates/ or affines. However, all the men, women and their unmarried children in a household work independently or collectively for the maintenance of the common household. Division of labour among the members of the households is based primarily on age and sex. With the onset of monsoon rains in June-July the men of the household start carrying manure to the fields. Their women also assist in the carrying of the manure and spreading it in the fields. Ploughing is tabooed to women and is the task of men. The levelling of the soil in the ploughed fields and the broadcasting of seeds are normally done by the men but in many cases women also perform the jobs in close collaboration with their men. Transplantation of the new seedlings is, however, invariably done by women. It is not tabooed to the men but they believe that the transplantation is performed better by the women. The Santal women, in fact, contribute much labour in agricultural operations.

During rainy days when men remain busy in ploughing, levelling and making the fields ready for transplantation, the women having finished their cooking and other domestic work carry meals and water to them and stay along with their men assisting the work in the fields. The children of 6-7 years old normally move about in the fields also assisting their parents in their work. Sometimes the children younger than the above are found to cling to their parents during their work in the field. These children are often left in a pool of water and mud to play about freely. The children in this way not only are exposed to different agricultural operations but also get acclimatized to the natural environment.

Small boys look after the cattle, sheep and goats of their respective households. Some also take the cattle of other households together to the fields to graze. These boys are locally known *bagal*. A *bagal* who works for others, normally gets one or two meals a day and one or two piece of clothes a year from the concerned householders.

The cattle-herders always move in groups. In the fields they allow the cattle to graze freely, and spend their time in a sportive manner by singing, gossiping and playing flutes (*tirio* or *murli*). They catch fishes and other games like rats, lizards, birds and the like from the natural water-pools and bushes in the surrounding ecology. They burn their catches on the spot and share the spoil among themselves for consumption. The sight of the *bagals* in the field would hardly give the impression that they suffer from the drudgery of the workload entrusted upon them by their elders. The parents of the boys also do not appear to nourish any feeling that they are unduly imposing work-loads on their minor wards. The work of herding the cattle by the small boys, in fact, appears to be institutionalized as a part of their life and culture. The job fits well to the usual playful disposition of the children and generates a spirit of work and cooperation among them from the very beginning of life and activity.

Old men and women of a household also do not sit idle either. They too work in the fields or stay at the house doing domestic work or looking after the small children. The old women, if necessary, also carry the small babies to the work-site of their mothers to feed them with breast-milk.

During the busy days in agricultural seasons many of the landless Santals move, along with wives and children, to the neighbouring district of Barddhaman to work as labourers. Barddhaman is an agriculturally prosperous area and the Santals who are considered expert in agricultural operations flock together to this area from many other places to work as hired labourers. The Santals from Mahisdal thus make temporary camps along with the other Santal labourers and stay there for two to three weeks. After the work is over they come to their village.

After the harvest of the crops the Santals turn their attention to other jobs that were kept pending so far: the repairing of houses, the erecting new huts or holding marriage ceremony, etc. The marginal landholders and the landless labourers, however, mostly engage themselves in non-agricultural labour-work for subsistence. Both the men and the women go out for work on daily wage in building construction, brick-kilns, rice-mills and also in the gardens of private households in adjoining area. When they do not have any such work, they go out for fishing in the river Kopai or in the surrounding natural water-pools. The women keep themselves busy in collecting *gugli* (shellfish) and small crabs. Some men and boys are found to move about with their bows, arrows, bird-traps and slingshots to hunt birds and other small games like rats, squirrels, porcupines and the like. Some people, especially the women and the girls are found to go out with small jute bags and brooms to collect dry leaves, twigs, branches and creepers from the surrounding jungles and the gardens for fuels. They collect these things for day-to-day use as well as store them for use during rainy season. It may be mentioned in this connection that except one or two households in the village almost every one has to depend on nature for firewood, and the Santal nowadays regret for not having a steady supply of firewood owing to depletion of natural forests in the area.

The Hindu caste as well as the Muslim peasants of the locality prefer Santal women for labour-work. One of the reasons for this is the low wage for women labour. There are also other reasons which are no less important than above. The Santal women, in fact, can perform almost all sorts of manual liking, collecting firewoods, digging soil and carrying loads on heads besides delicate handling of utensils and other household articles. The usual gay communicative and witty nature as well as the clean appearance make them particularly attractive. As a result, during lean seasons when many of the men remain unemployed, their women are found fairly engaged. In such cases the men of the household carry out the necessary household work including cooking. They also look after the children. This type of reversal in the division of labour is very common among the Santals.

The Santals leave their village for labour- work normally at 8.00 or 8.30 a.m. They always travel in groups and every one carries with him or her one aluminium tiffin-carrier containing rice and salt for lunch during their recess. In the work-site they retain their very cooperative spirit as well usual enthusiasm. A glance at the Santal labourers at work often gives the impression they work with pleasure. After the work is over, they leave in groups for their village at about 4.30 or 5.00 p.m. They walk along the street singing melodious tune of their usual nature, gossiping and also laughing all the time thereby surcharging the surrounding atmosphere with joy and gaiety. From a sight of such a group of people it is very difficult to think that they returning after their day's hard toil. The whole day's manual labour hardly tells upon their usual gay disposition.

The service-holders among the Santals do not stay away from their village. They regularly go to their work-site in the morning and come back in the evening and their income is spent for the common maintenance of their household. Except in a few cases of the cattle-herders all the collections of the natural products as well as fishes and games caught by the individuals are pooled together and shared by the members of the household. Normally the finance is managed by some elderly male member, specially the head of the household but the expenses are made in consultation with all the adult members of the household. Although the income of the members are pooled together, every member may, if necessary, keep some amount for his or her personal use but always within the knowledge of other members.

Normally, jobs like cooking, rearing the children, husking the paddy in the country made husking lever, collecting fuels, drawing water from wells and the river for drinking as well as cleaning, washing the utensils, cleaning huts and yard are specified for the women. But if the working woman is sick or happens to carry a baby in arms, her husband does the jobs for her. The author has come across, on many occasions, men to press chili and turmeric into powder, husk paddy in the husking lever, or to fetch fuel. They have also been found to look after the younger babies and help their wives carry out household work. Sometimes the elder sons and daughters also look after younger brothers and sisters thereby helping their mothers doing work.

Village

Although every household operates more or less as an independent production and consumption unit, it is highly embedded in the social and cultural matrix of the village *(ato)* and as such many of their economic decisions and activities are subject to the approval and sanctions of the village society.

The Santals say that in the past they used to own land communally. Some piece of land was allocated to the village officials, namely, the *manjhi haram, naeke, kudum naeke, jogmanjhi, godet* and *paranik*. This land was known as *manjomi*. This was meant for the subsistence of the officials as well as for the expenses of the village festivals. Due to the scarcity of communal land, this system is no longer in vogue. Instead, for communal festival subscriptions in cash/kind are raised from the households of the village. Each of the traditional officials are now paid annually Rs. 5/- to Rs. 10/- for their community service.

Although most of the people are either landless or marginal farmers, all of them have some amount of residential land which is owned by the village. Some of the householders are now found to have got their homestead land recorded in their name. In case of the homestead land owned communally, the householders have only the usufructory right. They can neither sell nor pass it on to anybody else without the approval of the village council. If a householder leaves he village, the land becomes the village property. But the man, in his absence from the village, may continue to have the right on his land of the village if he regularly contributes the subscription toward the village festivals. With proper approval of the village council he may also hand over his homestead land to one of his relatives who, in turn, contributes subscription for the village festival.

The different phases of the productive activities of the Santal are always accompanied by some rituals and ceremonies that are held communally in the village. The households of the village are permitted to perpetuate their independent productive activities only after these communal rituals and ceremonies are over. This kind of ritual sanction , in fact, acts as a moral force in binding the households of the village into a corporate productive unit and stands in the way of complete nuclearization or individualization of productive units. It is only after the festival *'erok'* held in the month of June that the villagers are ritually permitted to sow their seeds in their respective fields. Again, it is after the communal festivals *'iri gundli,* and *janthar* held in September and November respectively that some of their products are ready for consumption and secular use. During these festivals the new crops that are harvested at that time are ritually offered to their deities. *Sohrae* is another important village festival of the Santals. Although the festival is connected with their agricultural activities and primarily revolves round the cattle complex, it is, in fact, a ritual and symbolic representation of the whole range of their traditional productive activities. The festival lasts for six days and is held in the month of January after the winter crops have been raised by the villagers. Celebration of the *mag* festival in the month of February ends their agricultural calendar and it is after this festival that the villagers are socially permitted to bring the straw to their houses and use them for thatching huts or other secular purpose. On the day following the *mag* festival the village officials are ritually paid off for their sevices to the village for the year. On that day the annual contract labourers *(mahindar)* are also paid and new contracts are made in presence of the villagers.

An intimate probe into the ritual process and the behaviour pattern of the people during different village festivals reveals a consistent tendency towards reinforcing the village solidarity thereby arresting the apparent socio-economic differentiations among the villagers. For instance, on the second day of the *magh parab* a ritual is held at the *manjhi sthan*, the sacred place in memory of the first settler and leader of the village when all the villagers including the traditional officials ritually surrender their lands and offices to the present *manjhi haram* who represents the direct heritage of the first settler and leader of the village. Normalcy is, however, restored as soon as the ritual is over.

Besides cultural and religious beliefs and practices associated with their productive activities there are also norms of reciprocal interaction among the Santals reinforcing the corporate nature of their village society. There is a system of cooperative labour among the Santals. If a householder needs additional labour in his agricultural operations, he may seek the help of other householders in the village. Those who extend labour are not paid in cash or kind. They are simply entertained with rice beer *(handi)* and puffed rice *(khijuri)* and sometimes with meat curry by the man for whom they work. Obligation of the man towards these volunteers is not, however, over with the offering of rice beer *(handi)*. The man for whom the people work as free labour *(bagar)* is also supposed to render his free labour to them as and when they would require. People are, in fact, bound together to one another on mutual obligation and continue to reciprocate among themselves as and when they feel the need. This type of cooperative labour arrangement is also found in the construction of house and other non-subsistence spheres of activity. All the households of the village are, in this way, interwoven into a single social system.

Sometimes, a man may have a piece of land but no plough and cattle to cultivate. He may, however borrow the same from other cultivators who also feel it their moral obligation to help *(goro)* their neighbours. The partners involved celebrate such transaction through drinking of rice beer that is arranged by the borrower.

The normative reciprocation of goods, services and labour in terms of rice beer across diverse spheres of their life and activity binds the households of the village into a kind of moral community. Despite their economic articulation with the caste-peasants and market economy of the larger society, the Santals try to organize the subsistence activities within the social bounds of their village. There is a system of loan through which the landless Santals can be sustained in lean periods. Two varieties of loan are prevalent among the people: *delbari* and pancha. The former is given on a long-term basis, and some interest is charged for it. The second variety of loan is given on a short-term basis, and no interest is charged against it. In the *delbari* system the usual rate of interest is two to two and a half tins of paddy per five tins of paddy per annum. Many landless Santals, indeed, pass through their lean period by borrowing from their neighbours who normally do not decline to oblige their fellow villagers. This has almost become a normative practice of the Santals of the village. Once a land-owning Santal cultivator had to face the village council when he was about to sell away his surplus paddy before meeting the demands of the village people and subsequently, breaching the norm. Sometimes the Santals who need a large amount of cash may also procure the same through their institutionalized practice of *bharna* (mortgage). In this system, the loanee mortgages a piece of his land for one or two year as the case may be, to another Santal in exchange of money he needs. He temporarily gives up his right of cultivation in the concerned land for the period of contract. The loaner cultivates the land and takes the crops for the money he gives to the loanee. Afterwards the loanee gets back his land. If a man has plough-cattle but no land, he may lend the same to a man who need them. This is locally known as *banchei gai*. In exchange of the plough-cattle the owner gets twelve tins of paddy per year.

In course of our description it becomes apparent that there different occupational categories among the Santals of the village. But if we look deep into the aspects of interaction among these categories of people in appropriate context, it would reveal that this apparent differentiation among the people on the basis of their techno-economic positions does not create any perceptible social cleavage among them. In their day-to-day interaction, status based on their descent and affinity is given more importance than their economic positions.

The relation between a landowner and a landless mahindar *(guti kora)* is almost like that between two kinsmen. Though the mahindar is an annual contract labour and is paid in cash/kind, he is, in practice, always assured of the day-to-day subsistence for his family. Previously, the mahindars were also given by their landlords a piece of cultivable land for the maintenance of their household. In Mahisdal the mahindar of a householder was his wife's brother. The householder reports that his wife's brother has neither parents nor any brother of his own to live with and therefore, lives with him as a kin. It is his moral duty to orient him properly to their traditional work and culture so that he can be economically independent, get married and build up a household of his own. This kind of fostering orphans and poorer kin, and subsequently helping them for economic independence is a common practice among the Santals.

The contractual relation between a Santal householder and his *guti kora/guti kuri* is much embedded within the traditional jural and moral relations of the people. There is also quite a good number of songs describing the relations between the *guti kora* and their employers and subsequently, giving proper cultural meaning to the status relations.

In the changing techno-economic situation the traditional relation between the landless and their landowners is sometimes found to be constrained. Some of the mahindars also nourish a sense of deprivation. During my field investigation I came across a *mahindar* who gave up his contract in preference to work as a free casual labourer on daily wage basis. It was reported that he was constrained not simply by the non-fulfillment of his material expectation. From a further probe into the situation it was revealed the mahindar was more constrained by the breach of normative behaviour from the master. Such individual constraints are, however, counterbalanced by the jural and moral forces of the village society where the people, irrespective of their economic positions, are assured of social security as well as an arena for meaningful cultural communication.

It has already been mentioned that the Santals, besides agriculture, also pursue fishing, hunting and gathering. Here too, household is their primary production and consumption unit. But hunting among the Santals s also pursued collectively when a number of households participate together in the expedition. In case of their annual hunting *(disum sendra)* men of all the households of the village participate together in the expedition. The games hunted in such an expedition are shared among them. Previously the hunter who could hit the prey first with arrow got the hind limb *(madal)* of the game and the rest was divided equally among the other participants. The widows *(rendi)* who could not send hunters for *disum sendra* were also entitled to a share of the games. Though at present the nature of sharing the games has changed a little, broadly it conforms to the normative and cooperative spirit of working and sharing together. The traditional practice of the *disum sendra* is encapsulated in various myths and beliefs and is perpetuated symbolically through occasional religious and cultural practices. The participation of the Santals in such a communal expedition not only gives them pleasure but also reinforces their social and cultural cohesion thereby arresting the gradual nuclearization or individualization of their productive units. By sharing their hunts with others the successful hunters not only gain much prestige and honour to eyes of the villagers but also are able to overcome the constraint generated through the apparent socio-economic differentiation in the present situation.

Kinship and Social Relations

In connection with their observation on tribal society anthropologists, especially the British social anthropologists contend that economic and property relations of the people are embedded into their system of kinship and descent. To them it is the 'idiom' or 'morality' of kinship that motivates the actors in the ultimate patterning of their social relations (Beattie 1964, Fortes 1969, Strathern 1972, and Bloch 1973). Without any *a-priori* assumption we have, however, described so far the various techno-economic activities of the Santals of Mahisdal and tried to delineate the nature of organization of their day-to-day subsistence activities. In the following pages an attempt will be made to study the traditional kinship of the Santals and the nature of its adaptation to the present techno-economic situation.

In the course of our ethnographic description we have seen that the primary production and consumption unit of the Santals is the orak or household. However, a probe into the social composition of the households reveals a definite pattern of kinship. About 36 percent of the households are composed of nuclear families comprising husband, wife and their unmarried children while 14 percent of the households are built around joint families. In these households the vertically joint families where the parents and their married sons live together are more common than the lateral joint families where two married brothers live together. A little over 23 percent of the households are found to comprise nuclear or joint families with dependent consanguines or affines. Normally, widowed, deserted and unmarried men and women remain attached to some of their kin and help running a common production and consumption unit. In 14.78 percent of cases households are found to be composed of broken families while in 6.08 percent households are built around nascent family of husband and wife. In 3.47 percent instances households comprise families with sons-in-law *(ghar jawai)* while 2.6 percent are single-member households. From the nature of composition of their households it is evident that the basic production and consumption units of the people are built, and developed around the kin group, family.

The lineage of the Santal is locally known as *gusti.* Ideally, it is a descent group, the members of which can trace their actual geneaological connection with a common male ancestor. Among the Santals a male ego, his father's father and the male descendants are included into this ideal group. In Mahisdal all the members of a lineage do not live together to maintain a common household nor do they operate as a corporate property holding group. Lineages are now fragmented and, often dispersed over villages. The principal basis of unity among the member-households of a lineage is, however, centred around the worship of orak bonga (household deity). The ritual is initiated by, and held at, the house of the eldest male member of the *gusti,* and the expenditure is shared by all its household units. The ritual is held at the cattle-shed *(gai gora),* and two animals, one male and one female, are sacrificed to the deity or deities. The kind of sacrificing animals varies from lineage to lineage. The sacrificial meat of the female animal is then shared by the women of the group. A *sanga* wife normally is not entitled to share the sacrificial meal but she may have claim on the share if she has a male issue for the lineage. The sacrificial meal of the male animal is shared by the male members of the lineage. The excess meat, if any, is buried into the soil.

Immediately after the worship of the *orak bonga* at the cattle shed another ritual is performed inside the house of the head of the lineage, and animal sacrifices are made to the *hapram,* the ancestral spirits of the group. The sacrificial meat at that time is shared by all the members of the lineage, the males, their wives and also the affines and the neighbours.

If we look deep into the process of ritual we would notice that Santals do not use all sorts of animal for sacrifice. They sacrifice the domesticated animals like goats, sheep, pigs and fowls that they normally have to procure with cash from the neighbouring non-tribal peoples. Santals do not use these animals directly for cor ımption; they are ready for consumption after they are ritually slaughtered and offered to their deities.

Different descent groups use different animals for ritual slaughtering. Through this custom of animal sacrifice Santals seem to ritually regulate the use of some essential resources that are otherwise scarce to them and minimize individual competition.

Besides the unity manifest in the ritual performance of *orak bonga* the lineage unity of Santals is also expressed in their cognitive use of the term, *gutie pera,* meaning one people. The term signifies the collectivity or oneness of the descent group, and involves the individuals' feeling of belongingness to a single social entity.

The Santals of Mahisdal have a notion of another kin group larger than gusti. This is locally called *khunt*. Ideally, a *khunt* consists of the lineages that count their descent from a common male ancestor. But the lineages of the *khunt,* like the households of a *gusti,* cannot trace their actual geneaological links. The kin group, khunt, also does not operate as property-holding corporate unit. Khunts are, in fact, their sub-clans, and their names clearly indicate their specific clan affiliations. For instance, *sada tudu, sindur tudu* and *dantelai tudu* are the *khunts* of the clan tudu. Each *khunt* has its own presiding deity, locally known as *abje bonga,* and differs from others in ritual performance. For instance, the people of *sada tudu* use *sada* (white) rice powder while those of *sindur tudu* use *sindur* (vermillion) in the worship of their *abje bonga*. The worship of *abje bonga* is held in the field located at the outskirts of the village and the sacrificial meal is shared strictly by the male members of the *khunt*.

The *paris* or clan is another kin group still larger than the *khunt*. Every man and woman inherits, on birth, the clan name patrilineally and uses it as surname. The women after marriage, however, use the clan names of their husbands. The clan solidarity is not normally observed except in the practice of clan exogamy and in the moral recognition of a common mythical ancestry by its members.

So far we have described the notions of their ideal-type groups and the nature of their solidarity. An attempt will now be made to study the actual functioning of the groups and the process of their adaptation in the changing contexts of techno-economy. It has been noted that the households, the principal production and consumption units of the people are built around nuclear family and modelled after the ideal-type lineages that are also termed as orak. A close probe into the development process of the household reveals that the present technoeconomic situation does not allow them to effectively perpetuate the corporate nature of their lineage group. The sons of a family, after marriage, build up new households either in the village proper or in other villages. The families of a lineage thus no longer operate as a viable local group. For labour and cooperation in the day-to-day subsistence activities the families of one lineage, therefore, have to make alliance with the neighbouring families related primarily through marriage.

The Santals of the village are now found to depend on their affines more than before. For instance, while the sacrificial meat in the worship of *orak bonga* is shared only by the males of the group along with their wives, the animal slaughtered in the ritual of *hapram* or the ancestral spirits is shared with other affines and neighbours in the village. This tendency becomes more obvious if we notice the exclusiveness of agnates in sharing the sacrificial meat ritually offered to the *abje bonga,* the presiding deity of the khunt, a descent group larger than the *orak*. In the context of the changing technoeconomic situation the people not only divide their kingroups into smaller units and breach the boundary of their patrilineal descent but also include affines and give them ritual recognition. For immediate and essential economic interaction they make alliance with their affines and neighbours in the village and form operational unity while for the ultimate social solidarity they turn towards the morality of kinship.

An ideal-type *khunt* is larger than a lineage and its unity is based on the morality of male-descent and hence agnatic relationship; embedded in the concept of *khunt* is also another aspect of social relationship. According to the social norm no individual can marry in his/her mother's *khunt*. This custom of *khunt* exogamy, in fact, reflects a recognition of cognatic descent.

It has been pointed out that the clans of the Santals are exogamous in nature. It is through the principle of exogamy that the apparently autonomous segments are bound together to maintain the structural solidarity of the tribe. Marriage involves not merely exchange of women between two groups; it also helps perpetuate a flow of exchange of gifts and services among the groups that have, besides ritual value, crucial economic and political significance. Traditionally the Santal have eleven clans of which only nine are found in the village. In the past the clans were said to have specialized occupations though the specializations are no longer found operative among the contemporary Santals. The exogamous nature of the clans is, however, very much in vogue and any violation of the norm is highly disapproved.

As pointed out earlier, women make substantive contribution to the household economy, and enjoy better social position in the community. The people have a custom of paying bride price *(ganam taka)*, and the amount of bride price is same for all grooms or their families irrespective of their socio-economic status. The transaction of bride is more symbolic in nature than material. At one point in the series of elaborate transactions the bridal party comes to the parents of the groom when the latter pay an amount of Rs. 11/- and five bags of paddy to the former. On the day of marriage the groom party again pay one rupee. Again, when the first child is born of the new couple, the groom's family offers a bovine calf to the natal family of the bride. The meaning underlying the process of transaction as understood from the people is that women constitute essential actors in the production and reproduction of their society, and the marital transactions reinforce their social significance.

The institutional practice of *ghar-jawai* is an alternative arrangement for the grooms who are unable to pay the bride price. In such instances the groom stays in the house of the bride's father and contributes labour in his household production for five years. Every year five bags of paddy are kept aside and after the completion of his service the marriage is finally performed. After the marriage is over, the accumulated paddy along with a plough and a pair of draft animals are given to the groom to form a household of his own. In some instances the groom is also offered a piece of cultivable land. The material transaction underlying the practice is of more social and cultural than economic. It is the complementarity as well as autonomy of the kin groups and not the hierarchy among them that is reinforced in the customary practice.

Inheritance and Succession

Ideally, property and offices of the Santal are transmitted patrilineally. If a man has a number of sons by a number of wives, the property is divided equally among the sons irrespective of their uterine relationships. Sons of the same mother by different fathers would inherit from their respective fathers. In one instance, it has, however, been noticed that two sons of a woman begotten by two different men are living together and running a common household. The younger of the sons, on the death of his father, built up a household on his father's homestead land along with wife and widow mother. He was a sharecropper. After some years he fell sick and became unfit for manual work. At his elder brother (uterine) came up for his help, and started living with him along with wife and children. It may be noted here that it is not the agnatic but the uterine relation that binds the two families to form a common production and consumption unit.

Though the ideal pattern of property transmission is patrilineal, the village elders, nowadays are found to distribute a portion of a deceased man's property to his widow also. In such cases the widow enjoys only the usufract on the landed property and on her death the sons of the deceased man get the ownership right. In the case of re-marriage, the widow may or may not continue to hold her usufract on the land. Considering the situation the village elders take decision about such cases.

The Santal have the usual practice of naming their children after their grand parents. Normally. The boys are named after grand fathers (on the mother's as well as father's side). The grand fathers and the grand mothers whose names are thus adopted become morally obliged to transmit some amount of their property to the inheritors of their names. The general notion is that through such adoption of names an image of their elders' self and personality is perpetuated by their living relatives even after their death. This is, in fact, a two-way process and the individuals belonging to two alternate generations are thus bound together in a reciprocal manner.

The practice of adopting names does not strictly follow the rule of biological descent. The meaning or spirit underlying such social transactions, however, remains the same. An instance may be cited here. Mongol Tudu married a widow who had a son. The widow, on marriage, moved to live with Mongol leaving her son in his father's land. Later, it was discovered after Mongol's death that he had recorded a piece of land in the name of his wife's earlier son as he adopted Mongol's name.

Adopted sons also inherit the property of their new fathers. Normally, the Santal adopt their brother's sons. Sometimes, a man who has no son but only a daughter may also keep the son-in-law permanently in his house and transfer all the property in his name.

In some instances, the man belonging to a particular clan or lineage may also be absorbed into another clan. This occurs specifically in the case of a widow marriage. If a man marries a widow with a son, the son is adopted into his clan. The adoption is performed through a ritual initiation locally known as *bonga tala*. After the ritual is over the son gets the right to worship the *orak bonga* of his new father.

A close observation on the nature of adoption and the pattern of property distribution among the Santals of Mahisdal it reveals that the people value more on social relations based on kinship and sharing of property than individual ownership and accumulation of assets. A strong sense of generosity and morality prevails among the people. The traditional boundary of unilineal descent group is now not as rigid as was normally thought of. There is a perceptible tendency among the people to include close affines related through wife and married daughters in the formation of social groups in their day-to-day activities.

10

System of Exchange in Tribal Society: A Case Study of the Santal

Introduction

Exchange is a panhuman phenomenon of giving and receiving; human beings cannot survive without exchanging their labour and services with one another. However, the pattern of exchange differs from one culture to another. Karl Polanyi identifies three distinct forms of exchange in human societies: reciprocal, redistributive and market exchange. According to him tribal societies are characterized by reciprocal form of exchange while marketless archaic and market-integrated industrial societies are characterized by redistributive and market forms of transactions respectively. Sahlins, however, opines that both the reciprocal and redistributive forms of exchange may prevail in tribal societies. He notes that the array of economic transactions recorded in the ethnographic literature may be resolved into two types. 'First, the vice-versa movements between two parties familiarly known as reciprocity. The second, centralized movements : collection from members of a group, often under one hand, and re-division within this group'. Though viewed analytically different types of transactions, both of them in a way involve reciprocity at their base. To him both reciprocity and redistribution involve flow and movement of material goods and services but are functionally related to different types of social organization. While reciprocity refers to transactions between two parties or groups, redistribution involves transactions within a group. In redistributive forms of exchange goods are pooled or collected together from the members of a group, often under a central authority and re-divided within the group. 'The material transaction that is pooling', he says, 'is socially a within relation, the collective action of a group. Reciprocity is a between relation, the action and reaction of two parties' (Sahlins 1965: 141). Cooperative food production, village councils, communal and ceremonial rituals and actions are some of the contexts of pooling in tribal societies. Considering material transactions in the context of socio-cultural organization of particular tribal peoples Sahlins thus identifies three forms of reciprocity: generalized, balanced and negative. Sahlins sees these forms of exchange more or less as a continuum. He observes that one can 'specify social or economic circumstances that impel reciprocity toward one or another of the stipulated positions, toward generalized, balance or negative reciprocity' (*ibid*: 149).

Some studies on tribal societies in transition reveal prevalence of multiple spheres of exchange. Bohannan (1955), for instance, identifies, among the Tiv, three spheres of exchange, each marked by institutionalization and different moral values. The subsistence sphere involves the exchange of gifts and agricultural and craft products. The exchange of goods in this sphere is characterized by a fair degree of bargaining and haggling. Bohannan's second sphere, i.e., the sphere of prestige consists of the exchange of slaves, cattle, houses, ritual offices, white cloth, medicine or magic and prestigious brass rods. The exchange involves no price; only rough equivalences are considered. The third sphere is concerned with exchange of rights in human beings other than slaves, particularly rights in women. Barth (1967) in his study on the Fur economy of the Darfurs, also identifies three spheres of exchange. The Fur economy involves three basic circles of flow. In the first circle, labour is converted into cash crops providing capital for the acquisition of more wives who, in turn, provide labour for cash crops. The second circle consists of converting cash into cattle and again cattle into cash (cash-cattle-cash). The third sphere involves the use of labour for the production of millet which is brewed into beer and used again for labour in millet production (labour-millet-beer-labour). Barth includes, in his study of exchange, material goods as well as activities or whatever people consider of value, 'all forms of circulation and transformation of value, whether by exchange, production, inheritance' (*ibid*:1967:15).

The identification of various restricted spheres and circles of flow and exchange of material goods and services by Bohannan and Barth reveals not only a direction of change but also persisting areas of traditional social and cultural interactions and values. In traditional societies economic behaviour can hardly be separated from their social and cultural behaviour. Even the changing tribal societies in India are highly characterized by social and cultural homogeneity, and economic differentiation among the people is seldom encouraged. Social and ceremonial relationships are valued more than economic or material relationships and objects of practical value are often found to be converted or transformed into objects of social and ceremonial value. In an earlier study of mine on the Birhor, Mundari tribe of Orissa, I found that the people, despite their regular economic interaction with caste-peasants and market economy of the larger society, were inclined much on keeping up a meaningful world of social and cultural interactions among themselves. Kin-based social relations were of more value to them and the nature of material transactions among themselves were qualitatively different from that of their material transactions with the neighbouring Hindu caste-peasants. The transactions of the Birhor with the larger society were primarily economic in nature while those among their kinsmen, affines and friends within the community were social and ceremonial in nature (Adhikary 1984).

The ancestral spirits, gods and their jungle environment were also considered part of their society. In the contexts of meaning of their interactions the Birhor were found to have conceptualized two sets of environment: one, 'a morally ordered gemeinschaft in disum, their own territory in the forest' and the other, 'a rationalist-utilitarian gessellschaft orientation in muluk, the territory dominated by caste-peasants and market economy' (Sinha 1984 : VI).

The Santhals of Birbhum, with whom we are concerned here, also belong to the Mundari family of tribes but unlike the Birhor they pursue agriculture and lead a sedentary village life in close association with the caste-peasants of the Hindu society. They are encysted by the dominant caste people and have almost no environmental terrain to retreat like the Birhor. From a preliminary study of the subsistence activities of the Santhals in the village of Mahisdal, it is, however, observed that the people still maintain a dynamic isolation from the dominant Hindu caste society and perpetuate a meaningful area of social and cultural communication. Though exposed to the money economy of the larger society, the circulation of goods and services also involves means other than money, that are embedded deeply into the social and cultural matrix of the people. Their household production, inheritance, marriage transaction, labour exchange, land transfer, etc., are guided mostly by the norms of the village community. Land, labour, paddy, cattle and even cash that are of much practical and economic value are manipulated and exchanged among themselves in a manner quite different from that in the larger society. For a meaningful understanding of the different spheres of exchange it is, therefore, essential to study the various aspects of circulation and transformation of values in the context of their total view on life.

The Santal: Their Land and Economy

Though the Santal are broadly designated as an agriculturalist tribe, their direct access to land is marginal. In this area they pursue agriculture mostly as tenant cultivators or hired agricultural labour in the land of the neighbouring caste-peasants. Some also work as labourers in non-agricultural sectors of the larger society.

Of 115 households in the village 77 are landless and only 38, own lands. Of these 38 landowning households 35 have less than 5 acres of land. Almost all these landowning households are marginal farmers and have to cultivate lands of the caste-peasants on share basis for their livelihood. It may be noted here that the total amount of land cultivated by the Santhal farmers in the village during 1983-84 was 233 acres while the amount of land actually owned by them was only 91 acres. The rest 142 acres of land were leased in by them from the Hindu peasantry of the locality.

Aspects of Economic Interactions and Exchange with the Larger Society

There were 55 Santhal households in the village, who cultivated the lands of the Hindu caste-farmers of the adjacent villages on annual contract. Considering their mode of exchange with the caste-peasants two categories of farmers were distinguished: one, the *bhagchasi* which involved 38 households and the other, the *kirsan* involving 17 households. The contract for the *bhagchasi* was that they would give their labour and bear the cost of ploughing the leased-in lands, and in return, would get 50 percent of the total products (in terms of paddy and straw). For the *kirsan,* the contract was that they would give only their labour for the cultivation of the leased-in lands, and in return, would get one-third of the total of the total products (paddy and straw). It may be mentioned here that all the farmers of the village under the category of *bhagchasi* had plough and drought-animals, while none of the *kirsan* had plough and drought-animals. Of the 38 *bhagchasi* households had also small plots of own land while only one kirsan family had a small plot of land. For share-cropping or tenant cultivation labour was, however, very important, and all the Santhal share-croppers, the *bhagchasi* as well as the *kirsan,* had to exchange their family labour with the lessors for paddy and straw. It may be pointed out in this connection that the Santhals in this area are considered expert agricultural labourers and both of their men and women can work equally in agricultural fields.

There were four Santhal farmers in the village who were found to remain tagged, as annual contract agricultural labourers, to the caste-peasants of the adjacent village, Taltore. They were locally known as *guti kora* or *mahindar*. For their labour and service they were paid in paddy and clothes. During the period of my field investigation each of these labourers was found to exchange his labour and service in exchange of 96 tins of paddy, two napkins, one *dhoti* and one *banian* (vest) per year. Unlike the *bhagchasi* and the *kirsan* who employed their family labour for their essential economic interaction with caste-peasants these mahindar employed only their individual labour for the purpose. It may be noted here that both the *bhagchasi* and the *kirsan* had more freedom and choice in the productive activities on their leased-in lands than the *mahindar.* The *mahindar* had to work primarily at the dictate of their landlords.

There was still another category of Santhal agricultural labourers in the village, who were locally known as nagare munish. These people borrowed, for their subsistence in lean seasons, paddy from the landed Hindu peasants of the locality to be paid back by imparting their individual labour in the fields of the Hindu peasants during peak seasons. In peak seasons the demand of labour in the locality is comparatively high, and both the Santhal and caste-peasants are aware of it. In the course of my field work I, however, got two such cases. They took loans in advance on the condition that they would work throughout the entire agricultural season only for their loaners. The caste-peasants who extended loans also felt assured of their labour needed for cultivation by entering into such a contract. Unlike the *mahindar* who had to work for the whole year, the *nagare munish* worked in the fields of their masters only for a part of the year.

Besides the Santhal farmers who exchanged their labour in lands and agriculture there were people who directly exchanged their labour primarily for paddy and sometimes for clothes and cash, the latter exchanged their labour and service mostly for cash. There were some landless men and women among the Santhals of the village who remained tagged to some Muslim and Hindu masons, and worked as labourers in the construction of buildings on daily wage basis. There were also seven Santhals who worked as permanent employees in the private and government concerns of the locality on monthly salary basis. The cash earned by these individuals were immediately converted into paddy, clothes and other consumable articles required for the maintenance of their households in the village.

Two employees were, however, found to purchase cultivable lands with their accumulated money. In one case, the widow of a man who was an employee of a local pipe factory, purchased a plot of land in the name of her son, Sukul Murmu, with a sum of Rs. 2500/- accumulated in provident fund account of the deceased. In the other case, Budhi Murmu, teacher in the primary school of the village spent an amount of Rs. 5,000/- for a plot of agricultural land of 5 bigha.

For iron implements like plough shares, scythes, spades, axes and knives the Santhal cultivators used to depend on *jajmani (jao)* relationship with some traditional blacksmith families in the nearby village, Seala. They used to procure new implements or get the ones repaired in exchange of paddy on annual contract basis. Now-a-days both the parties are, however, found to run their transactions preferably in terms of local price-market. Salt, oil, clothes, earthen pots, baskets, metal utensils and other necessary articles were procured from markets in cash. A few Santhal farmers were found to use chemical fertilizers, and they procured those from markets.

The Santhal farmers who had more than 5 acres of land produced paddy and crops like potato, wheat and mustard seeds. Crops like potato, wheat and mustard seeds were produced primarily for household consumption and to maintain social obligations among their kin, affines, friends and neighbours through gifts.. The paddy that remained surplus after household consumption was, however, sold in markets for cash. In all those cases the money earned was found to be invested partly in the improvement of land and agriculture and partly in procuring some luxury goods like radios, transistors, tape-recorders, bicycles, mopeds, etc. All those three farmers used chemical fertilizers, and purchased pumps for irrigation. It may be mentioned here that all those farmers also maintained three grocery shops in the village. But of those three only one shop is now in running condition and the other two are closed. On close observation I came to learn that the people had little commercial spirit. The prevalent mode of exchange in kind as well as the non-economic, non-profiteering motive of the people compelled them to close down the shops dealing with commercial goods.

Aspects of Economic Interaction and Exchange Among the Santhals

We have so far described aspects of interactions and exchange of the Santhals of Mahisdal with caste-peasants and market economy of the larger society. It was found that for land, one of the important means for agricultural production most of the Santal farmers of the village have to primarily depend on the Hindu peasantry of the neighbouring villages. It was in exchange of their labour and skill that the Santal farmers got their rights of cultivation in the lands of the Hindu peasants, and subsequently, a share of their products of paddy and straw. It may be mentioned in this connection that there is a general preference among the Hindu peasantry for Santal labourers in agricultural operations in the locality. A few men and women of the village were even found to be hired as labourers by the peasants in the neighbouring district Burdwan.

From our description in the preceding pages it is evident that the Santals of Mahisdal pursue agriculture either as tenant cultivators or as labourers on wage basis. Even the marginal landowners among them have to lease in lands from caste-peasants in the neighbouring villages. Their own labour and skill, therefore, forms the principal means of their agricultural production. All the members of a Santal household can, indeed, work in all spheres of agricultural operations, and there is, among them a simple division of labour in terms of age, sex and proficiency. In the village, seven or eight years old children were often found to assist their parents in the different spheres of their agricultural operations.

The Santal farmers of the village do not hire/purchase labour for their cultivation. Normally a Santal farmer cultivates his lands with the labour available in his family. If at any stage, he requires more labour he seeks the help of his relatives and friends from other households. The people who give there are paid neither in cash nor in kind; they are simply entertained with rice beer *(handi)* and puffed rice *(khijuri)*, and sometimes, with meat or vegetable curry by the man for whom they work. It may be noted here that the transaction of the man is not terminated with his offering of food and drink to the people. He is also expected to render his own labour and service in the fields of the people as and when they would require. These labourers are locally known as beggar (free labour). In the village of Mahisdal I observed five instances where labour and service were exchanged in this system.

Labour, among the Santal, is not looked as a commodity. To them labour has a social value and a man who is lazy or crazy is often ridiculed. They work for one another primarily as a duty towards the person who wants the work done rather than for material gain. In fact, individuals interact among themselves in the context of their social value, and exchange their labour with one another in this institutionalized practice of begar. The members of the party are only bound together on mutual obligation. There were five Santal mahindar in the village. But the relationship between a mahindar and his Santal employer is almost like that between two kinsmen. The payments of the *mahindar* were calculated not merely in material terms. Considerations of their needs for subsistence were also taken into account by their employers. Previously, the Santal *mahindars* were also offered a piece of cultivable land for maintenance of their families. In the village a Santal farmer had a young *mahindar* who was his wife's brother. The Santal employer reported that his wife had neither parents nor any other brother. Before they he lived together. The husband of the woman considered it his social duty to look after his wife's brother so that he could get married and build up an independent household for himself. This kind of fostering orphans and poorer kin, and subsequently, helping them having economic independence is, in fact, a common practice among the Santals of the village.

The contractual relation between a Santal farmer and his *guti kora/kuri* is intricately enmeshed into the traditional jural and moral relations of the people. There is also quite a good number of songs describing the relations between the *guti kora* and their employers and subsequently, giving proper cultural meaning to the status of the Santal *guti kora*. It may also be noted here that among the Santals the employment is not a personal contract for transaction but a socially approved custom of mutual exchange of labour and goods. On the day following *magh parab* that was held after the winter harvest in the month of February, 1984, I observed that the *mahindars* of the village were ceremonially paid off by their Santal employers and new contracts were made in the presence of the traditional village officials. The *magh parab* of the Santal, in fact, denotes the end of their agricultural calendar while the day following the festival signifies the beginning of the year.

There were certain institutional arrangements in the village by which the people could obtain wife, house and also land in exchange of labour and service. A man who was not in a position to afford the payment of the customary bride price used to stay in the house of the bride's father, and contribute his labour and service to the family for five years. During his stay he gets his food, drink and clothes. Besides these, five tins of paddy are kept aside for him every year. After the completion of his service the accumulated paddy along with a plough and a pair of drought animals are finally offered to by the bride's father. In some cases a separate house is also built up for him and his wife. In one instance the groom and his wife were also given a piece of land for cultivation.

Many of the essential economic transactions of the Santal were maintained by them within the village. My Santal respondents pointed out two forms of material transactions in the village by which they overcome the economic crisis during lean periods. In one form locally known as pancha, the people may take loans of paddy from the Santal farmers on a short-term basis. In another form known as *delbari,* loans of paddy may be taken on a long-term basis. In the case of pacha no interest is charged. But in the case of delbari when the people take loans for more than a year they have pay interest. The normal rate of interest is 2-2.5 tins of paddy per 5 tins of paddy. It may be mentioned here that in the course of my fieldwork I found only the cases of interest-free loans. I did not find any case in which interest was given in the payment of loans. In 1983 Sri Budhan Soren, one of my informants took 35 tins of paddy as loans from 9 different farmers. Sri Soren took the loans during the lean periods—September-October—and paid them back after harvest in months of December-January. He had to pay no interest for the loans. Indeed, I observed many landless Santals who were passing through their lean periods borrowing from their kin and affines living within and outside the village. The people who could afford it did not disoblige them. This kind of transaction is a normative practice among the Santals of the village. On one occasion a Santal farmer was found to be a subject of public ridicule when he sold away his surplus paddy in the market and refused loans to his villagers. He had also to face the traditional village council for the breach of the village norm. Sometimes a farmer who needs a large amount of cash may get the same through their institutionalized practice of *vorna* (mortgage). In this system the loanee temporarily gives up a part of his right over a piece of his land to the lender for a certain period of time. This land is then cultivated on share basis and as soon as the period is over, the loanee gets back his full right on the land. Sri Shyam Murmu, in 1982, took a loan of Rs. 500/- from Jyatha Murmu for the medical treatment of his mother in exchange of about half a bigha of his land through their traditional system of vorna. He gave 1/3rd of the products to Sri Murmu for two years and after that he got back his right on the land.

A Santal can borrow plough and draught animals from another farmer for the cultivation of his land simply in exchange of rice beer. This is, in fact, locally known as an act of *goro* (help), and the farmer who owns the plough and cattle can hardly deny to help for fear of public ridicule.

A few Santal of the village were also found to lend their draught animals for paddy. Normally, an owner gets twelve tins of paddy per annum for one draught animal. This system is locally known as *banchei gai*.

Discussion and Conclusion

It becomes evident from the preceding pages that the Santals of Mahisdal maintain two distinct spheres of interaction and exchange: one, with the Hindu caste-peasants and market economy of the larger society and the other, among themselves. In the former sphere the Santal exchange paddy, straw, clothes and sometimes, money and maintain an essential economic articulation with local peasantry. In the later sphere the Santals exchange gifts, labour, service, rice beer, cattle and paddy. In this sphere they seem to give more importance to the fulfillment of social obligation, thereby perpetuating a social order. They are well aware of the value of money but do not consider it an essential medium of exchange among themselves. The values of the material things that are used as media of exchange consist, in fact, in their 'social use'. Marriage is an important socio-cultural institution of the Santals, and it involves a series of material transactions between two kin groups among them. There is a custom of paying bride price *(ganam taka)* among the Santals. The bride price consists of both cash and kind, and the amount and the set of bride wealth are always the same for all irrespective of their socio-economic status. A close probe into the processes of marital transactions would, however, reveal that the transactions are more symbolic in nature than economic. At one point in the course of their elaborate transactions the relatives of the bride come to the parents of the groom when the later ceremonially offers a cash of rupees eleven to the bride's party. On the day of marriage the groom again offers one rupee more to the parents of the bride. The groom has also to give five tins of paddy to the bride's family. Exchange in terms of clothes, puffed and flattened rice is also made. Payment in odd numbers is, in fact, a socially prescribed norm of the Santals, which reflects their view of life. After marriage when the groom's family is blessed with a child, the groom again offers a calf or a cow to the natal family of the bride. The underlying meaning of these marital transactions is that on marriage, the bride's parents lose some potential labour force which is socially recognized and symbolically compensated with cash and kind by the groom's family. Again, with the birth of a child some new labour force is added to the family of the groom, and this is recognized by offering a calf or cow to the bride's natal group.

That the Santal, despite their essential economic articulation with the larger society, endeavour to persist in a distinct sphere of exchange among themselves can be understood meaningfully if we carefully probe the perceptions of the world in and around which they live.

In the course of their economic interaction with the larger society the Santals have come across a number of ethnic groups. All these ethnic groups are broadly categorized by them as diku or alien people. The Santals do not consider them a part of their community, even when they both live in the same village. In the village Mahisdal that I studied, the Santals and the Hindu caste-peasants live in two distinct hamlets. The Santals call their hamlet as *hor ato,* i.e., a Santal village which, in fact, functions as a separate socio-cultural entity. It may be pointed out here that though the Santals are known as an agriculturalist tribe, live within the broad framework of the agrarian economic structure of the Hindu peasantry, they are not considered good *chasa* by the caste peasants. The caste people also call their men and women as *majhi* and *mejhen*. The Santals are not happy with this notion. Some of my respondents even expressed their regret by saying that the term *majhi* is derogatory, and should not be used for them. They say that the term *majhi* means boatman and they are not boatmen; they are *hor* or man.

The economic world of the Santals, on the other hand, is much embedded into the socio-cultural matrix of the people. The economic activities of a Santal household can hardly be studied outside the social and cultural contexts of the village as a community. The Santal families pursue economic activities not merely to meet their requirement of food, clothing and shelter. Their economic activity is not an individual affair, it is a socialized and cultural response to the material needs for biological survival. The values they put upon their food and drink do not consist simply in its capacity to satisfy hunger but in the they make of it to convey and reinforce jural and moral relations with their kin, affines, ancestors and deities or bongas. The Santals of the village like many other tribal people in India, give more emphasis on mutual sharing of food and drink among kin, affines and friends. They also share food with their ancestral spirits and other supernatural deities who are considered an integral part of their community. Even the domesticated animals *(ato posu)* constitute a part of their village community. In many instances the cattle are found to live, under the same roof, along with their human masters. Goats, sheep, dogs and chicken are often found to share food with the Santals. The milching of cows is considered unethical since it would deprive the young ones of their essential feeds.

The Santals of Mahisdal have, indeed, a limited idea of good. Their desires and expectations in economic spheres of life are very limited. They hardly think of making a surplus production or earning more and accumulating for the future. They are concerned primarily with the present and desire for two square meals a day, a few clothes a year, a house to live in, and a disease-free gay disposition with ample scope for pleasures. The Santals have a genuine penchant for *raska* or pleasures. They crave for pleasures in the form of communal dancing, singing, drinking and feasting. This orientation towards pleasures which forms an important aspect of their outlook on life and society, indeed, stands in their way of individual saving and accumulation of wealth.

The Santals perpetuate an intimate relation with their ancestral spirits and bongas, and form a moral community with them. They make animal sacrifices and offer food and drink to the supernatural spirits who are thought to control the natural resources and look after their health and prosperity. Every Santal conceives of his 'self' in the wider context of his position in the clan-lineage based structure of the society. These social segments are considered divine in origin. They are sacred and preside over by some supernatural spirits. The social segments are, in fact, the appropriate cultural constructs in the context of which they organize their transactions meaningfully.

The flow of material goods as well as the mode of exchange among the Santals is therefore to be understood in the wider context of the structure of participatory relations with the Hindu caste-peasants and the markets of the neighbouring society as well as the natural and supernatural phenomena or entities around them. The Santals seem to have a close affinity with surrounding natural ecology and the supernatural world of their cognition; their transactions with them are geared in a spirit of affectivity. Among the people of their community the exchange is geared with a sense of altruism and more value is given on gift and mutual help as a social necessity.

11

Tribal Groups of Eastern India: Changing Aspects of their Land and Economy

I

The early ethnographers in India were concerned with an overall description of social and cultural life of the tribal peoples, and most of their studies were intended primarily to reconstruct an archaic base of Indian Civilization. Later on, anthropologists focused on the study of particular aspects like the political life, religious life or the economic life of the tribal people. It is, perhaps, during this period that we find some ethnographic studies and observations on the changing conditions of their land and economy in particular and culture in general. The phenomenon of land alienation of the tribal people and historical incidence of several uprisings among them as protest to non-tribal encroachment on their ancestral territory also drew the attention of ethnographers, historians and administrators.

However, we still lack systematic study on the nature of land tenure and economy of the tribal groups under different productive systems and ecological conditions. According to 1971 Census there are 427 Scheduled Tribes in India comprising about 7 percent of her total population. The numerical size of these groups ranges from as many as a few millions (e.g., the Gond, the Bhil, and the Santhal) to as less as a few individuals only (e.g., the Onge, the Great Andamanese). Occupationally, these people live at different levels of techno-economy ranging from hunting and gathering to settled plough cultivation. Though land is an important means of production, it is not utilized uniformly by all the tribal groups in India. There are a number of tribal groups who do not show any direct concern with a particular piece of land as such but with a wider geographical territory and the natural resources in it. A careful study of their origin, myths, beliefs and the history of the locality would, however, reveal that most of the tribal groups are not autochthones of their habitat. There have been enormous internal migrations of the people in the country, which, in turn, have brought about change not only in the mode of their land use and economy but also in their social and cultural life. In this paper my purpose would, therefore, be to briefly describe the pattern of land utilization and economic activities of some of tribal groups, broadly following their mode of livelihood in Eastern India. Instead of dealing with aspects of change in their land system at any particular point of time in history, I will focus, primarily on aspects of variations in the pattern of land use, and economy of the tribal groups at different levels of economy. A study of variations among the groups would help us in understanding the nature of change in the tribal life in general with respect to land and economy. For illustration I will depend on my own studies on the Birhor, a hunter-gatherer group, the Juang, a shifting cultivator group, and the Santhal, a settled cultivator group living in Orissa and West Bengal respectively, as well as on the studies and observations on other tribes made by other anthropologists.

II

Before coming to a detailed description of the situation I would like to say a few words as to what is meant by the concept 'tribe' in anthropology. Normally, the term 'tribe' is used with reference to the list of Scheduled Tribes in India. To anthropologists the use of the term , 'tribe' refers to 'two realities, two fields of facts'—one, 'a type of society' and the other, 'a stage of evolution' in human society (Godelier 1977 : 70). Though conceptualized separately they are linked to one another. The anthropologists in India initially looked at the tribal people as a 'stage of evolution'; later on they are found to show more interest in the nature and type of tribal society in relation to the caste-based Hindu society in India. The term 'tribe' is, therefore, found to refer to a group of people who are characterized by a series of social and cultural features distinct from those of the caste society. Considering the persistence of a distinct socio-cultural identity among the tribal groups in India in the context of modernization, Sinha prefers to view 'tribe' both as a 'system of social relations' and a 'state of mind and cultural tradition' characterized basically by isolation and lack of stratification (Sinha 1965).

Bailey is, perhaps, the pioneer in considering land and economy in the conceptualization of tribal society in India. Bailey contends that tribal lands are vested in clans, the members of which together share a common productive territory. He observes that the tribal society is segmentary, and all the component groups or segments of it are more or less autonomous having similar function and status. The clan territory and the constituent villages are not hierarchically arranged, nor are they interdependent through economic specializations. With reference to the Kondhs of Orissa, among whom he worked Bailey says that they have localized clans and 'membership of the clan is, under this system, a condition of holding and exploiting land in the clan territory. A right to land is not achieved by subordination to any one else, but by equality as a kinsman' (Bailey 1961: 11-12). According to him direct access to land is the main feature of tribal organization and 'the larger is the proportion of a given society which has direct access to land the closer is that society to the tribal end ...'(*ibid* : 1: 14).

While studying the nature of 'economic interdependence and *jajmani* relationship' among the contemporary tribal groups in India Mahapatra observes the 'the tribal economy is basically a self-sufficient, subsistence oriented economy, not characterized by specialized roles or hierarchical relationships' (Mahapatra 1982 : 108). He says, 'ideal-typically, each family and each village in a tribe engages itself in basically the same types of activities as other families or other villages do respectively. The resources whether of the forest , or of the land, or of the water, can be exploited by each family as more or less equal partners. These rights are derived from their being pears in a kinship-bound society, with no specialization and division of labour beyond those based on proficiency, age, sex of the individual' (*ibid* :). Considering the technology and economy of the tribal groups in India Fernandes (1965) makes an important observation on the nature of tribal society. He opines that the hunting, gathering and shifting axe cultivation represents tribal technology. The economy is characterized as tribal when agricultural production is mainly made for household consumption, that is, not with an eye towards cash market. According to Farnandes there is a large number of tribes at present whose technology is no longer tribal but whose economy and perhaps other socio-cultural features may be considered as 'tribal'.

In the course of his analysis of the tribal life in India Sinha (1958) makes an important observation on their economic values. He points out that the tribal people are much oriented towards the life in the present, and show little concern for distant future. To these people saving and planning for future are of no economic value. In brief, Sinha characterizes the tribal worldview characterized by a this-worldly 'hedonistic' pleasure-orientation.

We, therefore, find that despite variations in habitat and economy the tribal groups are conceptualized by anthropologists as having a kind of socio-cultural tradition and outlook on life distinct from the hierarchically based dominant caste society in India.

III

There are 20-22 distinct tribal groups in India, who still pursue hunting and food gathering for their livelihood, though they do not constitute even one percent of her total tribal population. The numerical strength of the group ranges from a few individuals to a few thousand only, and their distribution is mostly along the forest-clad regions of north-east and southern India. They are also found in central-east regions of India, and beyond the mainland in the Andaman and Nicobar Islands. It may be pointed out here that the hunters and food gatherers in Andaman Islands are or until recently were more or less isolated and self-sufficient in their economy, exploiting the resources either of the forest or the coastal sea or both, while those in the mainland India, primarily based on jungle crafts, maintain a regular economic symbiosis with the plough cultivators in their neighbourhood.

For the present purpose we will describe here the situations of the Birhor and the Hill Kharia of Eastern

India. Bose (1956) points out that 'the Birhor (literally, men of jungle) of southern Bihar and northern Orissa have practically become an appendage of the rural economic system of the caste villages'. He observes that the Birhor, having come in contact with the plough cultivators of the neighbouring villages, have specialized themselves 'in some industries based on jungle produce'. They are now converted into a 'nomadic caste' and form a complement to the land-based agrarian economic structure of the Hindu caste society. This kind of caste-like occupational specializations based on jungle resources among them were also noticed by Sinha (1968) and Fox (1968). With specific reference to the Birhor as well as the Hill Kharia, Sinha observes that those are secondary hunters. In the past, they practiced shifting cultivation combined with hunting and gathering in the forests on the hill slopes. With the encroachment of the settled Hindu peasantry from the plains they find their traditional mode of shifting cultivation untenable and adopt hunting and gathering mode of production. It may be mentioned in this connection many of these hunters and food gatherers are, in fact, offshoots of larger ethnic groups.

Whatever may be the historical past as regards their land use and economy, a study (Adhikary: 1984) on the Birhor of Sundargarh district, Orissa, reveals that the whole range of their economy is centred around the collection of natural products in jungles and the maintenance of a regular economic interaction with the village peasants and markets. They operate between two ecological terrains, one, a natural ecology comprising the jungles and the other, a social ecology comprising the settled peasantry. Their access to the jungle resource is now much limited. The jungle ecology on which they have to depend for the resources is also exploited by the members of the neighbouring village communities. The Birhor ,therefore, exploit jungle resources in a selective and calculative manner. Of all the resources, they are now concerned mostly with the collection of a jungle creeper, namely, Bauhinia, and the hunting of wild monkeys that are seldom exploited by other people. They prepare different kinds of ropes and rope-made articles from the barks of the creepers, and have specialized themselves in this profession of cottage industry. They exchange their products with the villagers for cash, paddy and other consumable articles. Besides this, some of the Birhor are found to act as magico-religious experts, and sell various kinds horns, bones, skins and other parts of rare dead animals to the villagers. In this job they heavily depend on their close and intimate relation with, as well as traditional knowledge of, the jungle environment. A careful study on aspects of world view of the Birhor reveals that they clearly distinguish a world, dism, their own territory in forest from muluk, a world of the larger society. Subsequently, they have developed adaptive strategies of social interaction in the context of two sets of environment : a morally ordered gemeinschaft in disum, their own jungle territory and a rationalist-utilitarian gesellschaft orientation in muluk, the territory dominated by the caste-peasants and market economy' (Sinha 1984 :vi).

In order to perpetuate their present state of economy the Birhor have adopted a nomadic way of life. They normally move and camp in small bands of 5-10 related families, the members of which together exploit the natural resources of a common territory. They encamp on the fallow lands of some villagers, preferably at the outskirts of forested hills. The Birhor collect resources in terms of their availability in the neighbouring jungles as well as their demands in the larger society. When they feel shortage of resources in a jungle or find demands of their products and collections diminishing in the villages and markets they move to another territory.

When the Birhor of a local group or band feel that there will be no more collection of natural resources in the proximal jungles they either extend their area of exploitation still staying at the place or shift their camps to anther area. If there are good markets and big peasant villages around, they try to extend their area of exploitation in forests or, if they feel, may shift to a nearby convenient place but never far away from the markets and villages.

When a market is found to visited by the members of more than one or two bands living in proximal distance or together at one place, the demands of their ropes and rope-made articles may diminish. In such a situation some of them either visit other markets or simply withdraw from the site and move to other places. Sometimes, over-crowding at a place is solved by splitting a band into 2 or 3 smaller units and dispersing in different directions.

There is no fixed territory for any band or household of the Birhor, but they always move along known routes. The area the members of a band would like to move about is decided primarily on mutual understanding of the people and there is no central authority in any band guiding their movement. If a band moves along a particular area, it does not come back to it immediately. Instead, it passes through another area. During their occasional meetings in villages and markets, information is exchanged among the individuals and subsequently, the Birhor come to know which area is worth-moving and which is not.

The places a Birhor band is usually found to move about in a year are not confined to any single administrative zone. A cycle of movement of a Birhor band covers areas of different police stations, or of different sub-divisions and districts or even of different provinces.

Unlike the Birhor of Orissa, who still perpetuate an effective hold over the natural resources of forests, the Hill Kharia of Purulia district in West Bengal 'find themselves in a situation where they have been thrown at the door-step of the peasant societies as landless dependent communities' (Sinha, D. 1984 :85-86). The Hill Kharia of this area have experienced, over the years, a gradual decrease of resources in forests, and subsequently, there has occurred an erosion of technology and knowledge of ecology' among the people. The Hill Kharia now lead a sedentary village life along with various peasant castes and communities, and are very much tagged to the economic and socio-polotical networks of the larger village society.

In order to cope with the depleted condition of the forest they often work as casual and contract agricultural labourers to the villagers and prepare handicrafts like broomsticks and fish traps for sale and barter. Mention may be made of their specific adaptation to the collection of paddy grains from the rat-holes in the harvested fields of the peasants. Though the Hill Kharia have little effective grip over the resources in forests, they are found to spend much of their and energy in hunting, fishing and gathering in the surrounding natural ecology with which they still seem to have an intimate and moral relation. They realize that the jungle resources are more or less exhausted, but they find it easier to adjust with the jungle ecology by means of their cultural idioms (*ibid* : 52).

IV

Shifting cultivation in India is practiced by 2.6 million tribal people who constitute about 8.7 % of the total tribal population. Under this type of agriculture about 10.8 million hectares of land are cultivated (Report of the Commissioner : 1955). There is quit a good number tribal groups in north-east India and a few, in central

India, who practise swidden cultivation. In Orissa alone there is a number of groups, namely, the Juangs and the Bhuiyans of Northern Orissa, and the Saora, the Gadaba and the Kondh of southern Orissa who practise shifting cultivation. The Saoria Paharia of Bihar also practise shifting cultivation.

Unlike the symbiotic hunters the shifting cultivators lead more or less a sedentary life in villages, and instead of depending primarily on the natural produces of jungles they use patches of jungle land for cultivation, and produce crops for subsistence. The swidden cultivator tribes are found to have not only a definite territory of their own but also an elaborate organizational structure over it.

In this method of cultivation a patch of land is selected on the hill side, and the wild growths on it are slashed down by axe. The felled bushes are burned and the ashes are allowed to be mixed up into the soil by rain water. The seeds are then sown. Under this method a single plot of land is cultivated normally for two or three years and then is abandoned for some more years to regain the fertility. The period of recovery may range from 4 to 10 years or more. In the following pages a brief description may be made of the situation of the Juangs of Orissa among whom I worked for sometime in 1977. In 1961 census the total population of the Juangs was 21,890. The original habitat of these people is in the district of Keonjhar from where they have migrated to the districts of Dhenkanal, Koraput, Mayurbhanj and Cuttack. The land or the territory of the Juangs in Orissa is broadly known as Juangpir; it includes the entire hill tract of Keonjhar bordering Dhenkanal and Sundargarh districts. The Juangs and their land Juangpir were initially under the jurisdiction of the former princely estate of Mayurbhanj. The then capital of Mayurbhanj was at Khichching near Juangpir. Later on, the king shifted his capital to Badipada which is situated far away from the land of the Juangs. At this arrangement the Juangs found it difficult to attend the annual dussera festival at the king's palace. They, therefore, felt for a king of their own in a nearby place. There runs a story among the Juangs, as to how they formed the princely state of Keonjhar:

Once the Juangs kidnapped a son of the king of Mayurbhanj and kept him under a *kendu* tree near a stream *(jhara)* in the plains. They carefully brought him up. When the prince grew young, the Juangs ceremonially declared him their King of the state of Kendujhar, later known as Keonjhar.

Whatever may be the authenticity of the story it becomes apparent that the Juangs and their land have, since long, been exposed to the socio-political as well as the economic systems of the princely states of the region.

However, the Juangs of Keonjhar divide their country called Juangpir (i.e., land of the Juangs), into six *pirs* (divisions), namely, *(1)* Jharkhanda *pira*, comprising 12 villages, *(2)* Rebena *pira*, comprising 16 villages, *(3)* Kathua *pira* comprising 12 villages, *(4)* Satkhanda *pira* having 7 villages, *(5)* Charigarh *pira* with 6 villages, and *(6)* Hunda Dandapat *pira* with 11 villages. Each of these *pira* has one headman called *sardar*, the job of whom is to mediate almost all kinds of inter-village affairs. The *sardar* performs his job in consultation with the headmen of the villages under his jurisdiction. It is said that the institution of *sardar* was first created by the King of the State. During that period, the *sardar* of a *pira*, besides looking after the land and economy of the locality, used to collect revenue for the king. Every year at the time of *dussera* festival the *sardar* had to collect goats from his villages and present those to the king. In the Bengali month of *Pausa* they collected the local crops, *rasi* and paddy, and sent them to the king's palace. Normally, they had to give 25 *pai* of *rasi* to the temple of the State and 11 *khondi* (440 kgs. Approx.) of paddy to the king as revenue. In the Bengali month, *Asad* they had to supply the coir required for pulling the sacred cart of the State. Actually, the King used to give one turban *(shiropa)*, one dhoti and one shirt to each of the Sardar for their service to the State.

However, for day-to-day economic activities the Juangs of Keonjhar organize themselves in villages, with 140-150 persons. Each village among them represents one clan, the members of whom share a common productive territory. For the purpose of cultivation one has to clear jungles and prepare the land on the hill slopes. The amount of land a man is able to clear is owned by him. There are, almost in every village, some jack and mango trees that are of much economic importance to the Juangs. They are normally considered the property of the village community. There are, however, some trees that are owned collectively by a group of families related agnatically.

The normal state of land and economy of the Juangs as well as the corresponding socio-political organization has undergone considerable changes. The structure of their traditional territorial organization has been attenuated to a great extent, and almost in every Juang village on the hill slopes there have been considerable immigration of various caste groups from the plains. The villages also are, no longer, uniclan, and members of more than one clan are found to live together in one village. In some instances it was also found that the members of a village migrated to another place on the hill slope and established a separate hamlet with the name prefixed by an adjective denoting the nature of the land. In Dhenkanal as well as in Keonjhar district the Juang now practise both hoe and plough cultivation. In most of the areas of Dhenkanal district the Juangs have switched over to taila (shifting) cultivation in high lands and wet plough cultivation in low lands.

The Juangs of Pallahara (formerly, a princely state, now a subdivision of Dhenkanal) have almost given up shifting cultivation under the restriction of forest legislation. Now they have switched over to wet cultivation. But owing to low yield most of them are found to take recourse to basketry as their main source of economy.

The Dongria Kondh on the Niyamgiri Hills of Koraput district in Orissa are found to combine their shifting cultivation on hill slopes with the maintenance of orange and plantain gardens. Some sections of the Kondhs have, however, switched over to plough cultivation in the plains, and moved away from their complete dependence on shifting cultivation on hill slopes

Recently, Bose (1967) made a study on the carrying capacity of land under shifting cultivation among the Juangs. He studied the Juangs in three villages of Keonjhar. It is found that in the Juang villages of the district 'where 22 –27 persons can be supported, the actual density varies from 11-81. In most places the pressure has crossed the critical point; and that explains why the Juangs have either become landless labourers working in other people's fields in neighbouring villages, or taken to the plough themselves where it has been possible to do so' (Bose 1971:271). Some sections of the Saora tribe of southern Orissa are now found to build terraced fields on the hill slopes for growing paddy with the aid of plough.

V

We have seen in the preceding pages that many of the shifting cultivator tribes have already taken to or, are still taking to settled plough cultivation in the plains. At present about 60 percent of tribes in India are found to pursue settled dry cultivation as their primary mode of food production (Singh 1977). The Santhal, the Munda, the Oraon and the Kisan or Nagesia are some of the numerous agriculturalist tribes in Eastern India. Unlike the shifting cultivators the extensive cultivators are found to live in larger communities. Normally, they live in partially isolated hamlets within the jurisdiction of some multi-ethnic revenue villages.

With the aid of their land-based economy some of the tribes in Eastern India e.g., the Bhumij of Barabhum, the Mundas of Chotanagpur and the Bhuiyans of Orissa even developed elaborate state like socio-political structure over a wider territory (Sinha 1962). In the context of the various forces of modernization there has, however, been a mounting incidence of land alienation among the agriculturalist tribes, and the number of cultivator workers has fallen from 68 percent (1961) to 57.56 perent (1971) while that of agricultural labour has gone from 20 percent to 33 percent. The average landholding among the tribals is only 2.5 acres.

In the following lines I will briefly describe the situation of the Santhal land and economy. A careful study of their myths of origin and the ethnic history of the people would reveal that the Santhal had experienced a lot of internal migrations covering a wider territory within the country. They practiced shifting cultivation combined with hunting and food gathering in the hilly forests of central-east regions of India. With the encroachment of permanent settlement for land tax and the gradual extension of village by landed peasantry from the plains the Santhals were uprooted from their home-base in jungles, and subsequently, were drawn into the technoeconomic fold of the settled Hindu peasantry. Their knowledge of jungle ecology, and expertise in bringing waste land under cultivation by cleaning the jungles were made use of by the peasants. The landed peasants imposed rent and taxes over the lands reclaimed by the Santhals, kept them at the outskirts of their village and looked down upon for their 'primitive' life style. It was told that for fear of rent and tax they used to withdraw from one place to another. The entry of the Santhal to the economic fold of plough cultivation was, therefore, primarily as agricultural labourers and tenant cultivators. Their access to land as cultivators was indirect, and like the Munda and the Bhumij they could not develop a stable and permanent attachment to any particular territory.

From my study on the Santhals in a village of Birbhum, West Bengal, I find that majority of the people in the area are landless labourers; only a few are owner cultivators with an average holding of even less than 2.5 acres. Of the 115 households in the village the members of 55 households work as sharecroppers in the lands of the neighbouring caste-peasants, while members of 44 households earn their livelihood primarily as agricultural labourers in the fields of non-tribal peasants. During the period of my field investigation (1984-85) I found that the total amount of land cultivated by the Santhals, on share-basis, was 142 acres while that of owned land was 97.3 acres. Some of the Santhals of the village are also found to have switched over to the non-agricultural sector for their day-to-day livelihood.

VI

Following the mode of livelihood of the tribal people in Eastern India I have described them into three broad categories. With the specific reference to the nature of their land use they may, however, be grouped into two categories, e.g., *(i)* those do not cultivate land but primarily depend on the natural produces, and *(ii)* those who earn their livelihood from the cultivation of land. It may be mentioned here that though hunting and gathering groups in this area are economically dependent on the products of land, they themselves do not cultivate land but essentially, operate at the periphery of the peasant villages. Though the tribal people in general are conceptualized as having a distinct type of society, the groups in particular exhibit variations and changes in the nature and levels of socio-cultural organization in the context of their land and economy.

However, it becomes evident from our description in the preceding pages that most of the tribal groups in Eastern India were, in the past, shifting cultivators on the lands of the forest-clad hilly regions, characterized by a segmentary social system based on elaborate kinship organization. This mode of livelihood was or is always used in combination with hunting and gathering in jungle ecology. In the context of their land and economy we, therefore, find that among some of the groups, e.g., the Birhor of Orissa and the Hill Kharia of West Bengal, the hunting and gathering mode of production that was once a subsidiary one, has now become the principal one. Keeping in consonance with their knowledge and skill they have only shifted their emphasis from one technology to the other. We have already seen how selectively and calculatively the Birhor exploit forest resource by means hunting and gathering technology still perpetuating an effective link to the jungle habitat. Even the Hill Kharia of West Bengal who have to depend, for both habitat and rights of hunting and gathering, on the lands of the peasant villagers, still retain an emotional and moral relation with forest. Though under the limiting conditions of their land and economy they cannot even optimally operate the clan-lineage based segmentary system of their society, they organize their society broadly in terms of the social and cultural idioms of kinship.

Many of the shifting cultivator tribes have already switched over from their complete dependence on shifting cultivation on hill slopes, to settled agriculture in the plains while a few of them still continue the practice in combination with plough cultivation on the terraced fields in the hills. Some of the people are also found to operate as caste-like occupationally specialized groups within the broad framework of the economic structure of land cultivation. Though some of the agriculturalist tribes in Eastern India are found to build state-like socio-political structure based on their surplus agricultural production, in the contemporary life situations most of them have only a marginal access to land, and operate primarily as tenant cultivators or agricultural labourers in the lands of the non-tribal peasantry of the locality.

12

Ethnic Plurality, Nation-States, and the Changing Tribal Identities in India

I

India has, since long, been known to the world at large for her characteristic 'unity in diversity'. Despite geographical, ethnic and linguistic diversities India developed a cultural unity based on religion, social systems and a more or less uniform body of laws. There was no state organization with sovereign power of administration to maintain political order among the diverse population groups of the land. Ethnic groups of both exogenous and indigenous origins were slowly absorbed in the comparatively advanced socio-economic structure based on *varna-jati* model of group formations developed by the Indo-Aryans. The normative structure of society and polity prevalent in ancient India is well depicted in the *Dharmashastra* of Manu and *Arthashastra* of Chanakya.

In common usage a nation is viewed as a community of people sharing certain commonness of culture and living in a common territory under the common administration of one government i.e., a State. In this sense India was hardly a nation before the British rule in the country. The Mauryan king, Ashoka in Ancient India and the Mughal emperor, Akbar in the medieval period, had, however, made attempts to bring a large portion of the land and her peoples under one polity. It is said that during the reign of Ashoka, the Mauryan State became one of the largest states in the country, and its fame went far beyond the confines of the territory. Akbar too built up a big empire and brought in diverse ethnic and culture groups under one administration. Moreover, Akbar tried to build up a unified culture of 'Hinduism' by making a synthesis of elements from the two dominant cultures of the land : Moslem and Hindu. All these attempts were, however, only transient phenomena in the political history of India.

The Aryan-speaking peoples in ancient India developed a system of principalities, kingdoms and states, co-existing and interacting with one another. Mention may be made of the Solar and the Lunar dynasties that developed in the Ganges valley during the Vedic period. One of the kings of the Lunar dynasty, Bharata whose name had been mentioned in the *Rig Veda,* built up his kingdom over a large territory in northern India that was later known as Bharatvarsha after his name. During the Epic period there evolved, in eastern India, the States of Koshala (with capitals, Ayodhya and Shravasti), Kasi (with capital,Varanasi) and Videha (with capital, Mithila). To the south of Bihar was developed the State of Magadha (with capital, Girivraja, and later, Rajagriha), and to the west, the State of Avanti (with capital, Ujjayini). In the later Vedic period the country was divided into three parts: Aryavarta (the land of the Aryans), the northern kingdom, Madhyadesha, the middle kingdom and Dakshinapatha, the southern kingdom (Antonova et al 1979).

It may be noted here that in the process of their developing the elaborate socio-economic structure and the State-systems the Aryan-speaking peoples not only brought a large part of the territory under their techno-economic control but also incorporated multiple ethnic groups with their distinct ways of life within the broad framework of their society and polity. The various tribal ethnic groups who had long been settled in the country were found to be slowly absorbed into the economic and political structure of the *varna-jati* based Hindu society of the Aryans. In his anthropological studies on the structural dynamics of civilization in India Bose pointed out the manner and the way the various tribal groups were drawn into the regional productive systems of the hierarchically arranged caste society developed by the Aryans. Towards the early twentieth century Bose observed that the Juangs of Keonjhar and Pallahara, the former princely states of Orissa, were switching over to the settled plough cultivation and village crafts in the plains from their traditional productive technology of hoe cultivation on the hill slopes. Bose interprets this process of tribal absorption not only in terms of the superior productive technology of the Aryans but also in terms of their non-competitive productive systems with ample scope for economic security and cultural autonomy of the groups, guided by a general norm of economic interdependence and inter-ethnic tolerance (Bose 1941,1956,1968).

The princes and the kings of ideal-typical principalities and kingdoms were Kshatriyas or Rajputs. This Rajput-Kshatriya model was also emulated by many of the tribal groups in the formation of principalities and states in the forest regions of eastern India, of course after having attained the requisite productive base and economic surplus. Sinha observed that Chotanagpur Raj, ex-princely states of Orissa and Mallabhum were evolved by the tribal groups after the Rajput-Kshatriya model of Chhattisgarh and Garhjat Orissa (Sinha 1962,1987). In the epic literature many of the tribal kingdoms were mentioned as *atavika rajyas, mahakantaras,* or the great forest regions, and *pratyantadeshas* or the forest regions on the fringes of the agriculturally developed areas.

There were both large-scale and small-scale principalities in forest regions. Smaller ones often developed as vassals to some larger kingdoms. Recent studies reveal that the ex-principalities, Pachakot and Bishnupur in eastern India had several such forest kingdoms as vassals. The vassal chiefs or princes normally did not have to pay rent; they simply used to lend support to their kings in warfare or played the roles of buffers and mediators between large kingdoms. It is reported that Laksmi Sura, in the 10th century, supported the sovereign king Rampal of Eastern India in the expansion of his power base in the outlying forest regions. The princes or kings of ex-principalities and States were, however, not always engaged in warfare; they were also found to maintain marital and other contractual relations with one another. The kings brought Brahmin priests, and in the case of the State in north-east India, Buddhist-Lamaist priests, to their courts, and encouraged multiple ethnic groups including service and artisan castes and peasants to settle in their territory. Sinha (1987) identified four levels of tribal polities in pre-colonial eastern and northeastern India: Small chiefdoms (Mizo chieftaincies), Evolved Chiefdoms (Khasi Siyems), Principalities in forest regions of eastern India (Ex-princely States of Orissa, Chotanagpur Raj and Manbhum) and the Archaic States of north-east India (Ahom, Jaintia, Manipur, Dimasa and the frontier Himalayan State of Sikkim). Sinha further observed that most of these tribal states were secondary formations and significantly influenced by the cultural ideology of Brahminical Hinduism, Vaisnavism or Buddhism. The Hinduized Rajas who controlled polities were also held at apex of the societies—both tribal and caste. The role of the king in a State was, indeed, like that of a 'patrimonial head' of a big joint family-estate. The Rajas of ancient Indian states also used to patronize and organize local rituals and festivals at their palaces and carried an aura of sacredness. They were regarded as preservers of both political and social-moral order of their territory (Mahapatra 1987). It is thus evident that the state formations in ancient India not only involved a process of confederating diverse ethnic groups, languages and faiths in one polity but also provided a process of generating a regional pattern of 'relations of participatory interactions' between the social-moral order of the peoples and the administrative political order of the states.

During the pre-Muslim and the pre-British period numerous federal states had been co-existing and interacting with one another within a common ideological structure evolved by the Indo-Aryans. The primordial loyalties of the diverse local ethnic groups were meaningfully integrated with the administrative order of the States. The Brahmans and the Kshatriyas, the important social groups in the dominant varna-jati based Hindu society, had also significant roles in the development and functioning of the States. The Kshatriyas were rulers or kings while the Brahmans were the royal priests and legal advisors to the kings. The Brahmans who enjoyed higher ritual and social status were, in fact, peoples' recognized representatives of both State and Society. In every ancient State, monarchical or republican, administration was carried out in close association with the local caste and tribal councils or assemblies, as well as other public bodies that were, in ancient literature, recorded as *parishad, gana, sangha, sabha,* and *samiti*. These bodies embraced a wider range of public, and acted as important 'organs of power', bringing tangible influence upon the *rajas* (kings) their policies.

Even the king of a monarchical State had to dispense with the cases brought to the court in consultation with the Brahman priests and the democratic bodies of the locality. It may be noted here that the non-monarchical republican system of polities flourished the land in ancient India with smooth administration and a higher of culture (Antonova et al. 1979).

II

The above structure of intra-State and inter-State relations started breaking down fast from the time of the Muslim rule in the country. The people of India soon felt the presence of an alien power structure imposed from above. A new structure of relations in terms of super-ordination and subordination was in the process. The Mughal rulers notionally included many kingdoms and principalities in the forest regions of eastern and north-eastern India and granted their chiefs and kings tributary status as Penkash Zamindars. Chotanagpur (Kokrah), Panchakot (Panchet), and Mallabhum (Bishnupur) in eastern India and Koch Rajyas in northern India were, in this way, brought directly under the revenue system of the Mughal administration.

Under the stress of increasing demands of revenue by the Muslim rulers the princes and the kings of the States extracted surplus from the tribal and caste-peasant subjects, with almost no return to the peoples in terms of redistribution that was the normal practice in earlier times. The kings gradually became more and more exploitative and coercive in their dealings with the people. This process that was set in towards the end of the Muslim rule gained further momentum during the British rule in India, subsequently creating a substantial erosion in the political integrity of the traditional States and their chiefs.

After the Mughal, the British entered the scene, first, as traders and then as rulers of the country. While the

Mughal, for the expansion of their economic and power base in the land, made a notional inclusion of the princely States into their jurisdiction and granted tributary status of Zamindars to the kings, the British tried to entrench themselves into the dominion of India by doing away with the princely States and kingdoms. They, therefore, first adopted the policy of 'lapsed estates'. According to the policy of 'lapsed estate' a king would not be allowed to pass on his state power to his foster son, the custom that was prevalent at that time. In this way, Satara, Nagpur, Jhansi, Sambalpur and many other states were brought under the direct administrative control of the British. This policy of the British and subsequently, their demands for increased revenue created severe discontents not only among the dispossessed princes and kings but also among a large section of Indian population, including the tribal and caste-peasants of the country. Peasant uprisings, on frequent occasions, were even led by the dispossessed landlords. It is also reported that there occurred several solidarity movements among the tribal peoples all over India in response to the massive taxation imposed their land by the British administrators.

In this context of upsurge and turmoil the power structure of the British in India was reorganized by the British Parliament and Government, subsequently, leading to the modification of the structure of their power relations with the traditional principalities and states in India. They made a sharp cleavage among the existing states of the land by introducing a strategic policy of 'divide and rule', and entered into alliance with some of the principalities and states. The Britishers made generous gifts, offered honorary titles and pensionary benefits to some chiefs and kings and obliged them to render their active support towards the suppression of the local uprisings and other anti-colonial activities

This was essential for the consolidation of their power

structure and administrative apparatus in India. The States of Tehri-Garhwal, Kolhapur and Dhar that had been confiscated were returned to the adopted sons of their former rulers. With regard to the tribal dominated forest regions in north-east India the Britishers, however, adopted the tenets of 'indirect rule', and the Nagas, the Khasis, the Garos, the Mizos, the Kukis and other hill tribes in north-east India were administered liberally. The Hos or Kolhas of Kolhan and the Santhals of Santhal Parganas were similarly brought under the special administration. The activities of Christian Missionaries in these regions also helped the British coloniers in this process of their administration.

All these administrative measures of the British could not, however, check the rebellions organized by the peoples of India; they only widened the gap between the 'primordial and civic sentiments' of the people, and induced them to reinforce the primordial ties to their land and tradition. Subsequently, segmented primordial loyalties were consolidated and raised to the level of the country or nation as a whole that was manifested in various organized movements launched against the British administrators for the liberation of India. Ultimately, India was freed from the political clutches of the British in 1947.

III

After independence the Indian National Congress, the dominant party of the time, took over the charge of administration in the decolonized 'new state' of India. After taking over the administrative power the leaders of the ruling party felt it urgent to accomplish the task of integrating the numerous princely states into Indian Union. Of 601 princely states 555 were integrated into India and the rest became part of Pakistan. The princes were granted pensions, and allowed to retain rights to their property, personal and real. The military personnel and the civil servants of the former states were gradually absorbed into the regular army and Civil Service of the 'new state' of India.

The integration of the princely states took three forms (Antonova et al 1979):

i. 216 states were incorporated, as separate districts, in the neighbouring provinces: Bombay, Central Provinces, Orissa and others;

ii. 70 states were incorporated, either with their former boundaries (Bhopal, Manipur and Tripura) or as groups of princely states (Himachal Pradesh, Kutch, Vindhya Pradesh);

iii. 269 of the princely states were integrated as federal units or unions of states (Pepsu—the Patiala and Eastern Punjab States Union, Rajasthan, Sourashtra, Madhya Bharat and Travacore-Cochin) or as separate States with former borders (Hyderabad, Mysore, Jammu and Kashmir).

According to the Constitution of India the country was divided into 28 States, and the ex-princely states were integrated to this system as administrative units of some of the state governments, as union of states administered directly by the Central Government, or as separate States with their former boundaries. This arrangement of States within the country as well as the centre-state pattern of government and administration simply reflected the territorial divisions and the administrative system that the Britishers developed and adopted for their colonial rule in India. While organizing the state-system in India the leaders did hardly consider the historic fact that there had grown in the country, over a long period of time, a federal system of states, integrating diverse ethnic, linguistic and geographical elements into the 'civic order' of the states. Instead, the leaders of the 'new state' were in a hurry to build up the 'nation' through rapid economic and political modernization which, in turn, created new categories of political elites and pressure groups. These elites and pressure groups, in process of modernizing civil politics, became instrumental in organizing many mass movements through the mobilization of the peoples' primordial sentiments to language, ethnic identity, ecological contiguity and the like in different parts of the country. Thus soon after the initial task of organizing the States was over, there came a violent demonstration from the Telegu-speaking people with demand for a separate state of their own. Following the demonstration in 1952 Andhra Pradesh was carved, for Telegu speakers, out of the existing states—Madras, Hyderabad and Mysore. Similarly, Kannada speakers and Marathi speakers also came up with demands for separate statehood on linguistic lines. Maharashtra for Marathi speakers and Gujarat for Gujarati speaking people were created in 1960; Haryana was carved out of the Punjab Subha in 1966 for the Hindi speakers who were numerically dominant in the locality. Subsequently, many states were created out of the existing ones. But there are still pressures from different corners of the country for separate statehood. Uttarakhand, Jharkhand, Chattisgarh, Gorkhaland, Bodoland, Vidarbha and Telengana are some of the states, the demands for which are yet to be settled by the Government of India. In the meantime, the States Re-Organization Committee (SRC) of 1956 had been in force to ensure that the states, created on linguistic lines be economically viable, and enhance the national unity; several constitutional arrangements were also made to give either a degree of self-governance or some special economic assistance to the peoples demanding for autonomy. Mention may be made here of the Autonomous Hill Councils in Karbi Anglong and Bodo areas of Assam and in the Darjeeling hill district of West Bengal, or the regional development boards set up for Vidarbha and Marathwada in Maharashtra. However, neither of these could be worked out effectively, and the nation-building in India still remains in flux.

IV

In the preceding pages an attempt has been made to describe briefly the development process of the state-systems and nation-building in India in the context of her manifold 'plurality'. The observations made here are based, primarily, on the available historical and anthropological findings. 'Plurality' which is basically a natural phenomenon, is not, however, new to humanity, and man has, from the very beginning, been living with situations of plurality, yet maintaining a harmony or a meaningful order of shared understanding. The phenomenon of 'plurality' has, however, emerged as a crucial impediment to the socio-political harmony in complex state societies, and subsequently, led anthropologists and other social scientists towards its various conceptualizations. The political and structural integrity or harmony in most of the modernizing 'new states' of the world with diverse population groups has been in a flux. There is noticed not only a chasm between the primordial sentiments of the population groups and the civil politics of the states but also a lot of pressure from the groups asserting separate identity and striving for political autonomy or separate statehood, thereby keeping the existing nation-state harmony in a perpetual threat. The plurality of these situations is often described in terms of 'ethnic groups', and the dynamics of separate identity formations against nation-states, as a process of 'ethnicity'. The term 'ethnic group' is used by the scholars to broadly designate a population group in terms of its distinctive biological and cultural features, in terms of both objective and subjective criteria while 'ethnicity' is viewed as process of a group's identity formations based on its 'self-image' in the context (Barth 1969;

Despres 1975; Danda 1993; Shils 1957). Danda (1991) in his study of national integration in India further observed that the concept of ethnicity 'as a dynamic process' would help us in delineating 'the boundary of both stable and transient identities' of ethnic groups. Ethnicity as a process, primordial sentiments and civil politics dichotomy and many other concepts have thus been put forward to interpret the ethnic plurality in the context of nation-state formations. Both 'nation' and 'state' are, in fact, two different attempts towards conceptualizing the phenomenon of 'collectivity'. While modern 'state' is basically a political institution to deliberately bring unity or harmony among the diverse population groups living in a common territory, a nation's solidarity involves an in-group sentiment based, among other things, on enormous psychological and cultural features. In both the cases it is, however, the peoples' loyalty that counts much in the realization of solidarity. For a proper understanding of 'ethnic plurality' in the modernizing 'new state' of India, it is, therefore, essential to make a careful anthropo-historical study of the population groups and their contemporary political formations in appropriate social and cultural contexts.

It is evident from the preceding description that India has, since long, been in a situation of 'ethnic plurality' and it was never an impediment to the development of elaborate state-systems in ancient India. The primordial sentiments of the diverse population groups were meaningfully integrated to the civic politics of the Indo-Aryans in the process of evolving their state-systems in the land. There was no centralized government with a sovereign power of state administration over all the polities and states of the country though several kingdoms flourished the land covering large parts of the territory. Despite differences, there were federations of states and princedoms, and marital and other kinds of bonds often reinforced the federal structure. All the states, large or small, followed a uniform body of laws and administration, and operated broadly within an All-India framework of socio-economic structure and cultural ideology. The tribal-folk polities in the countryside of hills and forests were in continuity with the polities and states developed in urban areas. The various traditional cultural media provided a mechanism through which the unifying ideology of the ancient sages and philosophers were brought to the distant peoples in hills and forests thereby enabling them to share the spirit of a common grand culture. Both primordial and civic sentiments were bound together to form polities and states. Precisely speaking, the socio-cultural systems of the ethnic groups were well articulated to the state and political systems of the land in ancient times. It may be noted here that the elaborate varna-jati based socio-economic structure on which the state-systems were evolved was essentially a federal system of diverse ethnic groups or jatis, both of indigenous and exogenous origins. The term jati was used to denote any social group with reference to this socio-economic structure. The *jati* that was, in fact, a 'culture construct' modelled after this socio-economic structure was subsequently found to be used to refer to any ethnic group. In ancient literature, we also come across another term, jana that was used by the Indo-Aryans to refer to communities of people, specifically the numerous tribal peoples living in forest regions. It may be noted that many of these *jana*s were gradually accommodated into the techno-economic structure of the Indo-Aryans, with the generic identity as *jatis* (Roy 1972). In post-independent contemporary India also the term jati or jat is often found to be used to denote any ethnic group having the practice of endogamy and certain culturally distinguishable features including a traditional vocation. The *varna-jati* model of social system seemed to have influenced the Muslims of Bengal in rural areas of Bengal, and Bose (1949) identified numerous *jati*-like occupationally specialized groups among the Muslims of erstwhile East Bengal, now Bangladesh.

The diverse ethnic groups with their manifold primordial loyalties had thus meaningful positions in the larger spheres of the economic and political systems of the state and society. They had also ample scope for mobility through socially approved process of sanskritization, hinduization, rajputaization, kshatriyaization and universalization; syncretism of multiple faiths and cultures at regional levels was very common, and exploitation remained to its minimum through cultural mechanism of redistribution of surpluses and recycling of the ritual positions (Sinha 1962; Srinivas 1972; Marriott 1955). The phenomenon of inequality, exploitation and poverty generated from ethnic plurality in terms of status, wealth and power in the society and polity in ancient India seemed to have been in a natural state of cultural equilibrium, and there was hardly any ethnic upsurge in this respect.

It was, however, during the Muslim and the British rules in the country when the existing equilibrium structure of the peoples' economy, society and culture was disrupted to a large extent. The Muslim and the British with their superior military powers tried to build up their empires in the country. The economic structure and the state-systems were forcibly or tactfully brought under their control, subsequently dividing the peoples into the 'rulers' and the 'ruled'. During the Muslim rule several uprisings from the peoples of the land were noticed. Various tribal ethnic groups and caste-peasants rose to rebellion and launched social movements. Some Rajput kings also fought to preserve their political and cultural integrity against the onslaught of the Muslim invaders. Most of these movements during the Muslim rule were primarily revivalist in nature, and the peoples' loyalties to their traditional societies and cultures were emphasized. This kind of social and cultural movement continued throughout the nineteenth century when the British were in power. These social movements turned out as political movements towards the later part of the British rule when there was noticed a tendency of aggregating large number of traditional ethnic groups to form bigger units in terms of a common loyalty to economy, territory and cultural tradition of the land.

In the decolonized 'new state' the Indian National Congress Party, the main instrument for mobilizing the peoples, to fight in unison for national liberation, came to power in 1947. Soon after assuming the power the Party divided the country into several linguistic provinces with a centralized government at the apex. But almost in no time it was discovered that the united spirit that was evolved during freedom fight, is fragmented into 'narrow loyalties, petty jealousies, and ignorant prejudices'. The loyalties of the peoples to the country as a whole or the 'nation' were narrowed down to some immediate spheres of social existence: language, religion, regional economic resource base, tribal or other ethnic group identity and the like, that generated organized movements from different corners of the country for political autonomy or separate statehood, putting the national unity at stake. The nation-wide development and welfare programmes as well as the liberal administrative policies adopted by the 'new government' of India, intended for an immediate alleviation of poverty and social backwardness of the ethnic groups, further led to the creation of new, adhoc categories of peoples and eco-cultural zones such as Scheduled tribes, Scheduled Castes, Other Backward Classes, Minority Groups, and Scheduled and Reserved Areas. These policies and programmes, formulated and induced from above added a new dimension of artificial 'plurality' and widened the hiatus between the 'civil order' of the nation-state in India and the primordial sentiments of traditional ethnic groups, subsequently, heightening the shared feelings of the groups at their immediate spheres of social existence.

A careful study of the contemporary solidarity movements in the appropriate contexts of the peoples' socio-economic organizations, cultural traditions and world views would, however, reveal that they are not as disruptive to the national harmony as they seem to be. In most of the cases, the ethnic groups have been trying to carve out a meaningful arena, not outside the country, but within the very confines of the land itself. In the process of nation-state formations in post-independent India the leaders divided the country on linguistic basis, and made ad hoc categorizations of ethnic for rapid economic and political modernization, with almost no consideration to their social systems and cultural heritage. The political divisions of India and her peoples were, in this way, imposed from above on the prevailing divisions of the country based on social organizations and cultural traditions of the peoples. The kind of uniformity based on economic tradition of *varna-jati* based social system that grew up in ancient India 'between the geographically or even ecologically distinguishable regions of India' was also ignored (Bose 1950). Mention may be made, in this connection, of a few more anthropological observations on the socio-cultural basis of the country's division. Iravati Karve (1956), for instance, in her extensive study of kinship organization in India, observed that the country was divided into two zones: the Aryan North and the Dravidian South. Similarly Bose (1956) pointed out a division of India into North-West and South-East zones based on some important items of material culture in common. Bose (1961), while analyzing 'the structure of Indian Unity' that he analogically compares to a pyramid, gives a clear picture of the ethnocultural situations of the land. For convenience I am quoting him at length:

> If regionalism is in evidence to a certain extent in relation to the material arts of life, it is apparent already that the degree of differentiation is less in respect of the country's social organization ...if one rises to higher reaches of life confined to ideals or faiths or art, the differences.. ...become feebler and feebler. They are eventually replaced by a unity of beliefs and aspirations which gives to Indian Civilization a character of its own.

In the larger sphere of the modern nation-state organizations in India, the people thus feel not only the lack of their 'personal significance' but also a meaningful arena of participatory interactions and socio-cultural communication. A pertinent observation of Geertz may be worth-noting here. Geertz (1973) notes that 'the peoples of the new states are simultaneously animated by two powerful, thoroughly interdependent, yet distinct and often actually opposed motives—the desire to be recognized as responsible agents whose wishes, acts, hopes, and opinions 'matter', and the desire to build an efficient, dynamic modern state'. He further observes, 'it is a search for an identity, and a demand that the identity be publicly acknowledged as having import, a social assertion of the self as 'somebody in the world'...it is a demand for progress, for a rising standard of living, more effective political order, greater social justice, beyond that 'playing a part in the larger arena of world politics', of 'exercising influence among nations'.

A close probe into the organizational process of the various solidarity movements occurring in the country, over time and space, would reveal that there is developing a tendency among the peoples to expand and mobilize the social and cultural base of their movements by implicating multiple traditional groups to form larger units, to project an identity and shift the term of reference from narrow local to a greater sphere of the civil of the country. A tendency towards cultural universalization at the regional level is already in the process. The movement for the state of Jharkhand in eastern India, for instance, involves not only the aggregation of several tribal caste-peasant groups but also the strife for carving out a separate political territory from the existing provinces of Orissa, Bihar and West Bengal. The leaders of the movement are also trying to universalize the regional political institutions and religious ideologies at a higher level of synthesis. Bose would call this a trend of 'sub-nationalism', and attribute the spurt of such movements to the unequal forces generated through the induced development and welfare programmes in the modernizing 'new state of India (1967). Similar trends in the expansion of the social base through the aggregation of 'independently defined', diverse primordial groups and asserting political autonomy, are also noticed in the case of the Uttarakhand movement in northern, and the Chattisgarh movement in central India. The solidarity movements in connection with the former states of Nagaland, Meghalaya, Manipur in the earlier period of India's independence as well as the on-going movements for the statehood of Bodoland and Gorkhaland in the hilly regions of eastern India also reflect the tribal peoples' desire to evolve state by coagulating segmentary kin units of one or more tribal groups. Roy Burman would like to label these movements as a phenomenon of 'infra-nationalism'.

A cursory look from above may, however, give one the impression that the contemporary revolutions the ethnic groups are disintegrative and against the national interest of India, but a deeper probe into the situations would reveal that the peoples are trying not only to assert their personal identity and gain justice in the developing civil order but also to participate as 'somebody publicly recognized' in the nation-building process of India. In the case of the aforesaid sub-nationalistic and infra-nationalistic movements also the peoples' term of reference in not merely the local scene but the civil politics in the larger sphere of nation-states in India. Diverse ethnic groups unite together to build, protect an identity with 'personal significance' in the modernizing context of India. The solidarity movements of the ethnic groups involve a process of new group formations with wider social and cultural base, and do not reflect a mere parochialization of primordial sentiments, a simple shifting of loyalties from one sphere to another, or a clash between the primordial and civic sentiments. Implicit in all the uprisings there is, indeed, a tendency among the peoples to raise their economic and political status, and universalize the 'self-image', and not for cessation but for a meaningful articulation with the modernizing process of the nation-states in India. The solidarity movements in the 'new state' of India imply, to quote Geertz, a 'progressive extension of the sense of primordial similarity and difference generated from the direct and protracted encounter of culturally diverse groups in local contexts to more broadly defined groups of similar sort interacting within the framework of the entire national society...' (Geertz *:ibid*). It is true that various centripetal and centrifugal forces have been operative In the mobilization of diverse ethnic sentiments for solidarity movements. Nevertheless it can hardly be denied that a process of new social formations with a broader cultural base has already been set in, generating a spirit of loyalty, to a higher level of socio-political order.

Questions may, however, be raised as to the genuineness of the contemporary social formations as well as the integrity of their leadership. It is, no doubt, essential to identify the 'genuine' and integrative formations, and differentiate them from the 'spurious' ones before arriving at any firm conclusion. It may be noted here that in India as well as other decolonized 'new states' all over the globe there is emerging a 'nationwide system of ethnic blocs engaged in total relations with one another' and inclined to integrate themselves to the 'developing civil order'. Tribal, communal, ethnic and other principles of primordial solidarity are often transcended over the narrow and local loyalties and universalized, and the new social formations are set on a profoundly rooted 'consciousness of kind'. The leaders draw in new experiences and symbols from the larger world, weave them with the old ones to form a total view of life and action, and reinforce the new group identity for an appropriate recognition in the modernizing context of nation-state in India. The phenomenon of ethnocentrism is, however, not done away with such integrative movements. 'An integrative revolution' Geertz observes, 'merely modernizes it'. Our task would thus be to acknowledge and integrate such social formations into the process of nation building in India. The extent to which we are able to identify, and integrate genuine social formations with the developing civil order, our task of building up a new nation in India will be successful.

13

Ritual and Cosmology of the Birhor, a Hunter-Gatherer Tribe

Introduction

Semiotically, the category ritual may be viewed as a system of symbols involving the classification of the phenomenal world in and around which a people live, and as having, as its distinctive feature, a tendency toward certain forms and structures of communication. Ritual is a cultural construct and spans over sacred-secular, and natural-supernatural domains. A society's principal cosmological notions are held together as sacrosanct and perpetuated through multiple media of ritual performance. The discourse of ritual unlike that of science involves a language of emotions and affective participation in the world of phenomena, and also a traditionalizing effect.

The phenomenal world of the contemporary hunter-gatherer groups is undergoing changes and the people are constantly constructing idioms and sacred symbols to form a meaningful world of their own. Ritual acts are public, and serve as a key to the understanding of cosmology. Every people has a primordial motive for self-identity, and ritual helps to attain the end through its multiple media of communication.

In this paper I will try to describe the structure of the universe as conceptualized by the contemporary Birhor and note the process of their ritual construction that helps them form and maintain an integral structure of cosmos.

The Birhor

The term Birhor means 'jungle man' (*bir*. jungle, *hor*. man). They are best known, however, as adepts in ensnaring monkeys with charms. Consequently, in Orissa the Birhor are called Mankria, Mankar-khia-kol, or Mankirdia, which refer to their habit of sharing and eating monkeys. In Orya, *mankar* means monkey and *khia*, eating.

The Birhor have a close affinity with large agriculturalist tribes, the Santal and the Munda of the region. They use Santali and Mundari words in their speech, and often mix with them the dialects of local Hindi, Orya and Bengali. Originally, the people belonged to the Mundari groups of tribes who, in the past, practised shifting cultivation combined with hunting and gathering in the hill-slopes of Chotanagpur plateau. With the encroachment of settled peasantry from the plains and subsequent deforestation, they found shifting cultivation untenable and adopted hunting and gathering as their primary mode of subsistence (Adhikary, 1989). Hunting and gathering among the Birhor is thus considered a case of 'devolution' or 'secondary primitivization' (Sinha 1969).

The Birhor among whom the present author worked move around the jungle land in eastern and central regions of mainland India. The jungle land around which the people predate forms a continuous geographical corridor across the provinces of Orissa Jharkhond, West Bengal, Madhya Pradesh, and Maharashtra.

The climate in this area is characterized by heavy rainfall in the wet season, severe cold in winter and extreme heat in summer. The ecology is rich in flora and fauna of a tropical climate. In these hilly-forested regions there are many valleys and cultivated plains dotted with clusters of tribal and non-tribal peasant hamlets, including weekly and bi-weekly market centres. The peasants also collect forest products. The Birhor depend both on the forest ecology and the agricultural products of the settled peasantry. The Birhor hunt games and collect roots, tubers, creepers, fruits, honey and some rare articles from the jungles and rice, oil, salt, cloth and some iron implements from the villages and markets. The Birhor women prepare ropes and rope-products with bark fibres of Bauhinia creepers and sell them in markets and villages; their men act as magico-religious experts to the peasants.

The economy of the Birhor thus involves, on one hand, a selective exploitation of the forest resources and on the other, the maintenance of an essential economic articulation with the settled peasantry and the markets of the larger society (Adhikary 1974).

The Birhor and Their Universe

The Birhor do not have any crystallized idea about cosmological matter. They never spoke, on their own, about the origin and the structure of their universe. From their day-to-day conversation and behaviour it reveals that they divide their universe into *rimil,* the sky and the *utaye,* the earth. The earth is a circular plane while the sky is a hollow concave overarching it. The structure of the universe as presented by the Birhor is very similar to the conical structure of their leaf huts.

The Birhor are more concerned with utaye, the earth. They divide their universe on the earth into disum and muluk. By *disum* they mean the region of hills and forests, their own territory, and by *muluk,* the peasant villages and the markets, the territory of 'other people'. The Birhor have developed adaptive strategies of participation and social interaction in these two sets of environment: a morally ordered gemeinschaft in *disum* and a rationalist-utilitarian gesellschaft orientation in *muluk* (Adhikary 1984).

The Natural and the Supernatural

The Birhor do not make any semantic distinction between the natural and the supernatural. They, however, use the words, *hanapuri* to refer to 'that world' and *noapuri,* 'this world'. The *hanapuri* is inhabited by supernatural entities while the noapuri sustains both disum and muluk. To the Birhor all natural and visible things are animated and presided over by invisible personified supernatural entities. Though they posses a profound practical knowledge of natural phenomena, they feel neither the need nor ability to dominate or harness these phenomena. The meaning of the ultimate reality lies in the supernatural.

The Birhor broadly identify three categories of supernatural entities: *bonga, hapram,* and *churgin*. The bonga includes all personified supernatural entities of nonhuman origin, while the *hapram* are the spirits of their ancestors. Both are benevolent. All the evil spirits or the ghosts are classed together as *churgin*.

The Birhor think that the whole universe is created, and presided over by sing bonga, the sun deity and his wife chandu bonga, the moon deity. *Sing bonga* is considered the Supreme. He is benevolent and does not interfere into the domains of other gods and goddesses. *Dharti mai,* a female deity is in the charge of natural resources and creatures on the earth. She provides food to all creatures and looks after their well being like a mother goddess. *Sing bonga* and *chandu bonga* are worshipped together in January-February. A white cock and a white he-goat are sacrificed to *sing bonga* while to *chandu bonga* a black hen is sacrificed. *Dharti mai* is worshipped in November-December when the winter crops are sown in the locality. A black hen or a black she-goat is sacrificed to her.

The Birhor further conceptualize two other deities: *Lugu Haram* and his wife *Burhi Mai*. Lugu Haram resides in the east while Burhi Mai, in the west. These deities are also worshipped together annually in January-February. This couple has seven sons each presiding over a particular natural phenomenon. For instance, *hanuman bir* presides over the langur (*Presbytes entellus*) and *bandra bir*, over the monkey (*Maccacus rhesus*). *Nanda bir* presides over wind while *paban* or *hoyo bir* presides over rain and storm. *Bagh bir* is the presiding deity of tigers. The bear is presided over by *hundar bir* and thunder and meteor, by *babsha bir*.

Red fowls are sacrificed to both *hanuman bir* and *bandra bir*. *Nanda bir* and *hoyo bir* are worshipped with black cocks. Cocks of mixed colour are sacrificed to the deities, *bagh bir*, *hundar bir* and *babsha bir*.

The *hapram* live in the supernatural world along with the *bonga*. Two categories of *hampram* are identified: *bura burhi* and *chowrasi*. The *bura buri* refers to the spirits of the ancestors who are remembered by name while the *chowrasi* are those who are not remembered by name.

The relation of the living with their *hapram* is both contractual and ethical. A Birhor joins the *hapram* in afterlife only after having lived community values to the hilt. Living relatives initiate the departed souls into the *hapram* world. The *hapram* in turn look after their descendants' well being. For the worship of *hapram* the head of the animal is beaten *(kutam)* till death while for the bonga it is severed *(bonga)*.

When a man dies, his son or in his absence, any male member of the lineage buries the corpse and constructs a leaf hut over the grave. After one or two days the departed soul *(jiu)* is called back to rest on asthan, a sacred altar. The son then gives the soul food and drink. The belief is that if the son does not perform the ritual the soul will remain a 'wanderer' *(bhulah)* and would not get entry into the world of *hapram*. This calling-back ritual initiates the spirit of the deceased to the status of a hapram. The altar, *asthan* is symbolically preserved in a basket and carried by the people on shoulders when they shift their camps.

The term *churgin* denotes, in a generic sense, all malevolent spirits. The Birhor, however, believe that normally the spirits of the people who die in an unnatural manner become churgin. The idea of unnatural death is, however, not based on any strong sense of morality. The souls of these people are not called back to the sacred altar nor are they initiated to the world of *hapram*. They are 'evil', but not in the strong sense of the term.

They may, at times, be good and benevolent. The people remember them on all ritual occasions, offer oblations and ask them to live in peace and harmony.

The Birhor identify eight such spirits, namely, *daini, pangri, churni, draha, khut, bhulah, bhulah chandi,* and *baghat*.

The *daini* live under the creepers in jungles. The *pangri* are blind and live in the bank of rivers or streams. The *churni* inhabit rubbish dumps. *Draha* and *khut* dwell under big trees or big boulders while small bushes are abodes of the *bhulah* and *bhulah chandi*. The *baghat* live in deep jungles.

In the supernatural world the Birhor place the *hapram* at a lower plane than the bonga.

The *lugu haram, burhi mai* and their sons are placed between the *hapram* and the *bonga*. All these supernatural entities signify social power and authority and are held in high esteem by the people as their patron or guardian deities (Adhikary 1996).

Birhors are in a relation of contiguity and shared affinity with all the animals, plants, and trees in forests as well as the invisible phenomena, and maintain a structure of participatory relations with their world of perception. They tell that the animals like tigers and bears would not attack a Birhor if his relationship with them remains in a natural state. The people consider them as personified supernatural entities. One informant of 50 years of age told me that he had not seen any case of snakebite among them in his lifetime. Snakes often move around their camps and the people simply drive them away with mild scolds as if they are pets. Their children are sportive with snakes in their camp.

'Human relations with the non-human environment are modelled on the same principle of sharing that applies within the human community' (Bird-David 1992). When trees in the jungle start blooming in March and April, the Birhor strictly avoid cutting them. This they do simply not because they would bear fruits for them but because they feel communion with nature's ecstasy. This feeling of communion with nature is overtly manifest in their *baha parab* (flower festival) when the men, women and the children of the camp decorate themselves with various flowers and make merry through communal dancing and singing. They dance, sing and drink merrily the whole day and celebrate the nature's ecstasy.

Self and Society

The people normally ascribe themselves as 'men of jungle' (*bir,* jungle; *hor,* man). As to the origin of their identity as Birhor the people often narrate the story as follows:

Once upon a time there was a Kherwar king in Chotanagpur, who had two sons. After the death of the king, the princes started quarrelling over the throne. Then the elders of the State came forward to mitigate the dispute. They asked the princes to run a race on horseback and told that the throne would go to the prince who would win the race. Accordingly there was a race and the younger prince won. The elder prince was delayed because his turban stuck to the thorns of a bush on his way. The younger prince became the king of the State while the elder one took to a wandering life in the jungle.

The people trace their descent from the elder prince who took up jungle as his abode and consider themselves as birhor or men of jungle. In the story mentioned above the Birhor also note that they had a glorious past as well as definite territory of their own. The Birhor of Orissa divides their society into a number of clans (killi), each of which has its traditional home either on one or more mountains in the jungles. These mountains are located in Chotanagpur area of Bihar and Jharkhand States, and presided over by a deity, called *buru bonga* (mountain deity). For instance, the deity *bisrapat* of *gicksiria* clan resides on the *kuku buru, dal buru, hangar buru, ranga buru* and *matha buru;* the deity *nasan* of *hembrom* clan lives in *gnan buru,* and the *kokodhara* of *lakhurchuta* clan inhabits the *tamda buru.* In the context of their present life-situations the clans of the Birhor can no longer operate as localized corporate units. The members of a clan are dispersed over a wider territorial region. The mountain deity *(buru bonga)* is, however, held as an emblem of unity. They worship and make animal sacrifices to *buru bonga* facing the direction in which their traditional home sites are located. The clans are identified by the kind of animal they sacrifice to their *buru bonga.* The members of *gicksiria clan* sacrifice goats *(merom)* while those of hembrom sacrifice pigs *(ghusuru)* to their mountain deity. This cognitive structure also involves effective as well as affective relationship between the social and the natural world of the Birhor. The kin groups and the elements of nature are made sacrosanct through ritual acts and affective participation. The clan, the mountain and the animal together constitute an integral entity reinforced by shared understanding through ritual communication among the people.

Bansa or *jat* is another kin group smaller than the clan. It is, indeed, an exogamous lineage. The members of a *bansa* distinguish themselves from those of another primarily by their mode of worship and the kind of animals they sacrifice to their orha bonga or household deity. Like the members of a clan the members of a *bansa* too do not form a local group. They are dispersed into nuclear families over a wider region. The members of a lineage *(bansa)* feel themselves united if they find that the ritual sacrifice to their orha bonga is uniform.

Every Birhor, man or woman, has a name and a surname by which he or she is normally referred to, or addressed. The names of father's father, father's mother, mother's father, mother's mother are normally used in naming the children of a family. Small children are generally termed as gidre. The words, *kora* and *kuri,* are prefixed to *gidre* to denote respectively a boy and a girl. An adult male is referred to as *sanre* while an adult female, as *enga.* Individual identity of a Birhor is, however, embedded into the social matrix. As a child grows its self gradually loses its individuality into groups, like *orha, killi, birhor,* and ultimately, the world of *hapram.* To attain the status of *hapram* one needs to conform to the prevalent social norms and customs that emphasize the maintenance of good relation among camp members. Individual autonomy and mutual sharing are simultaneously valued. The band *(tola)* among the Birhor is a meaningful and secure social ambience (Bird-David 1994:599) and the people, 'in the conduct of their mutual relations...demonstrate the possibility of a perceptual orientation toward the social environment that is direct,..' as in the case of natural environment (Ingold 1999:408).

The people identify two broad categories of human beings: *hor* and *dikhu*. They ascribe themselves as *hor* (man) of *bir* (jungle) i.e., *birhor,* while the Santhal, Munda, and the Mundari tribes of the locality are ascribed as *horhon*. They are not *dikhu,* and the Birhor feel a close affinity with these peoples.

The various ethnic groups under the category, *Diku* are specified in terms of their occupations. In peasant societies occupations of the groups are hereditarily ascribed. Some of the occupations are considered pure while others, polluting. The groups pursuing polluting occupations are ranked low in the local hierarchy; the people who eat beef are also looked down upon by the Hindu caste-peasants. The Birhor carefully maintain socio-ritual distance from these groups and try to move about as clean as possible. The Birhor eat beef but when asked if they eat beef, they would normally say, 'no'. The peasants believe that the Birhor are expert in magical and mystic activities and this also helps them to enter into bond-friendship and *guru-sishya* (master-disciple) relation with the peasants in the villages. The social-cultural idioms of the neighbouring people as well as their impressions about them are strategically manipulated and conventionalized as a model of the community.

The Birhor conceptually distinguish the hierarchically-characterized society of the peasants from that of their own, and their ceremonial friendship and *guru-sishya* relationship with the caste-peasants simply act as social insurance of economic transaction. The Birhor's participation in the world of muluk is instrumental and lacks any affective attachment. Their experiences in muluk, indeed, help them reinforce their jungle identity.

Ritual and Cosmology: An Interpretation

Cosmology involves the study of classification of phenomena and provides the framework of concepts and relations, which treat the universe as an ordered system. The genesis and functioning of the existing phenomena are studied normally under the conceptual framework of cosmogony. In this paper I have, however, made no analytical distinction between the two concepts but more or less studied all the aspects together under rubric of cosmology. I have thus narrated the origin myth of the Birhor and their society and the classification and function of various phenomena in and around which they live. Some of my observations on their 'sayings' and 'doings' are also noted. Myths, sayings and doings in context often involve meaningful ritual communication and help maintain the structure of the cosmos.

The Birhor like many other hunter-gatherer groups in India and elsewhere do not hold elaborate ritual performance. They organize their day-to-day experience and conceptualize the phenomena of the cosmos both existentially and emotionally. Many of their performances in the changing context are guided by unstated assumptions of tradition and collective conscience. New experiences are woven together with the old ones and constructed symbolically so as to make them unquestionably acceptable to the community.

There are two distinct yet complementary modes of ordering our cosmos: religious and scientific. Religious mode involves participation and scientific mode, causality. 'Much of the discourse of participation is framed in terms of sympathetic immediacy, performative speech acts and ritual action' while that 'of causality and positive science is framed in terms of distancing, neutrality, experimentation, and the language of analytic reason'. Participation emphasizes 'sensory and affective communication and the language of emotions while causality stresses the rationality of instrumental action and the language of cognition' (Tambiah 1990).

The division of their world into disum and muluk signifies the Birhor's cognition at an immediate level of abstraction. At a higher level of abstraction it reveals that the people feel a close affinity with disum, which is reinforced by their affective participation and emotional involvement. The Birhor, the forests, hills, animals, plants and trees in *disum* are in a relation of existential immediacy, contact and shared affinity. *Muluk* is peripheral to the core of their cosmology and does not involve affective communication. The Birhor's relation with *muluk* seems to involve a gesellschaft type of orientation while their relation with *disum* is characterized by a gemeinschaft type of orientation.

The various gods, goddesses, ancestral spirits, and ghosts are symbolic identification of natural and social phenomena. The people communicate with these supernatural entities through ritual acts. The colour and the sex of the sacrificed animal analogically reflect the gender and appearance of the personified deity. The lineage and the clan segments of the people are identified in terms of the kind of animal they sacrifice to their household *(orha)* and mountain *(buru)* deities *(bonga)*. Each of these kin segments has its own animal for ritual sacrifice. Animal sacrifice is nothing but a sacred hunting to the people. In sacrifice it is the blood of the animal that is offered to the deity, and blood signifies life. Life is the unifying substance among man, nature and the supernature. Man, nature and supernature are considered con-substantial.

The Birhor do not take the meat of any domesticated

animal before offering it to their deities. Wild animals like langurs and monkeys are considered sacred, and the people believe that they cannot catch the animals if they are not pleased. The Birhor, however, take their meat without sacrificing them to the deities. A monkey or a langur is sacred in forests but after it is slaughtered and the meat divided among the members of the camp for consumption, it is treated casually. With the change of context code switching occurs. A leaf hut becomes sacred when a corpse is buried inside it and consecrated to the ancestral spirit.

The Birhor, like many other foragers, 'have both their practical and conceptual consciousness focused on animals, plants, the landscape and seasons, and meteorological and astronomical phenomena'. At the metaphysical level they regard nature 'as pervasively animated with moral, mystical and mythical significance' (Guenther: 1999: 426). They know that the animal and plant resources in forests are exploited by the peasants but do not believe in scarcity of resources in forests. Nature is considered generous and morally bounded to them. They are aware of the natural causes of life and growth of plants and animals. They are, however, inclined more towards maintaining a structure of participatory relations with nature through ritual sanctification.

The Birhor adopt ideas from the neighbouring Hindu caste-peasants and weave them with their traditional ones to form a distinct cosmology of their own. The caste people think that hunting of monkeys is almost an impossible job. They say that the Birhor hunt monkeys by means of magical power. They utter spells, touch the trees, and the monkeys come down with folded hands to enter into their nets. The Birhor carefully keep up this mystic impression of the villagers and construct myth. They say:

Long ago Ram and Sita were trying to catch monkeys

in jungles, but they could not succeed. They used iron nets but monkeys broke through them. At last they came across the Birhor in jungles and asked for their help. The Birhor then prepared nets with ropes of chop fibres and trapped monkeys.

The stories of the Hindu Great Tradition are so narrated as to show their professional skill in monkey-hunting a divine sanction as well as meaningful.

The Birhor are aware of many more visible and invisible phenomena than are described here, and their world view may be 'thought of as something constantly in process: a fluctuating assemblage of more or less connected ideas that change as to focus, affective colouring perhaps, content and choice of connections and emphases' (Redfield 1962: 281).

Though the Birhor have to adopt diverse occupational strategies and maintain economic and social articulation with caste-peasants and markets of the larger society, they carefully construct a culture around their hunting and gathering in close association with forest ecology. Their relation with forests is reflexive and affective while that with the larger world is instrumental. Man, nature and the supernature are morally bound in their cosmology, and the Birhor forms a meaningful world of ritual communication with the natural and the supernatural phenomena in and around which they live.

The phenomenal world that the contemporary Birhor encounter and perceive is, however, constantly being modelled and communicated through construction of multiple media of ritual performance characterized by emotional and affective participation. Ritual, viewed semiotically, thus gives us a clue to the meaningful understanding of the cosmology as well as epistemology of the Birhor.

14

Gods, Spirits and Ghosts: A Study of Santal Cosmology

I

Most peoples on the globe conceptualize gods, spirits and ghosts as supernatural beings belonging to an Other World in contrast to their Social World. Man's concern with an Other World of supernatural beings is as old as man himself. There are, indeed, few peoples who do not believe in a world of the supernatural though the nature of perception of, and the relationship with, the supernatural varies from one culture to another.

The gods, the spirits and the ghosts that constitute the Other World have personal attributes; they do not, however, belong to a similar plane of existence in terms of origin, status and power. While the ancestor spirits and ghosts are of human origin, gods and other supernatural beings are of non-human origin. Ancestor spirits and ghosts are ethereal or non-material substance of human beings persisting even after death and decay of their material bodies while gods and other kinds of spirits are personified supernatural forces or powers presiding over various natural phenomena. In most cultures ghosts are, however, placed at a plane lower than that of the ancestor spirits. They are inimical, and lack the softer, 'human qualities' of personality. Illness and misfortunes are thus often referred to the interference of ghosts. Ancestor spirits, on the other hand, are benevolent, and live in communion with their living heirs. All supernatural beings are, however, immortal, and more powerful than the living human beings.

Anthropologists have so long perceived the supernatural as a projection of the social world on the cosmic plane, and considered the beliefs and the practices related to the supernatural as validating and regulating social relations. With reference to 'ancestor worship' Lienhardt thus notes that 'commemoration of the ancestor is affirmation of the range of relationships he created among the living, holding together of all those who count him important in their past' (1978 :144). A more elaborate statement was made by Edmund Leach. He observes,

> The concept of the Other World is generated by direct inversion of the characteristics of ordering experience. This world is inhabited by mortal, impotent men, who live their lives in normal time in which events happen in sequence, one after another. In this world we get older and older ... and in the end we die. The Other World is inhabited by immortal, omnipotent (beings) who exist perpetually in abnormal time in which past, present and future all coexist... 'Power', conceived as the source of health, life and fertility, political influence, wealth ..is located in the other world and the purpose of religious performance is to provide a bridge, or channel of communication, through which the power of the gods may be made available to otherwise impotent men (1976:81-82).

Robert Hertz, a French sociologist also notes of a symbolic transformation of the social world into the Cosmic World. He identifies two distinct phases of mortuary rites among certain population groups in Borneo. In one phase, the surviving relatives of the dead man live in a world of ritual seclusion from everyday social life. In another phase, the living are incorporated into their social world and the spirit of the dead man is sent to a new world at the supernatural plane. Hertz, however, interprets the phenomenon of death as rite of passage to a new status and observes that the after-life is invented to avoid death as final.

The above interpretations, though highly revealing, begin, in fact, with an *a-priori* assumption of social structure and view the supernatural as its projection on the cosmic plane. But the cosmic world, though often related to the social world, is essentially a 'culture-construct' of the people and all the supernatural beings—gods, spirits and ghosts—are conceptual categories developed in the contexts of their confrontation with social as well as natural events and phenomena. They may be experienced, revealed, borrowed or even created by particular individuals in the contexts of their life-situations, and then gradually get institutionalized and encapsulated in myths and legends forming a system and acting as a model for the entire community. They are symbolic creations of human minds. They not only heighten the intensity of shared experience of social communication but also reinforce the people psychologically to cope, at times, with illness, failures, death and crisis. The existential premise of the supernatural beings thus involves a process of creation by the people explaining their orientation to the cosmic world and motivating their social actions. The gods, ancestor spirits and ghosts, no doubt, reflect aspects of social structure of a people; but a careful probe into the genesis of their cultural constructions as well as their significance in the contexts of behaviour would also render the possibility of their acting as a model of the people's social action. The genesis of man and his universe as well as the ultimate meaning of inevitable natural happenings like birth and death, illness and decay, misfortunes and failures is often referred to the personified supernatural powers presiding over them. When their general experience of causal relationship amongst the natural phenomena fails, they tend to explain by relating them to an all-purpose idea of the supernatural. Cultural constructions of the supernatural have thus an intrinsic quality of two-way functions. Geertz has made this dual nature of human thought very clear in his article, Religion as a Cultural System. I quote him below at length:

> The term 'model' has ...two senses, an 'of 'sense and a 'for' sense.... In the first, what is stressed is the manipulation of symbol structures so as to bring them, more or less closely, into parallel with the pre-established non-symbolic system,...In the second, what is stressed is the manipulation of non-symbolic systems in terms of the relationships expressed in the symbolic,.. ...It is, in fact, this double aspect which sets true symbols off from other sorts of significative forms. ... The perception of the structural congruence between one set of processes, activities, relations, entities and so on, and another set for which it acts as a program...is the essence of human thought. The inter-transposability of models for and models of which symbolic formulation makes possible is the distinctive characteristic of our mentality (1973 : 93-94).

With this brief introductory remark I would, therefore, keep in abeyance any *a-priori* assumption of the structure of social world as such. Instead, I will try to focus on the structure of the cosmos, specifically, the categories of the supernatural entities, their genesis and symbolic manifestations as they appear in people's thought and action, note the possibility of generation of ideas, and delineate their relations to the ordering of the society.

II

The Santal with whose cosmology we are concerned here is one of the largest tribal groups in India. They are a widely studied Mundari group of tribes concentrated in central-eastern India. Unlike other Mundari groups the Santal has a more or less systematized cosmology compiled by Skrefsrud in *Hor Korean More Hapram Reak Katha*. This book was recorded in Santali dialect, and the story contained in it was told to the author by an old Santal preceptor, called Kolean Guru. The book was later on translated in English by Bodding. While talking about their norms and traditions the Santals, irrespective of their educational status and articulation with the larger society, often refer to this book. The norms and traditions contained in the book are presented as 'conscious model' for their social and cultural organization.

A careful study of Kolean Guru's narration recorded in the book would, however, reveal that the various supernatural entities were not conceptualized by the people simultaneously; they were created gradually in the course of the development of their society and culture. The Santal who are now broadly known as an agriculturalist tribe have, in fact, a long history of wanderings in jungles. Before they took up the sedentary life in the plains within the broad framework of the agrarian economic structure of the caste-based settled Hindu peasantry the Santals had been practicing shifting and terrace cultivation combined with hunting and gathering on the hill slopes in central-eastern India. The original habitat of the people was reported to be in Palamou and Ramgarh areas. Probably in the late eighteenth or early nineteenth century the Santals came to Birbhum from where they moved further to the Santal Parganas. The district of Birbhum where the present study was conducted is bound on the north and west by the Santal Parganas, on the east by Murshidabad and Barddhaman districts, and on the south by Barddhaman which is separated by the river Ajoy. The western part of the district is more or less a geographical continuation of the Santal Parganas where the Santals are, at present, mostly concentrated.

The promulgation of the Permanent Settlement Act for land tax and the subsequent extension of tillage by non-tribal landed peasantry from the plains were, indeed, responsible for the displacement of the Santals from their traditional home-base in jungles of Palamou and Ramgarh areas. The Santals were dislodged from their land and employed by non-tribal peasants as tenant cultivators or as wage labourers for reclaiming more waste lands under cultivation. They were engaged to ward off the wild beasts and guard the crops in the fields. 'They have, in fact, few equals in the work of reclaiming and clearing jungles', says O'Malley. The Santals have not only a fair knowledge of jungle ecology but also an intense love for it. This is well reflected in the following observation of Dalton:

> A country denuded of the primeval forest which affords them the hunting grounds they delight in and virgin soil they prefer does not attract them; and when through own labour the spread of cultivation has effected this denudation, they select a new site, however prosperous they may have been on the old, and retire in the backwoods where their harmonious flutes sound sweeter, their drums find deeper echoes and bows and arrows may once more be utilized (208-209).

This intense love for jungles, hunting of games with bows and arrows, the traditional practice of swidden cultivation on hill slopes as well as their crave for song and music are also encapsulated in their myths and legends. For instance, while reciting the origin myths during initiation ceremony the Guru says, 'we will burn and clear jungles'. Many of the Santals still remember the cereals and pulses like *janhe, jandra, gundli, iri,* and *irba* that their forefathers used to sow on the hill slopes in the past.

Traditionally, the society of the Santal is characterized by a segmentary system of kin groups like clans and lineages based on patrilineal descent. They are also reported to have, in the past, an elaborate territorial organization of *ato, pargana* and *disum*. This clan-lineage based system followed by a territorial framework of villages and parganas was also developed gradually in the course of their wanderings or to be more precise, before they took to plough cultivation in the plains. The santals sing:

In Hihiri Pipiri we were born

In Khoj Kaman we were called for

In Harata we grew up

In Sasan Beda we became septs.

(We were born at Hihiri Pipiri; and then called to Khoj Kaman. We grew and multiplied at Harata, and we were divided into clans at Sasan Beda.).

It appears from the mythic song that the Santals were born at Harata and as they multiplied and grew larger they divided themselves into clans. In their origin myth it is further told that Thakur Jiu created the first human pair, Pilcu Haram and Pilcu Budhi. They got united and subsequently, were blessed with seven sons and seven daughters. On the attainment of maturity the sons and the daughters were married to one another and then, divided into seven exogamous clans *(paris)*. At a later stage, excessive indulgence to drinking made them violate incest taboo, and consequently, the whole tribe, excepting the original pair, was perished by Thakur Jiu. Pilcu Haram and Pilcu Budhi again had children and when they grew in number, they were divided, first, into seven and then into five more clans. It is told that twelfth clan known as Bedea was lost in the course of their itinerary.

However, after Sasan Beda the ancestors of the Santal came to Jarpi country from where they moved further to other places. Afterwards when they were at Cai Campa, their social organization of clans and territory became more elaborate. It is told in myth that

> The Kiskus became the royal under the cognomen of Kisku Raj. The Murmus became the princely tribe and were named Murmu Thakur. Hembrom was ennobled and was known Hembrom Kuar. The Soren became the soldier tribe and were named Soren Sepahi. The Marandis were appointed the king's treasurers and stewards, and named as Marandi Kipisar. The Tudus took to music and received the title of Tudu Mundriya.

This traditional segmentary socio-political structure of the Santal is no longer operative in the context of modernization. The Santals of today are well exposed to the forces of regional and national politics of India and are found to be actively participating in the process. The traditional territorial and social segments are however, consecrated and held by them as idioms for a shared understanding of their social solidarity. The power attributes essential for the maintenance of social order are now held at the supernatural plane in terms of ancestor spirits and gods. The hilly and mountainous jungle territory locally known as Ayodhya hills signifies their country, *disum* and its significance in the ordering of the national identity is overtly expressed in their ceremonial annual hunting *(disum sendra)*. During this ceremonial hunting the Santals from the adjoining regions assemble together in the forests on the Ayodhya hills, not merely for hunting. This also gives them a common platform for social and cultural communication and community organization among the members spread over a wider region.

Despite their exposures to Christianity and emulation of elements from the Hindu religious culture the Santal seem to have remained predominantly animistic in their faith. All natural objects and phenomena are considered to have some supernatural powers or beings presiding over them. Most of their gods and other supernatural beings are intimately related to their ecology and life-situations. Instances of their earlier habitat, economy and society have been significantly encapsulated in myths and tales. The natural and social objects of myths have lost pragmatic importance in the context of modernization but the gods and other supernatural beings signifying them are still found effectively operative among them as concepts guiding their social actions.

III

The cosmologies of the tribal groups in India, despite enormous diversities, reveal certain common features. All the tribal groups believe in a supernatural creation of 'man and universe' and perceive a binary division of their universe into 'this world' and 'other world'. Though many of the groups seem to hold the notion of a 'supreme deity', they do not consider him as the ultimate reality. All of them have categories of supernatural beings presiding over things and phenomena of nature. All misfortunes, illness, diseases, good harvest, fortune, rain, storm and other natural and social phenomena and happenings are considered to have invisible presiding deities who live in the 'other world'.

The Santal like most other tribal groups in India also divide their universe into two broad domains: *hanapuri* and *noapuri*, meaning respectively 'that world' and 'this world'. By 'that world' the Santals mean the world of the supernatural while by 'this world' they refer to their own social world as well as the perceptible natural universe in and around which they live. The number of supernatural entities conceptualized by the Santal is quite large and elaborate. Even many Hindu gods and goddesses are included into their pantheon of supernatural beings. It is, however, reported that the Santal did not have, in the beginning, any god or *bonga*. 'In the primeval age we had no bongas' says Kolean Guru, the old Santal preceptor. In ancient times they had only one *bonga, Thakur Jiu* who created the earth, man, and everything on it. The term Thakur is, in fact, a popular regional word used both in Hindi and Bengali dialects; it means 'god' or 'godly', an attribute to divinity. The term 'jiu', on the other hand, is a Mundari word and it means 'life'. Collectively, the concept 'Thakur Jiu' would thus refer to the presiding deity of life. The first pair of human beings, Pilcu Haram and Pilcu Budhi from the Santal trace their descent and ancestry were also his creations. He is, indeed, considered the creator of not only the first human life but also all other sorts of life on this earth. The phenomenon of death and destruction of life and every other thing on the earth are presided over by him. Kolean Guru considers him the supreme deity of the Santal and inclines to look upon him as the ultimate source of all realities in life. The Guru further notes that there are, however, some people who confuse *Thakur Jiu* with *Sin bonga* or the sun deity and this is, he says, because of their traditional practice of worshipping Thakur facing the east wherein the sun rises. To the Guru, Thakur is not the sun; he is more than that. He is invisible, omnipotent and omnipresent and thus can hardly be reduced to any perceptible natural object or phenomenon. He is everywhere and presides over all things yet transcends them all.

The Guru, however, observes that the *Sin bonga* was

revealed to them as the sun or the Day Spirit when they were on the way to *Sin Duar* (the Sun or Day Pass). He along with her female consort *Ninde Cando* (the moon) presides over days and nights and gears the activities of the Santal on this earth. According to Kolean Guru "he is the dawn, he brings the evening; he gives us warm sunshine, he gives us rain; he is the man and the moon is his wife, and the stars are their children".

It may be noted here that Sin bonga is also held and worshipped as a principal deity by most of the Mundari groups of tribes in central-east India. He is, in fact, the source and sustainer of life on this earth.

After *Sin bonga* the other major bongas of the Santal were revealed to them one by one. Regarding the genesis of these bongas Kolean Guru says,

> Among the bongas the *Sun bonga* is our great bonga. After him comes the *Jom Sim bonga*; after him *Maran Buru* (his real name is Lita); after him *Jaher Era*, the Lady of the Sacred Grove, (her real name is Ram Salgi); After her *Moreko Turuiko*; after these *Gosae Era* (her Ladyship); after her *Pargana Haram;* after him *Manji Haram bonga*; After him the *(Orak)* House *bonga;* and after him the *Abge bonga*.

It is clear from the narration that all the *bongas* were not conceptualized by the people simultaneously. It seems that the *bongas* were created gradually in the course of their socio-cultural development. There is, however, a relation between the categories of the *bongas* and the socio-political structure of the people. *Sin bonga, Jom Sim bonga, Maran Buru, Jaher Era* and *Moreko Turuiko* are held at the level of the tribe as a whole. They represent the entire community as a nation. They preside over the tribe as a national communal entity, and stand as collective conscience or representative collective. They act, in fact, as emblems that signify their identity as one tribe. *Pargana Haram* and *Manji Haram bongas* represent the levels of their politico-jural structure on the cosmic plane.

Pargana Haram symbolizes the territorial framework of pargana while *Manji Haram bonga* that of the village. *Orak* or House *bonga* presides over their households or families while *Abge bongas,* their septs or sub-clans.

Sin bonga is the caretaker of life on the earth; he also takes care of lives in the 'Other World'. Thus when a man dies, his body is placed on the pyre turning his face towards the sun with the assumption that the spirit of the deceased man would continue to remain under the good care of the *bonga* in the after-life. This conceptualization of *Sin bonga* signifies not only their communion with nature and relations of participation but also their belief in the continuity of life.

Jom Sim bonga, another national deity, is worshipped at the community level. Literally, *jom* means 'to eat' and *sim* means 'chicken'. Collectively, *Jom Sim* thus refers to the deity presiding over the 'eating of chickens' or precisely speaking, the communal feast on chickens. It is told in myths that there was no such *bonga* in the beginning. In the past the male members of every sub-clan *(khunt)* used to assemble in the forest and worshipped the tutelary deity of their respective sub-clans. The sacrificial meals were then shared by the male members of the respective sub-clans. On the next day, all the consanguines, affines, friends and neighbours assembled together and sacrificed chickens to *Sim bonga.* The sacrificial meals were then shared by them all at the community level. This was locally known as *jom sim* festival. The Guru says:

> The *Jom Sim bonga* was not present in the beginning; at the *jom sim* festival they were offering only to the *Sin bonga.* They had, it is

told, had a sacrifice to their Abge. When they had eaten and were going home, they forgot a battle axe and left it there. When they remembered this on their way, one of them ran back to fetch it. To this man the *Jom Sim bonga* revealed himself; he was picking up and eating what was lying scattered there. While the *bonga* was eating, he was talking to himself: Oh, now I have felt pleased for the first time. Then seeing the man, he disappeared. He brought the battle-axe but he did not tell them of the *bonga* that had revealed himself. After this they got a good deal of fever, so that they were near dying. They they had some divination made for them. The ojhas told them : some *bonga* or other is revealing himself to you. Then the man who had fetched the battle-axe remembered what had happened to him, saying : really I saw him when I was fetching the forgotten battle-axe. I heard him say : now I have felt pleased for the first time. Therefore, they called this *bonga Ahan*. The ojha said to them : this bonga says : offer to me at the *Jom Sim festival*. From this time the Santals worship him (135).

Maran Buru is perhaps the principal of all deities conceptualized and worshipped by the Santals of the region. He is invoked and given offerings on all ritual occasions. *Maran Buru* is, in fact, the patron or guardian deity of the Santal. In the history of development of their society and culture the role of *Maran Buru* is manifold, and it has been encapsulated in their myths and tales. In one myth, *Maran Buru* is reported to have appeared before them as *Lita* who taught the first pair of their ancestors, Pilcu Haram and Pilcu Budhi, the art of brewing rice beer, subsequently inducing them in sexual intercourse. In a later myth the deity revealed himself as *Maran Buru*. At one stage of their life when the people were wandering about to find a suitable place to settle in, they came across a big mountain on their way. They failed to find a way out of that unsurmountable, magnificient mountain and made a vow to him ; 'O *Maran Buru* (O Big Mountain), if though lettest us pass through, we shall worship thee when we have found a country (to stay in)'. Thus was revealed *Maran Buru* to them.

We find *Maran Buru* again in another myth, and by that time the Santal had already taken to a settled life. Once the people having been dissatisfied with their wives approached Maran Buru with a complaint against them. Their wives were behaving badly; they were quarrelsome and disobedient. The men thus went to seek the counsel of *Maran Buru* as to how to subjugate and bring them under control. *Maran Buru* yielded to their request and agreed to teach them an art of enchanting their women. The deity then asked them to prick out some blood from their body and put it on sal *(Shorea robusta)* leaves. At this the men became a bit scared and could not take up any decision instantly. They, therefore, asked the deity to allow them some time to think over the matter. They further told the deity that they would come the next day having discussed the matter among themselves in the village. In the meantime, the women of the village followed the men to the forest and heard their conversation with *Maran Buru* from a hide. They hurriedly came back to the village and pretended to wait upon their husbands with food and drink. The men were very pleased; they ate and drunk to their heart's content and lay half-conscious on the yard forgetting their promise to *Maran Buru*. The women now played a trick over their husbands, and having dressed up as their men they approached Maran Buru and tactfully learnt the art of witchcraft. Now when the trick was disclosed, *Maran Buru* taught the men a counter-art of witchfinding through divination by their *ojhas*.

Maran Buru is thus considered a great patron or guardian deity.

No myth or story could be known as to the genesis of the deity of *Jaher Era*. Some of my Santal informants observe that she is the sister of *Maran Buru* but no mythical story was given in support of the statement. It is, however, not quite unlikely that *Ram Salgi* (the real name of *Jaher Era* as told by Kolean Guru) is a sister of *Lita* later known as *Maran Buru*. However, if we carefully study the symbolic manifestations of the deity and her worship, we may get the meaning. In every village the Santal maintain a sacred grove comprising varieties of wild trees and boulders. This sacred grove symbolizes the 'virgin forest' and Jaher Era presides over it. Jungles or forests are traditional base of the Santal's habitat and economy and the presiding deity, Jaher Era is regarded as their

Jaher Era is regarded as their 'mother goddess' or guardian deity on the home front. The brother-sister relationship between *Maran Buru* and *Jaher Era* is, therefore, not unilikely.

Literally, the term *Moreko Turuiko* means 'five-six' but it is considered as one deity, and worshipped as a collective entity. *Moreko Turuiko* is regarded as a national deity who looks after the welfare of their villages and controls rains and crops. This role of the deity is well reflected in their songs during *baha parab* (flower festival). *Maran Buru, Jaher Era* and *Moreko Turuiko* are closely related deities. In the *Jaherthan,* all these three deities are symbolically represented by three sarjom *(Shorea robusta)* trees and three boulders. During their *baha parab* or flower festival two sarjom trees almost of equal height are planted side by side in the *Jaherthan*. They represent respectively *Jaher Era* and *Maran Buru*. Another Sarjom tree comparatively smaller in height is planted a little off the first two, and it stands for *Moreko Turuiko*. Two huts are also erected, one of which is shared together by these deities. This close relationship among these deities is also reflected in the ritual expression of the people during the Flower Festival. A ritual is organized in the courtyard of the village priest *(naeke)* on the previous day of the festival. Battle axe, bows and arrows, bangles, necklace, bamboo basket, broom, and other essential articles are arranged and displayed there, and the ritual starts. Three men are possessed respectively by three deities, *Maran Buru, Jaher Era* and *Moreko Turuiko.* The man possessed by *Maran Buru* picks up the battle axe while the man possessed by *Moreko Turuiko* takes in his hand bows and arrows. The man who is possessed by *Jaher Era* puts on the bangles and the necklace and takes up the basket and the broom in hand. All these three possessed men then move to the *Jaherthan* and together make the Sacred Grove ready for the ritual performance. Arriving at the spot *Jaher Era* starts cleaning the grove-yard while *Maran Buru* assisted by *Moreko Turuiko* fetches branches of sarjom trees and other essential things from the forest.

As pointed out by Kolean Guru *Gosae Era* was revealed to the Santal after the four major deities. No definite information could be available about the role of this deity in their life and activity. My informants in the village of Birbhum, however, regard her as one of the major deities, and offer sacrifice and oblations during the Flower Festival at the *Jaherthan*. Of the two huts erected at the *Jaherthan* during the festival one is meant for *Gosae Era*. In the Sacred Grove she is represented symbolically by a matkom *(Basia latifolia)* tree and a boulder.

As to the genesis of this deity some ethnographers note that once upon a time a Santal boy fell in love with a girl of blacksmith family of the caste-based Hindu society. The parents of the boy did not approve of it; the boy, however, married her out of love and lived separately at the outskirts of the village. After the death of the lady her ladyship is consecrated and remembered with reverence as *Gosae Era.* In Santali dialect, *gosae* is a general term used to refer to *bongas*; the term *gosae* also means 'to entreat'; 'to implore' or 'to beseech'.

Every myth has a history. The present myth also has an 'incapsulated history'. Of all caste groups of the Hindu society the one with whom the Santal have been in essential economic articulation from beginning was, perhaps the blacksmith. Even now when the Santals are well exposed to many other caste-peasants and the market economy of the larger society they are found to maintain one or two blacksmith families in their hamlet. Considering the proximal relation with the blacksmith family it is not unlikely that there would be a wedlock, though not socially permissible. The Santal had a stable and elaborate social organization and in the case of stable social organization past events of importance are often commemorated. The wedlock of the Santal boy with the Blacksmith lady is no doubt a social incidence of historic importance.

Pargana is a traditional socio-political unit of the Santal developed for the maintenance of ordered relations among individuals and categories of individuals within a particular territorial framework. Some scholars opine that *Pargana Haram bonga* is a spiritual counterpart of the institution of pargana. Some say that it is the spirit of the first parganaite, the had of the territorial segment, *pargana*. Both the observations are correct if they are considered at different levels of abstraction. It is quite possible that the *bonga* was conceptualized as the spirit of the first parganaite and subsequently, generalized as a spiritual counterpart of the institution of pargana, specifically when this structural unit seemed to have lost its effective role.

On the occasion of the Flower Festival the *Manjhi Haram bonga* is invoked and worshipped at the Sacred Grove of the village along with the major national *bongas*.

It has, however, a special altar in the heart of every village, known as *Manjhithan*. In the *Manjhithan* the deity is worshipped by *Manjhi Haram,* the secular leader of the village while in *Jaherthan* the *bonga* is worshipped by the village priest, *Naeke*. There is a belief among the Santal that the man who settles first would be the secular head or *Manjhi Haram* of the village. Customarily, the first settler owns all lands and is considered the chief of the village; others living there enjoy only usufractory rights on the lands. The spirit of the ancestor of the first *Manjhi Haram* is regarded as the *Manjhi Haram bonga* who is still considered to have the authority over the village land. This is well reflected in a ritual act during *Magh Parab*. On the last day of this *parab* which marks the end of their traditional year all the villagers including the traditional village officials surrender their lands and even offices to the *Manjhi Haram bonga*. Normalcy is restored immediately after the ritual is over.

Manjhi Haram bonga thus originated as the ancestor spirit of the first *Manjhi Haram* of the village was subsequently, universalized as a symbol of power and authority at the tribal communal level. The worship of *Manjhi Haram bonga* along with other national bonga is a clear case of universalization from its particular contexts of the village.

Like their territorial segments the social segments of the Santal are also presided over by supernatural beings. People belonging to different clans *(paris)* distinguish themselves in terms of their distinct clan names that they inherit on birth. It is told that the clan segments of the Santal were divine creations, basically intended to avoid incestuous and rampant matings among themselves. It is also reported in their origin myth that the incestuous matings among brothers and sisters created god's wrath which, in turn, led to their social destruction. It was, therefore, essential for the people to harness one of the basic biological or natural needs of man and bring order in the society by dividing it into several exogamous groups. Each of these clans was again divided into sub-clans *(khunts)*.

Abge bongas are the tutelary deities of these sub-clans. It may be noted here that the social segments, clans do not have any tutelary deity.

Structurally, it appears that the *Abge bongas* are the spirits of the founder ancestors of their khunts. Ideal-typically, the members of a sub-clan perceive their descent from a common male ancestor and operate as a property-holding corporate unit; in the modern context the members of a sub-clan can no longer trace their genaeological connections nor can they operate as a localized corporate unit. The sub-clan is now fragmented into a number of small households that are dispersed over a number of villages. The member-households of every khunt, however, express their structural solidarity through the collective worship of their *Abge bonga*, presiding deity of their sub-clan. The adult males of the households of a *khunt* worship together their *Abge bonga* and share among themselves the meat of the animals sacrificed to the bonga. The female members of the group are not allowed to partake of the sacrificial meal.

The men of the group also keep the name of their bonga secret among themselves and do not let their women know of it. A strong in-group sentiment prevails among the agnatically-related members of the *khunt*. *Abge bonga* acts, in fact, as an emblem of the *khunt* and reinforces the unity among its members, which is manifested in their occasional social gathering around the worship of the deity. The unity of the khunt is also expressed in terms of its differential mode of animal sacrifice to the bonga. For example, the members of the *khunt* Chopoar Murmu worship their deity, *Sat Mopan Dana* with a spotless pig and a red cock while those of Sada Murmu sacrifice two cocks (one black and the other white in colour) and one she-pig of any colour to their *Abge bonga, Dhangara*. There are also some *khunts* that belong to different clans but worship the same abge bonga. They, however differ in terms of the mode of their sacrifice to the deity.

The term *'orak'* means a house; it also denotes a household. By the concept *'orak bonga'* the Santal normally refer to the presiding or tutelary deity of their house or household. Among the Santals of the area a household originates and develops around a family or patrilineage; it is, in fact, a localized kin group, the members of which work together for the common maintenance of the group. The solidarity of the group is manifested not only in the members' living and working together but also in their faith in a common tutelary deity, *orak* bonga. In the context of economic transformations there has been a gradual nuclearization of the primary production and consumption units, i.e. households or orak of the people. These smaller households express unity in their belief in a common *orak* cult. The worship of the *orak bonga* is now initiated by, and held at the house of the eldest male member of the group, and the expenditure is shared by all the households of the extended family.

The worship of the *Orak bonga* is held in two phases. In the first phase, the bonga is worshipped in the cattle-shed *(gai gora)* while in the second phase, it is invoked at the sacred altar inside the house, locally known as bhitar. In the *gai gora* the deity of the House is invoked along with *Maran Buru* and *Ghureya bonga,* the presiding deity of the cattle-shed. While performing the ritual inside the house the deity is worshipped along with *Maran Buru* and *Hapram* or ancestor spirits. In all these contexts animal sacrifices are made to the deity. But the identity of *Orak bonga* as well as the mode of its 'worship' differs from one lineage to another. The Santals of every lineage, however, sacrifice two animals to the deity of their House, one male and the other, female. The meat of the she-animal is shared by the wives and unmarried girls of the participating households while that of the he-animal is consumed exclusively by the men. This mode of worshipping the *Orak bonga* as well as the nature of sharing the sacrificial meal together signifies the structural solidarity of their household or extended family. The of a common *Orak* cult manifest in their ritual action helps the people reinforce their identity as one traditional House or *Orak*.

The Santals conceptualize two broad categories of *Hapram* (ancestral spirits): *Burha-Burhi* and *Purudhul*. The *Burha-Burhi* are the spirits of their immediate ancestors whose are still remembered by the heirs while the Purudhul refers to the spirits of those "white-haired' ancestors whose are lost in the oblivion. Of these two categories, the Purudhul seems to be placed at a higher plane than the *Burha-Burhi*.

Both the *Burha-Burhi* and the *Purudhul* are held in high esteem, and the Santals carefully preserve and maintain a sacred altar for their Hapram inside the house. The people consider the Hapram as an integral part of their household and family, and feel it obligatory to share their food and drink with them. Most of the adult men are thus found to put a few drops of their drink on the earth in the name of their *hapram* before they take it. The people call it *cadar*. On the occasion of every religious festival at the community level the Santal invoke their *Hapram* and worship them along with the national *bongas*. The ancestor spirits, in turn, look after the wellbeing of the living heirs and guide their activities. They keep constant vigilance on their relatives, guard them from the evil forces and powers of the supernatural world and bring them children and prosperity.

The spirits of all the dead individuals cannot, however, attain the status of *hapram* in the after-life. The soul of a man, on his death, is first called back and ritually installed by his son or any of his close agnates at the sacred altar inside the house. Then another ritual is performed after which the soul is finally sent to the world of *hapram*. The sacred altar bhitar is, however, maintained inside the house as the seat of the departed soul. The belief is that if the son does not perform the ritual of 'calling back' the soul and subsequently, rehabilitate it in the domain of the hapram, it would remain a wanderer or bhulah. The hapram are thus morally bounded to the living relatives of their former families and lineages. If any Santal is found to show negligence to his *hapram* and fail to perform his duty, calamity may fall on him and his family. It is not that the *hapram* are angry with them; it happens so because the moral relation between them is breached. The persons concerned as well as community at large consider the misfortune as a consequence upon the breach of the normal state of the jural-moral relations between the ancestor spirits and their living heirs. The *hapram* are basically harmless, and the misfortunes just help reinforcing their lineage/social harmony.

The eligibility of a soul for the admission to the world of the hapram also depends, to a certain extent, on the nature of death. Death, among the Santal, is not considered an end to life; it is only a phase of transition in the process of their life and activity. It mediates between the living of 'this world' and the haprams of the 'other world'. To the Santal, death is normal when a man dies in old age, having married and begotten sons and daughters. Normal expectations associated with natural death are satisfied when an individual dies after having lived a life to the full. In such cases, the souls are ritually sent to the world of hapram. But death in pregnancy or child birth or in pre-initiation (chatiar) ceremony or through suicide do not satisfy the Santal's normal expectation of natural death. The dead bodies in such cases are buried into the soil and the souls are denied appropriate death rituals. These spirits, locally known as bhulah are accorded a marginal position in the 'other world'. They are not called back to the sacred altar in their house nor are they sent to the world of hapram. These spirits are not totally harmless like the hapram. They are considered 'evil', but not in the strong sense of the term. They may, at times, be good and benevolent. The people, in fact, seem to nourish an ambivalent attitude towards these spirits. They remember them on all ritual occasions, offer oblations and ask them to live in peace and harmony.

It may, however, be noted here that the people, though seem to have an idea of 'bad' death obstructing the normal passage of the departed soul to the world of hapram, they do not wish that it becomes an 'evil' spirit in the after-life. For instance, when a pregnant woman dies, her soul normally becomes a *curin* or female ghost. But the Santal would not like her to be so. They would thus first take the foetus out of her womb and then burn the corpse on the pyre, or put a thorn of the date-palm tree into the left heel and dispose of the body as usual. This would, they think, break the spell of the 'bad' death and smoothen the soul's journey to the 'other world'.

IV

Cosmology broadly deals with the structure of the universe or cosmos. It involves the study of classification of phenomena and provides the framework of concepts and relations which treat the universe as an ordered system. The genesis and functioning of the existing phenomena of the cosmos are studied normally under the conceptual framework of cosmogony. In this paper I have, however, made no analytical distinction between the two concepts but studied all these aspects under the rubric of cosmology. In the preceeding pages an attempt has, therefore, been made to describe the major categories of supernatural beings, their possible genesis and function in the life and society of the Santals of Birbhum, as reflected in their mythical thought and social action.

The Santals view their supernatural world as *hanapuri,* and the entities prevailing there in, as *bonga*. Bonga is, in fact, a generic term, and in a broader sense it includes all the powers and entities of the supernatural world. These supernatural beings may be benevolent, malevolent or even ambivalent; they may also be personal, familial or communal. Though broadly branded as *bonga,* all the entities in the supernatural world do not belong to the same rank and order, specifically in terms of their genesis and function. A close probe into the life-situations of the people would thus reveal that they have a perception of several categories of supernatural beings arranged hierarchically. The categories of supernatural entities that may be identified from their conceptualization and ritual action are as follows: *Bonga, Hapram-Bonga, Saket Bonga* and *Baric* or *Dan Bonga. Thakur Jiu, Sin, Jom Sim, Maran Buru, Jaher Era, Moreko Turuiko, Pargana Haram, Manjhi Haram, Abge* and *Orak* may be grouped under the category of *Bonga*. The category, *Hapram-Bonga* includes all the ancestor-spirits of the people. *Saket Bonga* are the tutelary deities of their *Ojha* or medicine-men. All the malevolent spirits are broadly grouped under the category, *Baric-Bonga*. These are the deities borrowed by the people from the neighbouring Hindus.

There is a seeming hierarchy among the different categories of the supernatural beings conceptualized by the people. The *Bonga* category of supernatural entities is thus considered superior to that of the *Hapram* or *Hapram-Bonga*. Below them comes the *Saket Bonga*. *Baric* or *Dan Bonga* is placed at the bottom of all the supernatural entities in the people's cognition. The *Diku Bonga* are not their traditional deities. In some villages I have, however, found the people worshipping some of the local Hindu deities along with their traditional national *bonga.*

Both the *bonga* and the *hapram* are basically benevolent. They both are treated as 'gods', and there is a close affinity between these two categories of supernatural entities. A careful probe into the ritual practices of the people would thus reveal that Pilcu Haram, Pilcu Budhi and Purudhul who are considered and worshipped as *bonga* are basically ancestor spirits or *hapram* graded to the status of *bonga*. The Santal perceive a gradation of transformations from humanity to divinity. A Santal *(hor)*, on death, becomes a *hapram* who, in the course of time, transformed into a *bonga* or 'god'. All these entities are bound together to form a moral community.

There are four distinct modes of ritual sacrifice among the Santal underpinning further this conceptualization of the supernatural categories. They perform the 'bonga' mode of animal sacrifice while worshipping the deities belonging to the category, *bonga*. This mode of sacrifice involves the partial cutting of the throat of the animal till its death. The'kutam' mode of sacrifice is performed in the case of their hapram. Bul mayam is another mode of animal sacrifice, and it is followed when they have to implore the baric bonga. It involves the offering of human blood to the so-called spirits that are considered basically 'evil'. While making animal sacrifice to the dikhu bonga the people slash off its head by means of a sharp weapon. This is locally known as the 'mak' mode of sacrifice. This mode of ritual sacrifice is also is also performed while sacrificing big animal to their traditional *bonga*.

The relations of the Santal of noapuri with the bonga of hanapuri are maintained by their village priest, *naeke,* who invoke and worship the bonga on behalf of the entire community. The Orak and the Abge, though regarded as *bonga,* are not, however, invoked by the naeke at the community level. They are invoked and worshipped at the lineage and sub-clan levels by the elderly males of the respective kin-groups. The *hapram* or ancestor-spirits are invoked and worshipped by the living relatives of their former families. Kudum Naeke, the assistant priest of the village has to implore and placate the *baric bonga* or evil spirits through the 'bul mayam' mode of ritual sacrifice. The assistant priest pierces a thorn of the date-palm tree into his left thigh, mixes the blood oozing out of the injuries with *adwa* (sun-dried) rice and then offers the same to the *baric bongas* at the outskirts of the village. The people say that by making such a ritual sacrifice they 'bind' their village with spells and protects it from any intrusion of 'evil' spirits into the territory. It may, however, be noted in this connection that the *adwa* (sun-dried) rice and the human blood *(mayam)*, in their own perception, signify 'life'. They note, rice, when boiled, becomes 'dead' and 'impure' but sun-dried rice is 'pure' and 'alive'. The offering of *adwa* rice and human blood thus implies not a phenomenon of 'exclusion' but a phenomenon of 'inclusion'. Through this kind of ritual sacrifice the Santals seem to express a feeling of communion with these spirits of the 'other world', and maintain their relations with them through participations, not through exclusion or avoidance. There is, in every village, some *Ojha,* and the people, in the case of any misfortune and disaster, approach him for his power of divination by supernatural means. He is considered to have magical powers to exorcise evil spirits. During ritual performance the spirits often posses them and convey message to the people through the mouth of the *ojha*.

It has already been noticed in our previous description that the various supernatural beings were conceptualized by the people in their ecological and socio-psychological contexts they had experienced in the past. The deities were created either after some natural objects or some social events or institutions of historic importance. Thakur Jiu thus conceptualized as the original creator of Man and the Universe. The deity does not seem to have much concern now, with the life-situations of the Santals, specifically in the locality of Birbhum. He is, at present, held mostly as an idea signifying their ultimate meaning of life and death, creation and destruction. *Sin bonga* signifies the sun, a natural object but the meaning that is now signified by *Sin bonga* is the protection and sustenance of life both in 'noapuri' and 'hanapuri'. The term, *Maran Buru,* literally means 'big mountain' which is also a natural object. We have, however, learnt that as a concept it stands for an overall personified patronization and protection. The Santal now look upon this deity mainly as their great grand father and seek his counsel and help almost in all contexts of their life and activity. They even invoke *Maran Buru* along with the spirits of their original ancestors, *Pilcu Haram, Pilcu Budhi* and other ancient ancestor-spirits collectively known as *Purudhul,* and ask him to settle the souls of their dead men in afterlife. *Maran Buru* seems to be equated here with the so-called *Hapram-bonga* and ancestor-spirits graded to the status of *Bonga. Jaher Era* who is signified by natural objects, trees and boulders, essentially stands for the maintenance of the 'virgin forest', the traditional habitat of the Santal. The deity, commonly known as the Lady of the Grove, is now regarded as their guardian in the homefront, and this is clearly evident in the ritual performances during the Flower Festival of the people. It has already been noticed that supernatural beings, *Moreko Turuiko, Pargana Haram* and *Manjhi Haram bonga,* now worshipped at the communal level as national bonga, were conceptualized either after their traditional socio-political institutions or after the first office-bearers of those institutions. In either of the cases these deities would, however, give a clear reflection of the segmentary power structure of the people's society at the cosmic plane. Like the segmentary structure of the socio-political organization their social system based on patrilineal descent and kinship is also reflected in their conceptualization of the supernatural deities, *Orak bonga, Abge bonga* and *Hapram*. It may be noted here that the socio-political units signified as deities do no longer operate as an effective segmentary system in the present context. They are, however, held at the affective level and adhered to, as idioms or symbols of power which guide their actions at the societal plane.

The supernatural entities discussed above thus form a hierarchically-ordered system of ideas adapted to the changing contexts of the life-situations of the Santal. The entities of the supernatural world, when viewed discreetly, would no doubt, signify the particular structural units and ecological contexts of the people, most of which have undergone changes over time and space. Every society changes over time and space, and no society is indeed, ever static. But while changing, it tends to keep on organizing itself as a meaningful whole which is essential for its people's social security and identity. A close probe into the organization of the various supernatural entities conceptualized by the Santals in the changing contexts of their life and society would thus reveal that the entities form a system of ideas that not only reflects their man-man, man-nature and man-supernature relations but also reinforces their collective conscience.

15

The Tribal Worldview: Changing Perspectives

Introduction

Study of worldview and philosophic endeavours among the preliterate people is yet to gain adequate currency in anthropology, though its importance has been felt even by the early evolutionary thinkers. Evolutionists like Tylor and Frazer were concerned, among other things, with the study of the mode of thought of the preliterate people and their nature of relationships to the natural and supernatural phenomena. The foundation for a worldview study was, however, laid by Emile Durkheim and his nephew Marcel Mauss in 1903, when they established Annee Sociologique school in France. The scholars of this school devoted their attention to the study of ideas of peoples about themselves and the world around them, as well as the study of their representative collectives. In the concluding chapter of their book primitive classification, Durkheim and Mauss observe that 'primitive classifications are ... not singular or exceptional, having no analogy with those employed by more civilized peoples; ... they seem to be connected, with no break in continuity, to the first scientific classifications... like all sophisticated classifications, they are systems of hierarchized notions. Things are not simply arranged by them in the form of isolated groups, but these groups stand in fixed relationships to each other and together form a single whole. Moreover, these systems like those of science, have a purely speculative purpose.' They further note that the object of primitive classification 'is not to facilitate action, but to advance understanding, to make intelligible the relations which exist between things...such classifications are thus intended, above all, to connect ideas, to unify knowledge; as such they may be said ...to constitute a first philosophy of nature' (Durkheim *et al.* : 1963 : 81).

Unlike the English scholars, Tylor and Frazer who dealt with isolated customs and 'individual experiences' of preliterate peoples, the French scholars were interested in their whole complexes of ideas, beliefs and meanings. The English scholars approached the problem basically from an 'intellectualistic standpoint' and tried to reconstruct the nature of 'primitive thought' in terms of the scientific rationality, characteristic of Western civilization. They considered the 'logical relations between things' the prototype of social relations of men. Magicians in preliterate cultures classified things together because of their likenesses, and the procedure, Tylor observed, was precisely that followed by modern science. Magic contained a logical scheme of thought but it was a logic of association rather than one of cause and effect.

The English scholars contend that the reality which the primitive peoples confront in their daily life is the world of the natural and the supernatural, and the social relations of them are based on the logical relations between things in nature.

For Durkheim and Mauss it was, however, 'Society' that provided the model in the classificatory thought of primitive people. They say 'it is possible to classify other things than concepts, and otherwise than in accordance with the laws of pure understanding. For in order for it to be possible for ideas to be systematically arranged for reasons of sentiment, it is necessary that they should not be pure ideas, but that they should themselves be products of sentiment. And in fact, for those who are called primitives, a species of things is not a simple object of knowledge but corresponds above all to a certain sentimental attitude. All kinds of affective elements combine in the representation made of. They therefore observe that the differences and resemblances which determine the classification of things in primitive societies are 'more affective than intellectual' (*ibid* : 84-85).

Like Durkheim and Mauss, Lucien Levy-Bruhl, another French scholar also notes that the patterns of thought of the primitive people are social, and not psychological or intellectual. To him every society has collective representations and the collective representations of primitive peoples are pre-eminently concerned with forces, influences and actions imperceptible to the senses, and hence, 'mystical', 'symbolic' and 'allusive' in nature. 'The reality' he says, ' in which the primitives move is mystical. Not a being, not an object, not a natural phenomenon in their collective representations is what it appears to us. Almost all that we see in it escapes them or they are indifferent to it. On the other hand they see in it many things which we do not even suspect' (Levy-Bruhl 1912 :30-31).

Despite differences in conceptual and analytical framework all these early scholars were inclined primarily in the reconstruction of the nature of human thought in primitive world views.

Radin, on the basis of his field experience among some Polynesian tribes, observes that there is, almost in every culture, a small number of men and women who may be called 'thinkers', who indulge themselves in explaining all things and happenings rationally and find pleasures in some form of speculative thinking. As against this category what is called a 'reflective few' by him there is the mass of common people known as 'men of action'. He notes that the Polynesians have 'a clear-cut recognition of the pursuit of knowledge for its own sake. It differs only in degree from that search for knowledge for its own sake that characterizes the philosophic systems of our own thinkers.... It is not divorced from life, from the immediate interests of the present in the same degree that most philosophies since Plato have been....' (Radin 1957 :322). Durkheim, Mauss, Levy-Bruhl and even Tylor and Frazer did not consider this distinction for the study of primitive thought.

In a recent review Michael Kearney (1975) identifies four distinct periods in the developmental history of worldview study and theory in anthropology: *(i)* the formative, *(ii)* the transitional, *(iii)* the propositional and *(iv)* the systematic. The formative period is exemplified by the Boasian configurationalists who delineate a synthetic pattern from and among the diverse phenomena of a people's culture. Benedict's *Patterns of Culture* (1949) is cited as one of the best examples of this period. The transitional period is typified by the ethnographers' explicit and specific concern with 'worldview' per se studies. The writings of Sol Tax (1941), Hallowell (1955) and Redfield (1952,1953,1955,1956) fall in this period. The propositional period, which is marked by an analytic treatment of worldview, is best exemplified by the writings of Foster (1965), Hoebel (1960), Kearney (1972) and Kluckhohn and Strodtbeck (1961). During the systematic period the scholars show concern not only with the exploration of the nature of relationships among the various elements of a particular worldview but also with the nature of relationships of the world-views with their socio-cultural and geographical environments. Mary Douglas' *Natural Symbols* (1973) and Michael Kearney's concept of logico-structural integration' (1975) involve such an integrated holistic approach.

It is, indeed, Daryll Forde in Britain and Robert Redfield in America, who initiated, among the ethnographers, a tradition for the systematic study of worldview of 'non-civilized' peoples. In his *African Worlds* Forde compiles nine articles on the worldview of the tribal people of Africa. In his own words it is a 'collection of brief but systematic studies of the cosmological, religious, and moral ideas of a number of African peoples in the context of their material environment and social organization' (Forde 1954: ix). Redfield is perhaps the first anthropologist who discusses, in great detail, the concept of worldview and tries to explicate the nature of 'primitive' worldview. He also inspired a number of scholars (E.M. Mendelson 1956; Charles M. Leslie 1960; Calixta Guiteras-Holmes 1961) to undertake systematic and explicit study of worldview of particular cultures and individuals.

Redfield defines worldview broadly as 'the way a people characteristically look outward upon the universe'. While 'culture' speaks the way a people look to an anthropologist, 'world view' suggests how everything looks to a people. Worldview is the sum total of beliefs, ideas and notions an individual or a group of individuals have about the world in and around which they live. It gives the characteristic picture of a culture from inside. It, however, differs from the concepts like 'culture', 'ethos', 'mode of thought' and 'national character' dealing with the totality of group character in that 'it is an arrangement of things looked out upon; things in the first instance conceived of as existing'. It includes the 'conceptions of what ought to be as well as of what is'. It also involves the study of 'the characteristic ways in which experiences are kept together or apart—the patterns of thought—and the affective as well as the cognitive aspects these things'. A worldview cannot be conceived without some dimension in time and space. 'Self' is the axis of every worldview; it is, in fact, a 'stage set' and gives 'the picture the members of a society have of the properties and characters upon their stage of action'. It attends to 'the way a man sees himself in relation to all else and speaks of 'the properties of existence as distinguished from and related to the self' (Redfield 1962: 270).

Based on the available ethnographic literature on preliterate peoples and ancient civilizations, Redfield further postulates certain universal elements and the nature of their integration in the 'primary worldview'. Broadly these elements are man, nature and God. He observes that 'the separation of God from nature and of these two together from man is ...made in some degree and in some sense in every worldview' but in the 'primitive worldview' the man-nature-super-nature relationship tends to be 'unitary' and 'morally significant' (ibid: 271). In his subsequent studies Redfield (1953,1955,1956) is, however, interested in the dynamics of 'primary' worldview and the nature of its transformation in varying contexts of modernization. In an endeavour to delineate the impact of 'technological and urban revolution on primary worldview' he observes that the man-nature-super-nature relationship which is unitary in 'primary worldview' gets dissociated with the change of economy (1953).

Tribal Worldview Studies in India

With this purposive introduction on the conceptualization and nature of worldview and philosophic endeavours of the preliterate people we may now move on to the study of the tribal worldview in India. As per 1971 Census of India there are as many as 427 distinct tribal communities constituting about seven percent of India's total population. In terms of language, numerical strength and levels of economy these tribal groups exhibit a wide range of diversities among themselves though in contrast to the non-tribal people they appear to be a different kind of humanity specifically in terms of their characteristic outlook to life and state of mind. Although mostly concentrated in the hilly and the forested regions of India, they can no longer be found in the natural situation of their 'habitat, economy and society'. Many of them are now in perpetual contact with their neighbouring non-tribal communities, and are variously exposed to the forces of modernization. There are some communities who maintain a regular economic symbiosis with the dominant Hindu caste-peasant groups, operate as occupationally specialized caste-like groups and live at the periphery of the village society.

Since long these tribal groups have been maintaining their identities through various kinds of adaptive mechanisms in pre-colonial, pre-independent as well as post-independent situations in India. Many of the tribal groups are found also to construct meaningful world-views for the maintenance of their identity. There are also groups who are still asserting their tribal identity through various kinds of movements in the context of their confrontation with the socio-political forces of the larger society.

The tribal groups in India are, no longer, stationary, nor is their worldview static. With the passage of time they have come across various kinds of faiths, categories of people and their customs and institutions. In fact, there have been tremendous changes in the life-situations of the people, and with these, the elements of their worldview are also undergoing changes. The tribal people are, however, found to constantly adjust with the changing situations, trying to weave their new experiences with the old ones in a meaningful way, thereby perpetuating a 'characteristic outlook' to life. Their worldview is, indeed, 'constantly in process: a fluctuating assemblage of more or less connected ideas that change as to focus, affective colouring perhaps the content and choice of connection and emphasis' (Redfield 1962: 281).

In the present paper my purpose is to grasp the dynamics of worldview of the tribal people in India. I intend to understand their perceptions of the changing universe and the manner they confront it in the context of their life-situations. My approach will be not merely to describe the normal state of their ideas and beliefs relating to nature, other men and the super-nature but to bring into relief the 'focus' of their 'total view' as reflected from their thought and action. For this purpose I will depend primarily on my empirical study of the worldview of a particular tribal group, the Birhor as well as on my observations on a few other Mundari groups of tribes in central–eastern India. Relevant studies and observations on the worldview of other Indian tribes will also be used.

There are only a few studies specifically focused on the world-views of particular tribal groups though there are some observations on their religious philosophy. Materials on other aspects of tribal worldview are also not rare, but they are embedded mostly into the general ethnographic descriptions on the people. Based on the information available in the ethnographic reports Mehra (1977) makes an attempt to explicate the aspects of tribal worldview in India. He describes the worldview of the tribal groups in terms of their 'origin and creation', 'man-nature', 'man-super-nature' and 'man-man' relationships. The worldview of the tribal people is depicted here in terms of their place in 'nature and society'; it gives us more or less 'a stable and abstract picture' of their universe. Little attention is given to the nature of the people's perceptions of, and relations with, their changing universe.

The pioneer among the Indian anthropologists in this order of analysis of worldview and philosophic endeavours of the tribal people is Prof. Surajit Chandra

Sinha. Unlike his predecessors whose primary interest was to describe the 'fossilized persistence of an idealized archaic worldview', Sinha considers the tribal life of India as 'a quality of socio-cultural integration' as well as 'a state of mind' and deeply involves himself in understanding the dynamics of the tribal worldview in the contexts of their life-situations.

Nirmal kumar Bose, another Indian anthropologist, also notes that the world view of the tribal people is not a static phenomenon. He observes that there is, in every human group, 'a constellation of ideas and emotions' that forms the core of its culture and that it builds up its worldview by weaving immediate experiences with those of the past; to these are added the hopes and fears for the future. The worldview changes with the changes in the qualities of its elements, and also with the changes in the perceptions of the people themselves (Bose 1971).

Bose further makes a conceptual distinction between the worldview based on sense perception and logical construction of immediate experience and the worldview based on extra-sensory perception. He thinks it important to consider both these pragmatic and transcendental aspects for a proper understanding of the dynamics of people's worldview.

Mahapatra also thinks similarly and notes that worldview may be conceptualized on the sensory, extra-sensory and moral planes. 'In the sensory plane, along the dimension of space', he says, 'one has to consider the juxtaposition of the self and the other, the external world, animals, plants, men and women, material objects, other peoples, cultures, regions other than one's own. Along the time dimension, one could take up the historic past, present and future. In the extra-sensory plane, the space dimension may be concerned with supernatural beings, spirits, powers, heaven and hell etc., while along the time dimension one may analyze the concepts regarding the mythical past, continuous future (as revealed in the transmigration of souls), discontinuous future (unredeemed souls, or once-for-all dispensation into the heaven or hell etc.), or the cumulative future (as in the concept of *karma,* leading ultimately to re-union with Brahma after hundreds of re-births). In the moral plane, again, we may encounter the differentiation of good, bad and their gradations and combinations, the concept of the ideal man, of the virtuous and upright man etc.'

Mahapatra further describes certain methodological issues for the study of worldview of pre-literate peoples. In order that the concept of worldview is viable, one must make 'some conscious effort to bring about some coherence, convergence and integration of thought and action: conceptualization, speculation and thought on one hand, concerns and behaviour in the work-a-day life on the other. Both the thinker and the man of the world should find their place in the anthropologist's integral view of his people's worldview' (Mahapatra 1983: 295).

Mahapatra further describes certain methodological issues for the study of worldview of pre-literate peoples. In order that the concept of worldview is viable, one must make 'some conscious effort to bring about some coherence, convergence and integration of thought and action: conceptualization, speculation and thought on one hand, concerns and behaviour in the work-a-day life on the other. Both the thinker and the man of the world should find their place in the anthropologist's integral view of his people's worldview' (Mahapatra 1983: 295).

Sinha does not make any conceptual discourse on worldview, but he makes use of the concept explicitly and analytically in his studies on the tribal culture in India. In an endeavour to understand the tribal culture vis-à-vis the little traditions of Indian civilization he makes an appraisal of the aspects of worldview of the tribal groups in Peninsular India. He studies the tribal groups in the context of their habitat, economy and social structure and critically analyzes their worldview(s) in terms of their conceptualization of, and relations with the nature, other men and the supernatural.

Sinha observes that though the 'tribal cultures of Peninsular India do share certain characteristics common to primitive cultures all over the world', they have 'certain specific items' that are not 'universally shared by the primitive tribes in other parts of the world'. The specific items mentioned are: 'the existence of a hierarchic pantheon with the Sun god at the top; and the belief in re-incarnation and transmigration of the soul' (Sinha 1958).

He conceptualizes the tribal world view as characterized by a 'non-puritanical', 'this worldly', 'hedonistic' attitude towards life, and living for today having no thought for tomorrow. He points out divergences as well as convergences in the worldview of the tribal people and that of the Hindu caste-peasants in Peninsular India. He notes that there are some transitional elements in the economy and social structure of the tribal people though there is no element of transition from 'ethically neutral super-naturalism' to 'ethical super-naturalism'. He had, in fact, a persisting interest in conceptualizing the process of worldview construction among the tribal people in the changing contexts of their life-situations.

The encounter of the tribal people with Hinduism and other religious faiths in India had been primarily at the sociological level. Bose (1971) notes that though there are Christians, Muslims, Buddhists and even Hindus among the people animism has still been their dominant faith. Despite changes in their religious beliefs and practices there is a tendency towards retaining the focus of their magico-religious worldview. He notices that the tribal groups irrespective of their religious affiliations seek 'tribal identity', therein asserting the aspects of their worldview that seem relevant to them in the context of their present life-situations. S.C. Roy (1914) in an attempt to delineate the philosophic endeavours of the tribal groups in central-eastern India also emphasizes their magical worldview.

The Birhor Worldview

A systematic study of the worldview of the Birhor was made by the author in the context of their environment and techno-economic activities in the district of Sundargarh, Orissa. The fieldwork was conducted during 1971 and 1977, covering all the seasons of a Bengali calendar. They form a small group of people and are broadly identified as hunter-gatherers moving along the jungle of the locality. They cannot, however, subsist exclusively on the resources of the jungle. Rice that is produced by the settled peasants is their principal food. For rice and many other necessaries they thus have to depend also on the peasant villages and the market of the larger society. Having specialized in hunting, gathering and jungle-based crafts they maintain a regular economic interaction with the neighbouring caste-peasants and the market economy.

The Birhor collect barks of bauhinia creepers from jungle, manufacture different kinds of ropes and rope-products from their fibres and sell or barter them in the larger society. They also adopt occupational strategies like dealing in live-monkeys, jungle herbs and tubers of medicinal value and working as professional experts in magico-religious acts.

Linguistically as well as racially the Birhor belong to the Mundari family. But in the present techno-economic situation they cannot even optimally operate the clan-lineage-based segmentary structure of their society, the characteristic feature of the Mundari tribes. They organize their livelihood activities in terms of small households and bands and lead a nomadic way of life. Despite diversified subsistence activities and flexible social structure the Birhor have a strong in-group sentiment and a moral relationship with the jungle.

The above-mentioned life-situations of the Birhor inspired me to the probe deep into the minds of the people for a meaningful understanding of the world they live in. I was thus concerned with their ideas and acts, thought as well as action and grasp the people's characteristic outlook to life. Existential, cognitive as well as emotional dimensions were considered. Respondents were often asked about the meanings of their behaviour in contexts; and when the people failed to articulate, in speech, their feeling, attempts were made to get to the their unstated assumption through participant observation and empathic understanding of their behaviour in varying time and space dimensions.

The Birhor distinguish two distinct worlds: *disum,* their own territory in the jungle, and *muluk,* the territory dominated by caste-peasants and the market economy of the larger society. Birhor is a Mundari term and it means 'jungle man' (*bir,* jungle and *hor,* man).The people would also prefer to identify themselves as Birhor or 'men of the jungle'. The people other than own are broadly categorized by them as diku or aliens and in that context the people would use simply the term hor to denote their identity. The ethnic groups like the Mundari, the Bhuiya and the Kurmi Mahato are referred to as *horhon* that is, they are akin to *hor*.

The Birhor have also developed adaptive strategies of social interaction in the context of meaning in two sets of environment: a morally-ordered gemeinschaft in disum and a rationalist-utilitarian gesellschaft in *muluk*.

There is a significant continuity of the human world of the Birhor with the natural and the supernatural worlds they conceive of. They consider jungles their home and describe themselves as men of jungle. Their clans still claim to have their traditional habitat on forest-clad hills or mountains. Menifestation of the jungle is noticed in their settlement and in many other contexts of their life and activity. Every phenomenon of the jungle is considered animated and is presided over by some supernatural deity, called bonga. Although the Birhor have some practical knowledge about the utility of many plants and animals and are aware of the regular courses of many natural phenomena, they do not think that they can regulate them without any intervention of the supernatural deities. The ultimate power is considered to be with the supernatural deities.

In the supernatural plane the ancestral spirits *(hapram)* of the Birhor are placed next to the bonga. The ancestral spirits live in close association with the *bonga,* and are considered to have power to control many natural phenomena. The ancestral spirits act as agents between the supernatural beings and their living heirs; they protect the relatives from misfortunes, guide them in day-to-day work and look after their wellbeing. They continue to have their power and authority over their heirs at the supernatural plane. The relationships of the Birhor with the *hapram* and the *bonga* are jural as well as moral in nature.

The Birhor talk of a number of occupations like agriculture, basketry, pottery, blacksmithy, leather-work, weaving and three to four types of labour-work. They also know of a number of markets, villages and human categories. They have, however, little idea about the technologies of those occupations; they also think that they would lose their habitual freedom if they adopt those occupations. They can broadly tell about some seasonal operations in agriculture, like the sowing and the harvesting. They do not have any clear idea about the agricultural operations like transplantation, threshing, winnowing and storing. They note that the pursuit of agriculture and other occupations requires sedentary village life along with other communities. They also feel that almost all these occupations have a social stigma, and most of the people pursuing them are placed low in the local social hierarchy.

In direct confrontation with the socio-cultural environment of the larger society the Birhor have learnt that they are looked down upon by the people there and have little grip over culturally-defined meaning of life in the village society. They, therefore, turn back to their jungle terrain where they feel free and find a meaningful world of their own. Under the changing ecological and economic situations they thus often create myths around their activities and adopt occupational strategies keeping in consonance with their traditional knowledge of, and skills in, jungle ecology.

The villagers consider the Birhor expert monkey-hunters having exceptional mystic power in supernatural activities. They think that no other people except these mystic people would be able to lead such a simple life in the midst of jungles. The Birhor are well aware of these impressions of the villagers and strategically manipulate them to their ends, reinforcing their articulation with the jungle.

It is evident from the foregoing pages that in the changing contexts of modernization the techno-economic activities of the Birhor are extended, from their natural universe of jungle ecology, far beyond into the environmental ecology of the market-based larger society, and with these the elements of their worldview have also undergone changes. In the course of their confrontation with the larger society they have gathered much experience but these are not meaningfully integrated into their characteristic way of life. Instead, these new experiences help the Birhor reinforce their special relation with the jungle in the context of which the people find their life socially and culturally meaningful. It may be mentioned here that though there have been some significant changes in their nature of dependence on the forest ecology, the Birhor are still found to form a world of their own in which the jungle, the supernatural and the people themselves are morally bound together.

Other Illustrations

Unlike the Birhor of Orissa, who still have an effective ecological base in the jungle, the Hill Kharia, another hunter-gatherer group in West Bengal 'find themselves in a situation where their anchorage to the forest economic base has been rudely uprooted and they have been thrown at the doorstep of the peasant societies as landless dependent communities' (D. Sinha 1984 :85-86). The Hill Kharia of this area have experienced, over the years, a gradual decrease of resources in forests, and subsequently, there has occurred an 'erosion of technology and knowledge of ecology' among the people.

In order to cope with the depleted condition of the forest as well as the present situation of contact they have adopted various occupational strategies. In agricultural seasons they work as wage labourers in the fields of the neighbouring caste-peasants. They manufacture brooms and various kinds of fish-traps based on natural products for sale or barter in villages and local markets. They also resort to hunting, fishing and gathering in the surrounding natural ecology. Mention may be made here of their specific adaptation to, and skill in, the collection of paddy grains from the rat-holes in the harvested fields of the peasants. The Hill-Kharia take away the grains for their own consumption; they also kill the rats. The peasants allow them to do so with the assumption that they are making their fields free from the rat. They would also get the service of the people as and when necessary. The Hill-Kharia are, indeed, trying to carefully switch over, from their traditional jungle domain, to the common property resource base in the surrounding natural ecology of the village for survival and develop a structure of symbiosis with the caste-peasants in the locality.

In the past the enterprising Mahato peasants of the locality used to engage the Hill-Kharia against one another as robbers and plunderers. During the British administration they were thus notified as 'criminal tribe' and subsequently, were pushed out to the periphery of the village society. After Independence they were, however, de-notified; measures were also adopted to rehabilitate this 'ex-criminal tribe' into the 'civil order' of the locality. But the villagers still look upon them as a 'criminal' and mystic people. Though they live within the territorial boundary of the village, they do not belong to the 'moral order' of the village society; they indeed lack a meaningful arena of socio-cultural communication in the larger world. The Hill-Kharia, however, concede the mystic status accorded to them by the villagers, manage the villager's impressions for material benefit and carefully maintain a world of their own in close association with the natural ecology of the locality.

They spend much of their time and energy in foraging the resources of the locality and seem to find much pleasures to work in the forest. Although they realize that the forest resources are more or less exhausted, emotionally they find it more easier to adjust with. The forest and all of its resources are considered animated and presided over by the supernatural beings. The Hill-Kharia feel comfortable in the domain of the supernatural and hold appropriate ritual performance to communicate with the supernatural. Their relationship with the natural ecology as well as the supernatural is, indeed, morally bound and is reinforced through affective participation. From their nature of interaction and participation it is evident that the Hill-Kharia consider the forest and the natural ecology not only a domain for easier ritual and cultural communication and participation but also a secure arena for food and survival. They do not have any arena of meaningful social and cultural communication in the peasant society of the locality.

Morris (1981) has shown how the religious worldview of the Hill Pandaram, a hunting and gathering community of southern India, is integrated with their jungle habitat and economy in spite of their economic and cultural articulation with the neighbouring Hindu society. He describes the various gods and spirits as conceptualized by the Hill Pandaram and interprets their nature of relationship with them. He finds that 'the spiritual agencies recognized by the Hill Pandaram fall into three broad categories: the ancestral ghosts or spirits *(chavu)*, the mountain spirits *(mala devi)* and the gods of the Hindu pantheon. The spiritual agencies in the third category—and the myths and rites associated with them have little significance for the Hill Pandaram. The two principal supernaturals of the local villagers, Aiyappan and Karuppaswami, though part of their religious consciousness, have for the Hill Pandaram only a peripheral influence' (Morris 1981 :204). Though the Hill Pandaram religious system shows some ideological changes, the people make differential treatment to the Hindu supernatural. The Hindu deities are looked upon 'as alien spirits who have little concern' for the welfare of the people *(ibid* :214).

It becomes obvious from the preceding pages that many of the tribal groups in the mainland of India living at the level of hunting and gathering economy have now developed a symbiotic relation with the settled Hindu peasantry for their day to day subsistence. Subsequently, the elements of their worldview have undergone changes, and they have come across a world much wider than before. A careful probe into their world view reveals that the new experiences, though entered into their consciousness, lack meaning in the context of their life and culture and, as a result, do not get their emotional and affective support. The people, therefore, try to perpetuate their socio-cultural identity either by carefully preserving their knowledge of, and relations with, the jungle (as exemplified by the Birhor of Orissa and the Hill Pandaram of southern India) or by perpetuating a cover of 'mysticism' around themselves (as in the case of the Hill Kharia of Purulia). It may be mentioned here that the scale of society among these tribal groups hardly exceeds the level of a band, or a small hamlet, comprising a few nuclear families, and lacks any perceptible social differentiation in terms of education, wealth and power. The experiences and meanings are, therefore, shared by all the members of the community concerned.

There are, however, tribal groups who live at a higher level of techno-economy and are much intensely enmeshed into the larger society. They pursue agriculture and lead a sedentary village life in close association with different castes, communities, markets and urban centres. Many of these people are even exposed to the forces of modern education, industrial economy and power politics of our State, and consequently, have got education, employment, and also political party affiliation. These individuals with their new perceptions of, and relations with, the larger society, are in many instances, found to consciously build up a worldview for their respective communities. Orans (1965), based on his empirical study on the Santal in an industrial setting of Jamshedpur, Bihar, observes that the educated, employed and comparatively rich Santals emphasize on works, study and rank-attainment, and discourage their traditional involvement in pleasures or *raska*. A few Santal elites appeared to have been moving towards building up a great tradition for their community.

While studying the transformation process of the

tribal life in modern India S.C. Sinha (1981) observes that in the emerging situation of national economic development there has arisen a number of leaders and intelligentsia among the people. They are found to re-create and 'universalize tribal traditions at such a level as to appear authentic as well as prestigious to their own people as well as to the surrounding non-tribal groups in the contemporary situations. In this creative re-creation of tribal traditions the tribal intelligentsia and leaders often combine, in an ingenious manner, elements of tribal traditions with those of the Hindus and the Christians' *(ibid* : 121). Reviewing the tribal situation of Arunachal Pradesh, Sinha points out how the newly educated youths and leaders of the province, in the process of modernization, are consciously weaving their new experiences 'with their age-old traditions' and building up an integrated worldview for the community. Sinha further observes that 'in their search for, and preservation of, identity in their modern situation some of the tribal intelligentsia are not looking towards either Hindu or Christian model but are creatively universalizing the traditional mythology of 'Sun-Moon god' in a wide social arena' *(ibid*:133).

Changing Perspectives

The spectrum of worldview that has been described above is not an integrated picture of the tribal view, nor does it cover all the tribal groups in India. An attempt has just been made to bring into relief some aspects of their perceptions of, and relations with, the changing universe in the modern contexts. It becomes, however, evident from the above descriptions that the worldview of the tribal groups in India is not a static picture of their universe nor is it a closed system; it incorporates the changing perspectives of the world(s) which, in turn, guide their day-to-day life and culture.

With the change in the elements of the traditional

universe of their jungle habitat and self-sufficient economy there has not only arisen a group of educated and articulate intelligentsia among the tribal people but also occurred an expansion in their cognitive perception of the universe. Based on their experiences the young elites often develop a new outlook on life which, in turn, is placed as a conscious model for their community. Sometimes the leaders of different tribal groups, in direct confrontation with the socio-political forces of the larger society, are found to combine together as a united regional minority group and assert tribal identity. We are, however, yet to know to what extent the specialized experiences of the few educated tribal intelligentsia are articulated with the cumulative experiences of their community and subsequently, reflect the focus of the people's integrated worldview. It may be pointed out here that the aspect of worldview that the new elites build up in the modern context, besides having an urge for a meaningfully defined area of socio-cultural communication in the modern situation, has the notion of a progressive life in the future.

From our present state of knowledge on the worldview of the Birhor and a few other tribal groups in India we, however, find that the tribal peoples, regardless of their level of techno-economy and extent of contact with the larger society, perpetuate a 'quality of socio-cultural integration' as well as 'a state of mind' characterized by equality and representative collectives. The tribal people, irrespective of their numerical and techno-economic positions, are always constructing their world in which all the basic elements, man, nature and the super-nature, are meaningfully integrated. Their knowledge of the world in and around which they people live is derived primarily through affective participation than intellectual discourse.

The life and activities of the tribal people are primarily based on their immediate needs and desires. They are basically characterized by a 'this-worldly', 'pragmatic', 'non-puritanical', 'hedonistic' attitude towards life. They are also not loaded by ethical strivings. 'Although some of the tribes believe in a sequence of lives and others lay great store upon acquisition of social merit which raises the person's status in this life, in none of the tribal societies did we encounter the idea that moral choices affect a person's fate in future existence' (Furer-Haimendorf 1967: 168). A careful study of the day-to-day subsistence activities as well as the concept of good life in economic sphere of the Birhor of Orissa reveals that they are much concerned with the present, and do not have any idea of a future, far away from the present, though they often believe in a golden past. Most of the Birhor desire just two square meals a day, one or two clothes to wear, and a little drink. Although Birhors are aware that the resources of the jungle are not as abundant as they were in the past they do not believe in the scarcity of food items in the jungle as a normal state. Even the agricultural activities of a Santal household in the villages of Birbhum, West Bengal, are found to be deeply enmeshed into the social and cultural matrix of the village society. The normal security a Santal villager seeks lies in the fulfillment of his immediate needs and desires, in sharing his pleasures with kin and neighbours, and ultimately, in his conforming to the norms and customs of his society (Adhikary 1983). Personal upliftment of status by accumulating wealth or by attaining political power linkage to the larger society is not encouraged among them. It may be mentioned here that there are some traditional officials, and old men among the Santals who are considered and often referred to, as specialists having more knowledge about nature, supernatural phenomena, and the origin and creation of man and his universe. A careful probe would, however, reveal that these people are simply repositories of their traditional worldview that is integrated into their society and culture.

The Dafla and the Apa Tani of Subansari regions in Arunachal Pradesh though differ in their level of economy and social structure also 'subscribe to a worldview which, being basically utilitarian and prudential, is directed towards 'this worldly' goal, and lacks a belief in any link between moral and eschatological concepts' (Furer-Haimendorf 1967 : 82).

That the world view of a tribal people is not simply a metaphysical, philosophical activity of a few articulate people and that it is directed towards 'this worldly' goal and integrated into the work-a-day life of the people can also be understood from some recent observations on the Koya (Tyler 1976) and the Kota (Mandelbaum 1961). Tyler studies the conceptual categories of nature, supernatural beings inhabiting the earth and influencing their fate on the earth, land and soil, seasons as well as the relations of these categories with their actual practices of production, and finds that the podu (shifting) cultivation of the Koya is not merely a set of agricultural practices; 'it implies the whole nexus of Koyas' religious belief, self-image and tribal identity' (*ibid:* 17).

Mandelbaum, in the course of field investigation among the Kota of the Nilgiri Hills in the changing context of modernization, discovers that 'a Kota's main interest' lies 'not in his relations to the gods; not in his necessary dealings with plant and animal and matter but in his relations to other men' (*ibid* : 257). However, 'what seems typically to be in the forefront of a Kota's perception—that a man must struggle with man in defence of his social life. Gods are potent but not capricious: they can be dealt with effectively. Nature can be recalcitrant to man's efforts, but is not the centre of interest. The best man is one who does not allow himself to be deprived, one who responds vigorously to any threat of deprivation in social relations' (*ibid* : 244).

However, the whole spectrum of tribal worldview that is presented here reveals that the tribal people of India, though incorporate in their world view the perceptions of the modern universe, seem to lack there a meaningful area of social and cultural communication and, ultimately, show resilience to a world of their own in which their positions are socially and culturally defined, and morally ordered. Although most of the tribal groups in the modern contexts cannot perpetuate the techno-economy and the level of socio-cultural integration they had in the past, they retain, or try to retain, an outlook on life as well as a quality of social life which is morally significant and based on the idiom of kinship and sentiments. Altruism and generosity are still valued, and considered as the normative practice of life. The social world of the living is continuous with the world of their dead ancestors, and their relationship with nature and god is more or less unitary and morally significant.

Bibliography

Adhikary, A.K., 1984, *Society and Worldview of the Birhor: A Nomadic Hunting and Gathering Community of Orissa*. Anthropological Survey of India, Calcutta.

Adhikary, A.K., 1999, Birhor. In Lee, Richard and R. Daly (eds.) *The Cambridge Encyclopedia of Hunters and Gatherers,* pp. 248-51. The Cambridge University Press.

Archer, W.G., 1974, *The Hill of Flutes: Life, Love and Poetry in Tribal India, A Portrait of the Santals*. New Delhi: S. Chand & Co. (Pvt.) Ltd.

Barnard, Alan, 2001, *The Hunter-gatherer Peoples*. Fundacion Navarro Viola.

Basu, B.K., 1990, *The Onge : Negrito Hunter-Gatherers of Little Andaman*. Seagull Books, Calcutta.

Beattie, John, 1964, *Other Cultures*. Routledge & Kegan Paul Ltd., Broadway House, Ec.4.

Begler, E., 1978, Sex, status and authority in an egalitarian society. *American Anthropologist* 80.

Benedict, Rith, 1934, *Patterns of Culture*. A mentor book published by the New American Library.

Beteille, Andre, 1991, *Society and Politics in India: Essays in Comparative Perspective.* Oxford University Press, Delhi.

Bhattacharya, R., 1968, Social and cultural constraints in agriculture in three villages (Hindu, Moslem and Tribal) of West Bengal. *J. Indian Anthrop. Soc.* 3:79-108.

Bhanu, Ananda B., 1982, Economic organization of the Cholanaickans. In *Economies of the Tribes and Their Transformations*. K.S. Singh, ed., pp. 170-182. Concept Publishing Company, New Delhi.

Bhanu, Ananda B., 1982, The nomadic Cholanaickans of Kerala : An analysis of their movement. In *Nomads in India*. P.K. Misra and K.C. Malhotra, ed., pp. 215-226. Anthropological Survey of India, Calcutta.

Bhanu, Ananda B., 1989, *The Cholanaickan of Kerala*. Anthropological Survey of India, Calcutta.

Bhowmick, P.K., 1989, *The Chenchus of the Forests and Plateaux : A Hunting and Gathering Tribe in Transition.* Indian Institute of Social Research and Applied Anthropology, Calcutta.

Bichhieri, M.G., 1972, *Hunters and Gatherers Today : A Socioeconomic Study of Eleven Such Cultures in the Twentieth Century*. Holt, Rinehart and Winston, New York.

Bird-David, Nurit, 1982, 'Inside' and 'outside' in kinship usage : the hunter-gatherer Naikans of South India. *Cambridge Anthropology,* 7.

Bird-David, Nurit, 1983, Wage-gathering: socioeconomic changes and the case of food-gathering Naikans of South India. In P. Robb, ed., *Rural India.* Curzon Press, London.

Bird-David, Nurit, 1987, The Kurumbas of the Nilgiris: an ethnographic myth. *Modern Asian Studies,* Vol. 21.

Bird-David, Nurit, 1992, Beyond 'the original affluent society': a culturalist formulation. *Current*

Anthropology 33:25-47, (quoted from Ingold, T.: on the social relations of the hunter-gatherer band, In *The Cambridge Encyclopedia of Hunters and Gatherers*, ed. By Richard Lee and Richard Daly, Cambridge Univ. Press.).

Bird-David, Nurit, 1996, Puja, or sharing with the gods? On ritualized possession among Nayaka of South India. *Eastern Anthropologist* 49:3-4, 259-75.

Bird-David, Nurit, 1999, Introduction : South Asia. In Richard Lee and Richard Daly, eds. *The Cambridge Encyclopedia of Hunters and Gatherers*. Pp.231-237.

Bloch, M., 1973, The long term and short term:the economic and political significance of the morality of kinship. In Jack Goody (ed.) *The character of kinship*, pp.75-88. Cambridge Univ. Press.

Boas, Franz, 1938, (1911) *The Mind of Primitive Man* (revised edition). New York: Macmillan.

Boas, Franz, 1988, *The Central Eskimo*. Bureau of American Ethnology.

Bodding, P.O. n.d. *Traditions and Institutions of the Santals*. Oslo: Ethnographic Museum Bulletin: 6.

Bose, N.K., 1941, The Hindu method of tribal absorption. *Science and Culture* 7 :188-194.

Bose, N.K., 1956, Some observations on nomadic castes of India. *Man in India* 36 :93-98.

Bose, N.K., 1971, Land-Man ratio in tribal areas. *Man in India* 51(4): 268-310.

Bose, N.K., 1979, [1971] *Tribal Life in India*. National Book Trust of India, New Delhi.

Bose, Saradindu, 1989, Shifting cultivation in India. In Sinha, S., et al (ed.) *Man and Environment*, pp. 55-65. The Indian Anthropological Society, Calcutta.

Bose, S. *et al*, 1982, *Population Data Regarding Forestry Communities Practising Shifting Cultivation*. New Delhi: Inspector General of Forests.

Chandrasekhar, A., 1965, *A Monograph on Village Byrlutigudem.* Village monograph No. 33, Census of India 1961.

Childe, V. Gordon, 1951, *Social Evolution.* London and New York: H. Schuman.

Culshaw, W.J., 1949, *Tribal Heritage: A Study of the Santals.* London: Lutherworth Press.

Danda, A.K., 1998, Shifting cultivation in India. In Mishra, S.N. (ed.) *Antiquity to Modernity in Tribal India,* Vol. III:144-171, Inter-India Publications, New Delhi.

Dash, J., 1998, *Human Ecology of Foragers: A Study of the Kharia (Savara), Ujia (Savara) and Birhor in Simlipal Hills.* Commonwealth, New Delhi.

Dalton, E.T., 1872, *Descriptive Ethnology of Bengal.* Bengal Govt. Press, Calcutta.

Driver, W.H.P., 1888, Birhor. *Journal of the Royal Asiatic Society of Bengal,* 47: 12-38.

Durkheim, Emile and Marcel maus, 1963, (1903) *Primitive Classification.* Cohen and West, London.

Dutta-Majumdar, N., 1956, *The Santals : A Study in Culture Change.* Delhi: Govt. of India.

Douglas, Mary, 1973, *Natural Symbols: Explorations in Cosmology.* Penguin Books.

Dozier, Edward P., 1956, The concepts of 'primitive' and 'native' in anthropology. In William L. Thomas, Jr. (ed.) *Current Anthropology,* The University of Chicago Press.

Evans-Pritchard, E.E., 1940, *The Nuer.* Oxford, England: Claredon Press.

Evens, T.M.S., 1982, On the social anthropology of religion. *The Journal of Religion* 62 (4): 376-391.

Forde, Daryll, 1954, *African worlds.* International African Institute, London.

Fortes, Meyer, 1969, *Kinship and Social Order.* London

Foster, G.M., 1965, Peasant society and the image of limited good. *American Anthropologist,* 67:293-315.

Fowler, Catherine S. and Nancy J. Turner, 1999, Ecological/cosmological knowledge and land management among hunter-gatherers. In Richard Lee and R. Daly (eds.) *The Cambridge Encyclopedia of Hunters and Gatherers*, pp. 419-425. Cambridge Univ. Press.

Fox, R.G., 1969, Professional primitives : hunters and gatherers of nuclear South Asia. *Man in India* 49 : 139-160.

Furer-Haimendorf, Christoph von., 1943, *The Chenchu: Jungle Folk of the Deccan*. London: Macmillan.

Furer-Haimendorf, Christoph von., 1953, The after-life in Indian tribal belief. *Journal of the Royal Anthropological Institute* 83, pt. 1.

Furer-Haimendorf, Christoph von., 1969, *Morals and Merit: A Study of Value and Social Controls in South eastern Asian societies*. Weidenfeld and Nicolson, London.

Gardner, P., 1968, 'Discussion', part II. In Richard B. Lee and Irven DeVore, eds., *Man the Hunter*. Aldine Publishing Company, Chicago.

Gardner, P., 1982, Ascribed austerity : a tribal path to purity. *Man* 17 : 462-9.

Gardner, P., 1985, Bicultural oscillation as a long-term adaptation to cultural frontiers. *Human Ecology*, 13.

Gardner, P., 1991, Pragmatic meanings of possessions in Palyan shamanism. *Anthropos* 86: 367-84.

Gardner, P., 1993, Dimensions of subsistence foraging in south India. *Ethnology 32 : 109-84. Changing Identities in South Asia*, pp. 369-381. Paris: Mouton.

Gautam, Mohan K., 1977, The santalization of the Santals. In Kenneth David (ed.), *The New Winds: Changing Identities in South Asia*, pp. 369-381. Paris: Mouton.

Geertz, Clifford, 1993, *The Interpretation of Cultures*, pp. 33-54, Fontana Press, London.

Gordon, R., 1984, The Kung in the Kalahari exchange: an ethnohistorical perspective. In C. Schrire, ed.,

Past and Present in Hunter-Gatherer Studies. Academic, New York.

Guenther, M., 1999, From totemism to shamanism: Hunter-gatherer contributions to world mythology and spirituality, In Richard Lee and Richard Daly (eds.) *The Cambridge Encyclopedia of Hunters and Gatherers,* pp. 426-433. Cambridge Univ. Press.

Guiteras-Holmes, Calixta, 1961, *Perils of the Soul: The Worldview of a Tzotzil Indian*. Free Press, New York.

Horton, Rabin, 1962, The Kalahari worldview: an outline and interpretation. *Africa* 32:197-220.

Ingold, Tim, 1988, Notes on the foraging mode of production. In T. Ingold, et.al. (eds.) *Hunter-Gatherers II: Property, Power and Ideology*. Oxford: Berg.

Ingold, Tim, 1999, On the social relations of the hunter-gatherer band. In Richard Lee and R. Daly (eds.) *The Cambridge Encyclopedia of Hunters and Gatherers,* pp. 390-410, Cambridge Univ. Press.

Jones, W.T., 1972, Worldviews: their nature and function. *Current Anthropology* 13:1:79-109.

Kearney, M., 1975, Worldview theory and study. In Bernard J. Seigal et.el. (eds.) *Annual Review of Anthropology,* 4:247-72.

Kloss, Boden G., 1903, *Andaman and Nicobars : the narrative of a Cruise in the Schooner Terrapan with notices of the Island, their Fauna, Ethnology, etc.*. Vivek Publishing House, Delhi.

Kluckhon, Clyde, 1959, The philosophy of the Navaho Indians. In Morton Fried (ed.) *Readings in Anthropology,* vol. II, pp. 424-449. New York: Thomas Y. Crowell Company.

Kluckhon, F. and F.L. Strodtbeck, 1961, *Variations in Value Orientations,* Evanston, III., Row, Peterson and Co.

Kochar, Vijay, 1970, *Social Organization among the Santal*. Calcutta.

Kosambi, D.D., 1970, *The Culture and Civilization of Ancient*

India in Historical Outline. Vikas Publishing House, Pvt. Ltd.

Kroeber, A.L., 1925, *Handbook of the Indians of California.* Bureau of American Ethnology, Bulletin No.78.

Lathrap, Donald, W., 1968, The hunting economies of the tropical forest zone of South America : an attempt at historical perspective. In *Man, the Hunter.* Richard B. Lee and Irven DeVore, eds., pp. 23-29. Aldine Publishing Company : Chicago.

Leacock, E., 1978, Women's status in egalitarian society: implications for social evolution. *Current Anthropology,* 19.

Leach, Edmund, 1976, *Culture and communication:* the logic by which symbols are connected. Cambridge Univ. Press, Cambridge.

Lee, R., 1982, Politics, sexual and non-sexual, in egalitarian societies. In E.Leacock and R.Lee, eds., *Politics and History in Band societies.* Cambridge Univ. Press, Cambridge.

Lee, Richard B. and Irven DeVore (eds.), 1968, *Man, the Hunter.* Aldine. Atherton/Chicago.

Leslie, Charles, M., 1960, *Now We are Civilized: A Study of the Worldview of the Zapotec Indians of Mitla, Oaxaca.* Detroit, Mich.: Wayne Univ. Press.

Leuva, K.K., 1964, *The Asur:a study of primitive iron smelters.* New Delhi: Bharatiya Adimjati Seva Sangha.

Levi-Strauss, Claude, 1963, *Structural Anthropology,* Penguin Books, Levy-Bruhl, L.

Levi-Strauss, Claude, 1923, *Primitive mentality.* London: George Allen and Unwin Ltd. (Trans. By L.A. Clare).

Levi-Strauss, Claude, 1926, *How Natives Think* (English trans.). London. Lienhardt, Godfrey.

Levi-Strauss, Claude, 1978, *Social Anthropology,* (2nd Edn.). Oxford Univ. Press, London.

Mahapatra, L.K., 1989, Worldview, metaphilosophy and nature. In Surajit, Sinha, *et. al,* (eds.) *Man and*

Environment, pp. 291-293. Indian Anthropological Society, Calcutta.

Mahapatra, Sitakant, 1976, Ecological adaptation of technology-ritual conflict and leadership change:the Santal experience. In Kenneth David (ed.) *The New Winds: Changing Identities in South Asia*, pp. 357-368, Paris: Mouton.

Mandelbaum, D.G., 1961, The world and worldview of the Kota. In Mckim Marriott (ed.), *Village India*, pp. 228-60. Bombay: Asia Publishing House

Mehra, J.D., 1977, The worldview of Indian tribes. In S.C.Dube (ed.), *Tribal Heritage of India*, I: 58-84. New Delhi: Vikas Publishing House Pvt. Ltd.

Mendelson, E.M., 1968, Worldview. In David L. Sills (ed.) *International Encyclopedia of the Social Sciences*, 16, Macmillan Company.

Misra, P.K., 1969, Nomadism in India, *Journal of the Indian Anthropological Society*, 4:79-80.

Misra, P.K., 1977, Social transformation among food gatherers : a case study. In M.N. Srinivas, S. Seshaiah and V.S. Parthasarathi, eds., *Dimensions of Social Change in India*, Allied, Bombay.

Morris, Brian, 1981, Hill gods and ecstatic cults: notes on the religion of a hunting and gathering people. *Man in India* 61 (3).

Morris, Brian, 1982, *Forest traders: a socio-economic study of the Hill Pandaram*. London: Athlone Press.

Morris, Brian, 1999, Hill Pandaram. In Lee, R. and R. Daly (eds.) *The Cambridge Encyclopedia of Hunters and Gatherers*, pp. 265-68. Cambridge University Press.

Mukherjee, C.L., 1962, *The Santals* (2nd. edn.), Cacutta: A. Mukherjee.

Murdock, G.P., 1968, The current status of the world's hunting and gathering peoples. In Richard B. Lee and Irven DeVore, eds., *Man the Hunter*. Aldine Publishing Company, Chicago.

Myers, Fred M., 1988, Critical trends in the study of Hunter-gatherers. *Annual Review of Anthropology,* 17.

O' Malley, L.S.S., 1910, *Bengal District Gazeteers: Santal Parganas.* Calcutta.

Orans, Martin, 1965, *The Santals: A Tribe in Search of a Great Tradition.* Detrot: Wayne State Univ. Press.

Pandit, T.N., 1982, Economy of the Onge. In *Economies of the Tribes and Their Transformations.* K.S. Singh, ed., pp. 183-193. Concept Publishing Company, New Delhi.

Pandit, T.N., 1990, *The Sentinelese.* Seagull Books, Calcutta.

Pandya, V., 1993, *Above the Forest : A Study of Andamanese Ethnoanemology, Cosmology and the Power of Ritual.* Delhi: Oxford University Press.

Putnam, Patrick, 1950, The Pygmies of the Ituri forest. In *A Reader in General Anthropology.* Carleton S. Coon, ed., London : Jonathan Cape.

Radcliffe-Brown, A.R., 1922, *The Andaman Islanders.* Cambridge Univ. Press.

Radin, Paul, 1957, *Primitive Man as Philosopher.* New York: Dover Publications.

Redfield, R. 1953. *The Primitive World and Its Transformations.* Ithaca: Cornell Univ. Press.

Radin, Paul, 1955, *The Little Community: Viewpoints for the Study of A Human Whole.* Univ. of Chicago Press.

Radin, Paul, 1956, *Peasant Society and Culture: An Anthropological Approach to Civilization.* Univ. of Chicago Press.

Radin, Paul, 1962(a), The primitive worldview. In Margaret Park Redfield, ed., *Human Nature and the Study of Society : The Papers of Robert Redfield,* Vol.I, pp. 269-280. Chicago: The University of Chicago press.

Radin, Paul, 1962(b), Letter Michael Mendelson. In Redfield, M.P. (ed.) *Human Nature and the Study of*

Society: The Papers of Robert Redfield, Vol.I. The Univ. of Chicago Press.

Risley, H., 1911, *The People of India,* London: W. Tacker.

Rizvi, S.N.H., 1990, *The Shompen : A Vanishing Tribe of the Great Nicobar Island.* Seagull Books, Calcutta.

Roy, S.C., 1914, Magic and witchcraft on the Chotanagpur Plateau : a study in the philosophy of primitive life. *Journal of the Royal Anthropological Institute,* 44:324-50.

Roy, S.C., 1925, *The Birhor : A Little-known Jungle Tribe of Chotanagpur.* Man in India Office, Ranchi.

Roy Burman, 2003, Toward thinking about nature of human nature. *Journal of the Indian Anthropological Society,* 38(2&3): 333-340.

Sachchidananda, 1981, Study of primitive tribes : certain conceptual issues. In L.P.Vidyarthi (ed.) *The Profiles of the Marginal and Prefarming Tribes of Central-eastern India.* Government of West Bengal, Calcutta.

Sarkar, J., 1989, Breakthrough in Sentinelese contact: some emergency issues. *Journal of the Indian Anthropological Society,* 24.

Sarkar, J., 1990, *The Jarawa.* Seagull Books, Calcutta.

Seligmann, Charles G. and Brenda Z. Seligmann, 1911, *The Veddas.* Cambridge : Cambridge Univ. Press.

Sen, Amartya, 2006, *Identity and Violence: The Illusion of Destiny.* Allen Lane.

Sen, J., 1965, Ethnographic notes on the Birhor, *Bulletin of the Anthropological Survey of India,* 14: 45-58.

Service, E.R., 1962, *Primitive Social Organization : An Evolutionary Perspective.* Random House, New York.

Service, E.R., 1966, *The Hunters.* New Jersey: Englewood Cliffs, N.J. : Prentice-Hall.

Sherwill, W., 1851, Notes upon a tour through Raj Mahal hills. *Journal of Asiatic Society of Bengal* 20:544-606.

Singh, Bhupinder, 1998, Primitive tribal groups. In S.C.

Dube (ed.) *Antiquity to Modernity in Tribal India,* vol. 1, pp. 70-109. Inter-India Publications, New Delhi.

Sinha, D.P., 1958, Cultural ecology of the Birhor: a methodological illustration, *Journal of Social research,* 1: 86-96.

Sinha, D.P., 1968, *Cultural Change in the Inter-tribal Market: the Role of the Banari Intertribal Market among the Hill Peoples of Chotanagpur.* Asia Publishing House.

Sinha, D., 1986, *The Hill Kharia of Purulia : Impact of Poverty on a Hunting and Gathering Tribe.* Anthropological Survey of India, Calcutta. Bombay.

Sinha, S.C., 1958, Tribal cultures of Peninsular India as dimension of little tradition in the study of Indian civilization : a preliminary statement. *Journal of American Folklore* 71 :504-518.

Sinha, S.C., 1969 Urgent problems of research in social and cultural anthropology in India : perspective and suggestions. In *Urgent Research in Social Anthropology.* Behari L. Abbi and Satish Saberwal, ed., pp. 162-169. Indian Institute of Advanced Study, Simla.

Sinha, S.C., 1972, Tribal solidarity movements in India: a review. In K. S. Singh (ed.) *Tribal Situation in India,* Simla: Indian Institute of Advanced Study.

Sinha, S.C., 1973, Rethinking about tribes and Indian civilization. *Journal of Indian Anthropological Society,* Vol. 8(2): 99-108.

Sinha, S.C., 1977, Problems of diagonistic research and the strategy of development of pre-agricultural 'primitive' communities. In S.C. Sinha and B.D. Sharma (eds.) *Primitive Tribes: The First Step,* Ministry of Home Affairs, New Delhi.

Sinha, S.C., 1978, Co-existence of multiple scales and networks of a civilization : India. *In Scale and Social Organization.* Fredrik Barth, ed., pp. 122-132. Universitetsforlaget, Oslo.

Sinha, S.C., 1981, Tribes and Indian civilization: transformation process in modern India. *Man in India,* 61:2 :105-42.

Stegeborn, Wiveca, 1999, Wanniyala-aetto, In Lee, Richard and R. Daly (eds.) *The Cambridge Encyclopedia of Hunters and Gatherers,* pp. 269-273. The Cambridge Univery Press.

Steward, Julian, 1955, *Theory of Culture Change : The Methodology of Multilinear Evolution.* Urbana : Univ. of Illinois Press.

Strathern, Andrew J., 1972, *One Father, One Blood.* Australian National Univ. Press.

Tambiah, S.J., 1990, *Magic, Science, Religion and the Scope of Rationality.* Cambridge Univ. Press

Tax, Sol., 1941, Worldview and social relationsin Guatemala. *American Anthropologist* (new series) 43: 27-42.

Tyler, Stephen, 1974, Fields are for planting: swidden agriculture among the Koyas of south India, *Journal of the Indian Anthropological Society.* Vol. IX, No.1: 17-38.

Vidyarthi, L.P., 1981, *The Profiles of the Marginal and Pre-farming Tribes of Central-eastern India.* Bulletin of the Cultural Research Institute (Special series No.26), Calcutta.

Vidyarthi, L.P., 1983, [1976] *The Tribal Culture of India.* Concept Publishing Company, New Delhi.

Wilsmen, Edwin N. 1989 *Land Filled with Flies: A Political Economy of the Kalahari.* Chicago University Press.

Index

abje bonga 153-54, 238, 246, 254
Adhikary 37, 43, 47-48, 56, 68-69, 104, 162, 181, 214-16, 219, 276
African Worlds 259
Akbar 194
Antonova et al 194, 198, 201
Archer 132
Arthashastra 193
Arya 2
Ashoka 194
Asur 29
ato 139, 144
ato posu 174
babsha bir 217
bade behera 122
bagal 140
baghat 218
baha parab 219
bahinga 92
Baiga 29-30
Bailey 178-79
bak 119-20
Ban Rawat 27
banchei gai 171
bandhu bok 126
bandra bir 217
Baric-Bonga 250
Barnard 7, 31
Barth 161, 203
Basu 44
batu 136
Beattie 150
Begler 41
Benedict 19, 258
Beteille 3
bhagchasi 134-35, 163-64
Bhanu 28, 32, 50, 59, 70
Bharata 194
bharna 148
Bhattacharya 133
Bhil 177
Bhowmick 27, 52-53, 59-60
Bhuiyans 185, 189
bhulah 218
bhulah chandi 218

Bhumij 189
bichhieri 41, 63
Bidika Lachchan 116
Bird-David 26, 33, 43, 219, 222
Birhor 16-18, 26-28, 31, 33, 35, 37-39, 46-50, 54-57, 60, 67, 69, 73-75, 78-105, 161, 180-82, 191, 213-26, 266-70, 275
Birhor and Their Universe 215-16
Birhor World View 266-70
Bloch 150
Boas 22, 40, 63
Bodding, P.O. 132, 231
Bohannan 160
bonga 49, 105, 216, 218-19, 224, 239, 243, 251, 268
bonga tola 158
Bose 9, 45-46, 54, 66, 72, 76, 78, 88, 181, 188, 195, 209, 210, 263
Bose et al 8
British School of Social Anthropology 133
Budhan Soren 170
Budhi Murmu 166
Burhi Mai 217, 219
buru bnga 220-21
Census of India 1931 1
Chandrasekhar 27, 53
chandu bonda 216-17
changu 124, 130
Chenchu 6, 27-28, 33-34, 52, 58-59, 67
chharpatra 127
Childe 63
Cholanaickan 28, 32-33, 49, 56, 59, 70, 73
churgin 216
churni 218, 249
Culshaw 132
daini 218
Dalton 75, 132, 232
Danda 204
Dasyu 2
delbari 147, 170
Despres 204
Dharmashastra 193
Dhartimai 216-17
dhauri 90
digar kania 125
diku 48, 79, 86, 222
disum 48-49, 70, 224, 233
disum sendra 150, 234
Dombo 106-12
Dongria Kondh 106-16, 188
Dongria Kondh Development Office 113
Douglas, Michael 258
Dozier 15, 19
draha 218
drili 108
Driver 76
Durkheim 255-57
Durkheim and Mauss 20
Dutta-Majumdar 132
erok 145
Evans-Pritchard 20
Evens 21-22
Fernandes 179
Forde, Daryll 259
Fortes 150
Foster 258
Fox 16-17, 46, 67, 78, 181
Furer-Haimendorf 37, 40, 53, 63, 276-77
Gadaba 185
gai gora 152, 246
ganam taka 156, 172
Gardner 6, 27, 33, 35, 43

garisau 91
Garos 200
Gautam 132
Geertz 23-24, 209, 211-12, 229-30
ghar jawai 151, 156
Girijan Cooperative Society 59
Gisbert 16
Godelier 4, 178
godet 144
Gond 177
Gordon 18, 42
goro 147, 171
Gosae Era 242-43
Great Andamanese 25, 44-45, 56, 58
Guenther 225
gugli 142
Guiteras-Holmes, Calixta 259
gusti 151-52
guti kora 148-49, 164, 169
gutie pera 153
Habermas, Jurgen 11
Hallowell 36, 258
hanapuri 216, 235, 253
handi 147, 168
hanuman bir 217
hapram 49, 152, 154, 216-18, 221, 247-48, 251, 268
Hill-Kharia 17-18, 28, 50-51, 56, 70-71, 73-74, 180-81, 184, 191, 270-73
Hoebel 258
hor ato 173
Hor Korean More Hapram Real Katha 231
Hos 200
Hunter-Gatherers in the Context of Modernization 58-62
Ingold 58, 222
iri gundli 145
jagghi 89
Jaher Era 241, 250
Jaherthan 241-42, 244
jajmani (jao) 166
janthar 145
Jarwas 5, 25, 44-45, 56, 66
jati shabha 122-23, 129
jatra gudi puja 109-10
Jenu Kuruba 50, 56, 59-60, 62
jogmanjhi 144
joti 90
Juangs 30, 117-31, 185-87
jum sim bonga 238-39, 250
Jyatha Murmu 171
Kadar 16, 29, 58-59, 62, 67
kamandiria kania 124, 129
Karve, Iravati 208
Kearney, Michael 258
khijuri 147, 168
khunt 153, 155, 238, 245
khut 218
Kiratas 27
kirsan 134, 164
Kloss 25, 46
Kluckhohn and Strodtbeck 258
Kochar 133
Kolean Guru 231, 233, 237, 241
Kolhas 200
Kondh 30, 106-16, 179, 185
Kosambi 16
Kota 277
Koya 277
Kroeber 40, 63
kudum naeke 144
Kukis 200
Kung 18
kutum bok 126, 130-31
Lakshmi Sura 196

Lathrop 42, 64-65
Leach, Edmund 228
Leacock 41
Lee 7, 41
Lee and Daly 5-6
Lee and DeVore 40-41, 63
Leslie, Charles M. 259
Leuva 29
Levi-Strauss 22
Levy-Bruhl 20, 257
Lienhardt 228
Lugu Haram 217, 219
Magh Parab 169, 244
Mahapatra 132, 179, 197, 264
mahindar 135, 146, 149, 164, 168-69
majang 120
majhi and mejhen 173
Malhotra 60
mana mani 125
Mandelbaum 277
manjhi haram 144, 146
Manjhi Haram Bonga 243, 250
manjhisthan 146
Manjhithan 244
Mankria 75-87, 214
Manu 193
Maran Buru 239-42, 246, 250, 253
Mariott 206
Mauss, Maurice 255-57
Mehra 262
Mendeleson, E.M. 259
metta mirasi 27, 52
Misra 28, 50, 59, 97
Mizos 200
Mongol Tudu 157
Moreko Turuiko 241-42, 250
Morgan 63
Morris 26, 33, 37-38, 43, 53, 272
Mukherjee 132
muluk 48, 70, 224
Munda 48, 188-89, 214, 222
murli 141
Myers 18, 42
N. Dhora 110
naeke 144
nagan 119
nagare munish 165
Nagas 200
Nageria or Kisan 188
nayadi 16
Nayaka 26, 28, 31, 33-34, 67
Negroes 42, 64
Nicobarese 25, 46
noapuri 216, 235, 253
Nomadism 92-95
O'Malley 132, 232
Onges 25, 31, 34, 38, 44-45, 56, 58, 66
orak 139, 238
orak bonga 152-54, 158, 238, 246, 254
Orans 132, 273
Oraon 188
orha 101
pajenis 110
Palyans 27, 28, 33-36, 38
pancha 147
Pandaram 33, 37, 53, 272
Pandit 25, 44-45, 66
Pandya 33
pangri 218
pao behera 122
paranik 144
Pargana Haram Bonga 243, 250
paris 153

phul-saya 83-85, 92, 202
Pir Organisation 120-22, 186
Polanyi, Karl 159
Primary Hunters 44-46
Primitive Man as Philosopher 21
Primitive Tribal Groups (PTGs) 26, 30-36
Primitive Tribal Groups in India 24
Primitive Tribal Groups in Nation-State Contexts 36-38
Primitive World and Its Transformation 20
Putnam 42, 64
Pygmy 42, 64
Radin 2, 258
Raji 27
Rampal 196
Ray 76
Redfield 17, 20, 57, 226, 258-60, 262
Regional Systems in the Andaman and Nicobar Islands 25-26
rendi 150
Rigveda 194
Risley 76
Rizvi 25
Roy 205
Roy Burman 18-19, 210
Roy, S.C. 40, 63, 77, 87
Sacchidananda 14-15
sadar ghàr 111
Sahlins 160
Sahlins and Service 63
sai behera 122-23
sanga 152
Santals 132-75, 177-80, 188-90, 200, 214, 222, 227-54
Saora tribe 188
Saoria Paharia 185
Sarkar 57
Şecondary or Symbiotic Hun ers 46-53
Seligmann and Seligmann 40, 63
Sen 78
Sen, Amartya 3-4
Sentinelese 5, 25, 44-45, 56-57, 66
Service 41, 63, 100
Sherwill 132
shifting cultivation 8-10, 18, 32, 185-89
Shils 204
shiropa 187
Shompen 25, 44-46
Shyam Murmu 171
sikha 91-92
sing bonga 216017, 236-37
Singh 15, 188
Sinha 17, 29, 42, 44, 46, 51, 62, 64, 66-70, 73, 76, 78, 89, 133, 178, 180-82, 184, 189, 195-96, 206, 214, 263-65, 274
Skrefsrud 231
snai 115
Socio-cultural Distinctiion of the PTGs and Their Identity with the Forests 30-36
Sohrae 145
Sol Tax 258
Srinivas 206
States Reorganisation Committee (SRC) 202
Stegeborn 37
Steward 16, 41, 63
Strathern 150
Sukul Murmu 166
Surajit Chandra 262

surum kania 125
taile 118
Tambiah 224
tirio 141
tola 101
Tribal Life of India 4
Tyler 10, 277
Tylor and Frazer 256, 258
udung kania 125-26
United Nations 37
uthulu 89
Vedda 16, 37, 67
Vidyarthi 4, 16
Viswa Bharati 135
vorna 170
Wadaka Davoda 112, 116
White 63
Wilmsen 7